New World, New Earth

*Environmental Reform in American Literature
from the Puritans through Whitman*

Cecelia Tichi

New Haven and London, Yale University Press, 1979

Designed by Sally Harris
and set in IBM Press Roman type.
Printed in the United States of America by
Halliday Lithograph, West Hanover, Mass.

Published in Great Britain, Europe, Africa, and
Asia (except Japan) by Yale University Press,
Ltd., London. Distributed in Australia and
New Zealand by Book & Film Services, Artarmon,
N.S.W., Australia; and in Japan by Harper & Row,
Publishers, Tokyo Office.

Library of Congress Cataloging in Publication Data

Tichi, Cecelia.
  New world, new earth.

  Includes bibliographical references and index.
  1. American literature – History and criticism.
2. Ecology in literature. 3. Nature in literature.
I. Title. II. Title: Environmental reform in
American literature from the Puritans through
Whitman.
PS169.E25T5   810'.9'36   78-15809
ISBN 0-300-02287-5

Contents

Preface

Environmental "consciousness raising" has brought Americans a severe account of damaged earth, air, and water—and a nationally incriminating history lesson emphatic in such recent titles as *America the Raped* (1969) and *The Exploited Eden* (1972). Our collective *mea culpa* for environmental rapine, waste, greed, ignorance, fecklessness, and the like reaches backward, we are told, to the beginnings of settlement when those perennially blameworthy forefathers, the Puritans, misread Genesis and became what the late-nineteenth-century conservationist John Muir called "pious destroyers" of the landscape. Scholars and analysts alike tell us that Puritans ignored the stewardly obligations intended in Scripture's authorization of human dominion over all the earth, its flora and its fauna, and instead took "dominion" to mean carte blanche for promiscuous use of the New World resources. The Puritans' dangerous precedent, itself a longtime legacy of Western thought, apparently denied to man a harmonious balance with the rest of the natural world and established the pattern by which Americans have kept an adversary relationship to their New World environment. Over three centuries, it seems, arrogant Americans held themselves to be sovereign over the natural world. And while writers intermittently have urged historical sympathy for colonists and pioneers struggling for their lives in treacherous wilds, their indictments in the main fall to Puritans and Yankees, and especially to proponents of Manifest Destiny. As Perry Miller inquired of American thinking in the 1840s, "How could we at one and the same time establish our superiority to artificial Europe upon our proximity to Nature, and then view with complacency the rapidity of our despoiling her?"[1] The despoliation seems to have roots in values of imperious human power apart from (and at the expense of) those of environmental integrity. We were all, it seems, profligate of New World gifts.

By now this line of thought is as familiar as litany. And it suffers in the way of lip service paid even in the cause of real conviction. That is to say, the thesis has become a largely unchallenged assumption—which is regrettable because for the most part it is wrong.

A great deal of American writing from the seventeenth century onward suggests, on the contrary, that on the subject of the environment we are mistaking palpable present effects for past intentions. Just now, when values of environmental protection are institutionalized in a federal agency (a voice of conscience, if not of power) and when in connection with the environment the words *foul, pollute,* and *contaminate* ring with moral condemnation as never before, it is tempting to see in our environmental predicament a First Cause of ancestral sin. But, in fact, the writings of two centuries of those ancestors tell a story, not of arrogance but of driving aspiration to reform the New World environment conjointly with reform of the spiritual and political life of the nation. Writings from Puritans through the Revolutionary period and beyond to the Romantic era of the nineteenth century indicate that, far from heedlessly vandalizing the environment, early Americans saw its modification—in fact, its reform—as an ideological imperative that must proceed together with America's moral regeneration.

In this sense the phrase *environmental reform* means something different from the human restraint currently signified, say, in curbing industrial pollution, highway construction, and the like. Historically, the reform of the environment has meant instead aggressive topographical change, much of it thought to be "corrective" or "reparative" or a "refinement" of the natural landscape. It includes the destructive militarism in the outlook of the seventeenth-century Puritan and the nineteenth-century pioneer, and it encompasses the symbolic America of Whitman's *Leaves of Grass* as well as the social programs behind Frederick Law Olmsted's parks of grass. Largely, it has meant the orderly impress of civilization that defined amorphous space. But the ideology that gave transcendent meaning to dammed streams, cleared woodland, drained swamps, etc., was that of an America destined to a unique place in history. It derives less from Genesis than from the prophetic Book of Revelation which decreed a New Heaven and a New Earth. America promised to be the site of that utopian New Earth—though not in its original, benighted state. Enormous human effort was required to make the promise of a New

Earth become reality, and writers filled with reformist ardor addressed that huge task at hand. This then was no matter solely of aesthetics or of ego aggrandizement. The American spirit and the American continent were bonded ideologically. The spiritual biography of America required the reform of the New World into the utopian New Earth.

What follows is a close look, first, at the ideology of environmental reform in American writings from the mid-seventeenth to the later nineteenth century. Principally, it is the record of one national imperative, its development, its nurturance, its adaptation to changing modes of thought, and its vital endurance over centuries. John Seelye approaches this point when he writes that "there is a minority body of American pre-Romantic, which is to say colonial writing, that vibrates with an imperial necessity having a long trajectory into the nineteenth century. In that literature, exponents of manifest destiny evince a distinctly neoclassical sensibility,...a millennialism which...exalts the valleys, lowers the mountains, and makes the crooked straight."[2]

In part this millennial imperative emerges in mosaic pattern from writers who have left scattered and miscellaneous remarks in magazines, letters, diaries, verses, and fiction through more than two centuries. But historically we also recognize themes of environmental reform in Cotton Mather's sermons, in Jedidiah Morse's geography books, in James Fenimore Cooper's novels, in Daniel Webster's political speeches. They proceed in George Bancroft's United States history, in George Perkins Marsh's conservationist tract, and in Frederick Law Olmsted's writings on landscape design. Through the Puritan, Revolutionary, and Romantic periods we can observe the course of environmental reform in paradox and contradiction, in polemic and propaganda focused upon a nation at once destined yet provisional in its course toward global redemption.

To see urgent themes of environmental reform pursued in poetry, fiction, diary, history, travelogue, geography, sermon, and even in an early conservationist tract is to understand the cultural obsessiveness of the idea. It broke boundaries of genre, caste, and philosophical persuasion. Despite its initiation and predominance as a New England idea, it cross-cut regional lines and was endorsed by those now as familiar as Whitman and obscure as George Perkins Marsh. It emerged in popular as well as "literary" writings and is to be found in private, introspective observations as well as in public utterance. Consistently since the seventeenth century it has formed an integral and important part of our cultural and literary history.

There is, however, a most compelling literary reason to examine themes of environmental reform in American literature. For writers' engagement in the American New Earth tells a story of ideology realized, finally, as literary art. From the epochs of Colonial, Enlightenment, and Romantic America came single literary works in which the ideology of environmental reform became a major and fully stated theme. In the Puritan Edward Johnson's *Wonder-Working Providence of Sions Saviour in New England* and in the Early National writer Joel Barlow's *The Columbiad* we have epic programs for a millennial American New Earth. Absorbed both by the concept of environmental reform and by its implementation, Johnson and Barlow write as literary engineers at once eager to bring about the New Earth and unsparing of plans and specifications for it. (Not surprisingly, technological power is uppermost in their writings long before actual technological devices had been developed for use.) But only with Whitman's Romantic *Song of the Broad-Axe* is this ideology of environmental reform realized in literary art of uncompromised achievement. Earlier, Johnson and Barlow had revealed the brave attempt—and ultimate failure—of American writers to be both activist-reformers and litterateurs. Whitman, however, avoided the mimetic problems of these programmatic minds and, in the mimetic tradition of Mather and of Thoreau, brought the powers of the visionary imagination to bear on ideas of the American New Earth, which he conceived not as social programs but as symbol. To look in turn at these different writers' responses to the American imperative of environmental reform prompts appreciation for the complexity and the enduring cultural vitality of ideas on the American New Earth. More than that, it offers a lesson in aesthetic shortcomings and splendid achievement in American literature.

Acknowledgments

It is time now that in American literature imperative of environmental reform be recognized as one principal human response to the landscape of the New World. The body of writings in which this theme appears suggests that the American New Earth is as important conceptually in our literature as are the pastoralism and the primitivism associated with the edenic South, with the Appalachian frontier, or with the wilderness. These are concepts which have been examined profoundly in the work of Perry Miller, Henry Nash Smith, Charles Sanford, and Leo Marx, and more recently by Roderick Nash, Annette Kolodny, and by John Seelye, who recognizes the complementary relation of pastoralism with the American New Jerusalem. Every student concerned with the American landscape, this one included, is much indebted to the work of these scholars.

The particular impetus for this study, however, has come from scholarship specifically on the role of eschatology in American thought. Ernest Tuveson and Ursula Brumm have made important contributions in this area, although readers of the following study will at once recognize my special debt to the work of Sacvan Bercovitch, especially to his monograph, "Horologicals to Chronometricals," and to his more recent *The Puritan Origins of the American Self.*

I am thankful to Everett H. Emerson for his helpful suggestions for revision of three early chapters, and for the texts of Puritan letters which he generously furnished from manuscripts of his own work in progress. I am grateful, too, for his making available to me his transcription of an unpublished essay of Hector St. John de Crèvecoeur, "The Rock of Lisbon." Others too have been helpful. At an early stage of the writing Helen Vendler gave me valuable editorial advice, and for years Brom Weber's approach to the literature of American studies has been influential in my work, while further back Miss Eva Mae Brown, a rare teacher, was demanding and encouraging in her classroom. At home Bill Tichi has been consistently supportive, sponsoring this work in ways only a spouse can appreciate.

Funding for the research of this study has come from several sources. In 1972-73 I enjoyed a year of work concurrently as an American Council of Learned Societies Study Fellow and as a Fellow of the Radcliffe Institute. In the summer of 1974 I had the help of a summer stipend from the National Endowment for the Humanities. Twice, in 1970 and in 1973, the Graduate School of Boston University awarded me summer stipends, and has provided funds for the preparation of the typescript, a job seen to its completion by Melinda Douglass and by Donna Scripture, to both of whom I am very thankful.

Some portions of this study have appeared elsewhere, including a somewhat different version of the second chapter, published as "Edward Johnson and the Puritan Territorial Imperative" in *Discoveries and Considerations: Essays on Early American Literature and Aesthetics Presented to Harold Jantz,* ed. Calvin Israel (Albany, N. Y.: State University of New York Press, 1976). Too, some parts from the third and fourth chapters appear under the title "The American Revolution and the New Earth" in *Early American Literature* (Winter 1977).

Certain writings of Joel Barlow and his correspondents are printed by permission of the Houghton Library and of the Yale University Library. Portions of my writing on Edward Johnson are reprinted by permission of the State University of New York Press.

1: A Kingdom unto the World

> Lands found and nations born, thou born America,
> For purpose vast, man's long probation fill'd,
> Thou rondure of the world at last accomplish'd.
>
> Walt Whitman, Passage to India

The American impulse—in fact, it can be called our imperative—to re-form the New World landscape came first from the Puritans, whose writings reveal their belief that reform of the American land was divinely directed. Just now the Puritan motives for earthly reform are being overlooked as writers of cultural history consider instead the *effects* of this three-centuries-old mission. These effects are of course troubling to those who, like William Gass, believe that a "geographical history" is "the only kind [America] can significantly have."[1] Understandably, an awareness of a damaged America environment has led contemporary analysts to indict past generations as destroyers bent on plunder of the new land. Sensitive to ecological and aesthetic abuses of the American continent, writers (here, Richard Goodwin) cite these environmental sins of the fathers: "We tore wealth from the land with heedless greed and did not hesitate to obliterate those aspects of nature which were of no immediate use or which obstructed expansion." In this line of thought it is not only greed but fear that caused the obliteration of much American wilderness, itself "not a benign cornucopia but an enemy to our hopes, even to our survival." Thus "the necessities of conquest must always arouse the desire not merely to subdue but to destroy."[2]

Goodwin's remarks express the late twentieth-century conviction that, geographically speaking, we are hoist with our own petard—or, to put it in D. H. Lawrence's terms, that the first Americans prostituted their virgin land, leaving us to face the consequences of three centuries of environmental spoliation.[3] In fact, the social self-castigation in this backward glance at America's geographical history suggests that we have at hand yet another version of the jeremiad, that familiar literary mode of lamentation present in American literature since the seventeenth century. Yet Goodwin's geo-jeremiad is a pronouncedly twentieth-century expression. It deplores the sins of an arrogant people who from the start misread Genesis and, as Lynn White, Jr., reminds us, ignored Saint Francis as a model of human harmony with the natural world.[4]

But this geo-jeremiad really says much more about contemporary values and sensibilities than about those of the earlier Americans who are its subject and who are held responsible for what John Updike calls "cleaving and baring the earth, attacking, reforming the enormity of nature we were given."[5] Undeniably, the American colonists and their heirs did set about changing the New World, exploiting its resources and, whenever possible, making its topography conform with their needs and desires. Yet the national literature reveals beneath the surfaces of their actions a pattern of motives for which *ideology* is the apt term. Based in expectations of the Apocalypse, of the New Heavens and New Earth promised in Revelation, American literature from the mid-seventeenth century onward shows a commitment to change the New World landscape, literally to re-form it. From motives at once eschatological and polemical, cosmic and yet specifically American, our writers continued to reiterate this commitment to environmental reform. Alternately programmatic and visionary in their mimesis, they have left a rich and complex and always urgent ideology of imperative change to the American landscape. The national literature from the Puritan era onward suggests that, far from believing they had carte blanche for promiscuous exploitation of the earth, for being what one writer calls "breakers" of the earth, Americans have altered the New World from the conviction that reform of the land was a divine imperative that must proceed together with the spiritual reform begun during the Protestant Reformation.[6]

It is not surprising that themes of imperative reform of the New World land should emerge in the literature of Puritan New England.

Such themes would not come logically from writings of the South, a region described as a second Eden whose reform was, of course, inconceivable. These edenic reports are familiar from the propagandistic and promotional New World travelogues written by and for Englishmen and available from about the turn of the sixteenth century. Typical is that of Philip Amadas and Arthur Barlow, two of Sir Walter Raleigh's captains who in 1584 sailed along the coast of North Carolina and reported shoal water redolent of "some delicate garden." Barlow spoke of the incomparable abundance, "incredible to be written," but nonetheless wrote of pearl and cedar, of peas that grew fourteen inches in ten days, and of such natives as "lived after the manner of the Golden Age" in a Southland comparable to "the first creation."[7]

From others this same Eden emerges repetitively to form a pattern whose pastoral and paradisal qualities have been closely examined in scholarship by Leo Marx and Charles Sanford, and most recently surveyed by John Seelye.[8] Attributes of full sufficiency, abundance, fecundity, harmony in human relationships, political equilibrium, a congenial balance between man and the natural world—all appear to some degree in the promotional travel literature of the South. In his often quoted ode, "To the Virginian Voyage" (1606), Michael Drayton calls Virginia "Earth's only Paradise":

> Where nature hath in store
> Fowl, venison, and fish
>   And the fruitful'st soil
>   Without your toil

Cataloging the trees and without reservation invoking the "golden age" and "nature's laws," Drayton typifies the promotional celebrants of the South.[9]

For their part, however, the Puritans were unswayed by promises of new Edens or El Dorados in Virginia. Not that they were insensitive or indifferent to favorable reports about typography, natural resources, or climate in America, but the urgent conviction that they were descendants of that Adam who had been sent from the garden to toil and earn bread from the sweat of his brow would have made it both idolatrous and blasphemous for them to seek out ready-made Edens in the New World.

They were of course encouraged by reports of a habitable New England. From the earliest English eye-witness account, John Brereton's tract on Capt. Bartholomew Gosnold's voyage (1602), they had learned of abundant fish and fowl, of timber and fur, of rock and stones "fit for building," and of "fat and lusty" soil in which grains sown in May had "sprung up nine inches and more" in just two weeks.[10]

Of all such accounts, that best suited to the Puritan and Pilgrim temperament was Capt. John Smith's utilitarian *Description of New England (1616),* which asserts the necessity for hard work even as it evokes a sense of natural bounty. As an advocate of the freehold system, Smith envisioned the American settler touched with "virtue and maganimity . . . planting and building a foundation for his posterity . . . from the rude earth by God's blessing and his own industry." Smith's New England is free of debilitating institutions, of high rents, fines, or snarls of litigation. It is "ground as temperate and as fruitful as any other parallel in the world," its seas teeming with fish, which, with hard work, would make the colonists as prosperous as the seafaring Dutch. For Smith opportunity is instanced everywhere. And while he knew of obstreperous Indians, he hints that if "discreetly handled" they could be recruited for work in "fishing, planting, and destroying woods."[11] Consistently, Smith's exhortation is based upon an ethic of industry and not of edenic leisure. In brief he anticipates the Puritans' (and Pilgrims') own justifications for emigrating, his reasons favoring the colonization of New England so congenial to theirs that the Massachusetts Puritan patriarchs (as well as such proponents of the Plymouth Colony as Robert Cushman) virtually paraphrase and explicate the remarks of the Elizabethan promoter of New World development.

The Puritan—subsequently the American—ideology of environmental reform, however, came from another source. True, Puritans were heartened by favorable reports on the climate and soil of New England. And they were ready to confront hard colonial life. But the source of their imperative to reform the New World land was not the travel literature but Scripture. In the Bible they found authority for their civil rights to "this sayd ground" in New England, for their expectations of an imminent Apocalypse, and for their self-identification with the wilderness.

Significantly, the Puritans (and before them the New Plymouth Pilgrims) did have an a priori vision of America so strongly conceived through Scripture that it subsumed the physical geography of the new place. When their keels struck gravel, in 1620 and 1630, the configuration of the land did not matter, nor did each settler's personal optical report as he looked about him. "Sight is a faculty; seeing, an art," the pioneering environmentalist George P. Marsh would say a little pompously more than two centuries later.[12] The Puritans had learned the art—in England. And their imperative to reform the New World landscape came, not from the palpable Massachusetts wood, rock, and swamp, but from an America of the English mind's eye—or rather, the mind's *eyes,* an intellectual Argus of these separate but related views on land rights, the Apocalypse, and the spiritual wilderness. The writings of these seventeenth-century Americans indicate that the palpable geography of the country was of little importance as they projected instead a vision of a metaphysically transformed state of being that would characterize the prophesied New Jerusalem. Enclosing the New England Puritan period at its beginning and its ending, both William Bradford and Cotton Mather took up the idea of this transformed state which they represented in the literary ways of visionary minds. Between them, just at midcentury, one Puritan of a literal cast of mind, Edward Johnson, fused his beliefs in the Apocalypse, in colonial land rights, and in the wilderness and brought forth the polemical *Wonder-Working Providence of Sions Saviour in New England* (1653). As we shall see, Johnson wrote the first major work in American literature to embody several trenchant themes of Americans' imperative reform of the New World landscape. Edward Johnson and his Puritan confreres formed, by their ideas and assumptions, an archive of human values that largely determined what Americans did with their New World. But their own attitudes toward the New World were focused first through the lens of Scripture.

II

Unlike the Jamestown settlers, the Puritans sought exhaustive biblical authority for their emigration and land appropriation in New

England. Of course, when in his ode Drayton writes, "You brave heroic minds . . . go and subdue," his Anglican voice assumes the prerogatives of Genesis in which man is enjoined to replenish and subdue the earth. So does the Anglican John Smith when he speaks of subduing New England by "fishing, planting, and destroying woods." But in the main the Puritans' justifications emerge in a network of exhaustive explanation and biblical exegesis. In 1631 John Cotton wrote, "Where there is a vacant place, there is liberty for the sonnes of Adam or Noah to come and inhabite, though they neither buy it, nor aske their [Indians'] leaves."[13] As the proponent of emigration, John White remarked, "Colonies have their warrent from God's direction and command, who, as soon as men *were,* set their taske, to replenish the earth, and to subdue it, Gen. 1.28." White asserts God's commandment as binding throughout historical time as long as "the earth yields empty places to be replenished," and he suggests that the prospective colonists would in fact be disobedient and neglectful of God's command if they did not emigrate.[14]

Echoes of Genesis pervade Puritan colonial literature, including its verse. In "Uppon the First Sight of New-England, June 29, 1638," Thomas Tillam imagines the "lambe of God," Christ, saying,

> Come my deare little flocke, who for my sake
> Have lefte your Country, dearest friends, and goods
> And Hazarded your lives o'th raginge floods
> *Posses this Country* . . . [Italics mine][15]

Possession of an inhospitable environment is Michael Wigglesworth's emphasis in a verse whose speaker explains God's covenant with man and beast "in their desert haunt":

> So that through places wilde and waste
> A single man, disarm'd
> Might journey many hundred miles,
> And not at all be harm'd.[16]

Wigglesworth's faith is of course based in Genesis, as is that of the Puritan Richard Steere in whose poem about aesthetic attitudes we find suggestions additionally of the hierarchical Great Chain of Being.

Steere's man of the golden mean is "One, who can as he list Compel the World/To be his Servant." "This man," says Steere, "owns God as his Master, makes the World his slave."[17]

The extension of man's dominion on earth was, from the Puritan perspective, the enlargement of Christ's kingdom pointing toward the Apocalypse. The psalmist asks, incredulous, "What is man, that thou art mindful of him?" but sings exultantly of the excellence of the Lord's name on earth where man has "dominion over all the works of [God's] hands" and "all *things* under his feet: all sheep and oxen, and the beasts of the field, the fowl of the air, and the fish of the sea, and whatsoever passeth through the paths of the seas" (Psalm 8). The Puritan intention to include Indians in the realm of their godly stewardship led John Cotton to remind the embarking colonists to "offend not the poore Natives" but make them "partakers of your precious faith even as you partake in their land."[18] That philanthropic tone did not long endure in Puritan-Indian affairs, but from the beginning of colonization Puritan dominion over the New World space embraces a double imperative: God makes room there for his chosen people, but the saints are themselves responsible for an enlargement of Christ's kingdom.

Even war and pestilence seemed to be divine means of Puritan territorial expansion. One of Cotton Mather's wonders of the Invisible world was that God cast out the heathen (via a smallpox epidemic) to make room for his true Vine, the Puritan saints. Even after the horrible decimation of the English settlers in King Philip's War (1675–77), William Hubbard trusted God's hidden motive to rout the Indians from "many *rich and Fertile places* . . . whereby it may be gathered as we hope, that God is making way to settle a better people in their rooms, and in their stead."[19] And Increase Mather spoke of "the Heathen People amongst whom we live, and whose land the Lord God of our Fathers hath given to us for a rightfull possession."[20]

As recipients, however, the Puritans must actively expand Christ's kingdom. A contributor to the Eliot *Tracts* said of Puritan missionary work, "Hereby *the Kingdom of Christ is enlarged,* and the promise made unto him in the Covenant between him and his Father accomplished, his *Dominion shall be from Sea to Sea,* and from the floud unto the Worlds end, and therefore his designe is upon all the kingdoms of the Earth, that he may take possession of them.[21] In proper perspective, man took dominion in order that Christ's dominion could be assured. The Lord had created the earth, "not in vain," but "to be inhabited" (Isa. 45:18).

Before setting sail for New England the Puritans had anticipated the obvious objection that the land in their patent was not *vacuum domicilium* but long in the possession of the Indians who were, as John Cotton put it, "Proprietaries of the places which [the Puritans will come to] inhabit."[22] It was John Winthrop who most comprehensively answered the demurral with his favorite distinction between carnal naturalism and cultivated civility. He wrote that land "which lies common & hath never been replenished or subdued is free to any that will possesse and improve it," then explained that God had given men a "double right to the earth." one natural and one civil, the first pertinent to the nomadic life ("when men held the earth in common every man soweing, and feeding where he pleased"). But with the increase of people and cattle and the custom of enclosure "and peculiar manurance," God endowed men with a preemptive "Civile right." As for the New England Indians,

> they inclose noe land neither have any settled habitation nor any tame cattle to improve the land by, & soe have noe other but a naturall right to those countries So as if wee leave them sufficient for their use wee may lawfully take the rest.[23]

Others reinforce Winthrop's thesis. An anonymous essayist remarked that "Improvement of all his sayd ground . . . is one of the principall clauses of all that grand Charter made by the greate Lord of the wholl earth and King of Nations unto Adam: Replenish the earth and subdue it."[24] John Eliot had similarly remarked that "the whole bent of mens mindes, in such Exigents [of dispersal] are to build, plant, fixe, and settle themselves in the places of their desire."[25] Ostensibly Eliot spoke of the dispersion and resettlement of the Israelites after Nimrod's rebellion, but he really used the biblical events as a metaphor for the New Englanders fleeing England's own sectarian Babel.

Some New England colonists remarked on the Indian practice of burning the woodlands semiannually in spring and fall, and some of them regretted the scenes of black desolation. But for the most part Puritan writers kept silent on the implications of this Indian practice. Well they might, since the myth of the uninterrupted forest was necessary to Puritan planters justifying appropriation of New World lands on the basis of aboriginal failure to improve it. The Indians, as more recent geographical study has shown, did by Puritan standards "improve" the land by altering the forest cover far out of proportion to their numbers.[26] They burned underbrush in order to attract deer and other wildlife to the new green shoots, and, with incisions into sapwood, they deadened large trees whose thick foliage blocked sunlight necessary to a maize crop. Perhaps because the trunks and upper branches were left standing in a look of perpetual winter and the clearings themselves were abandoned by Indians after several seasons of a diminishing crop, the Puritans could avoid hard questions about Indian improvement of the land. They could assume that the Indian old fields, as they called them, were neglected from fecklessness of providentially abandoned when Indians died. Or they could view the Indian efforts as divine preliminaries to the Puritan planting ("The Lord mitigated their [Puritan] labours by the Indian frequent fiering of the woods"). The Puritan prerogative to take dominion remained intact, supported by Winthrop's warranty of private property.

These Puritan efforts to legitimate claims to New World land by promising to subdue and improve it surfaces in law and custom, too. An *Abstract* of the early New England laws says that the basis of land assignment was "partly by the number of beasts, by which a man is fit to occupy the land assigned to him, and subdue it."[27] *The Winthrop Papers* record enough tenant-landlord squabbles for us to understand that such improvement projects as fencing, tree pruning, and repair to thatch and clapboard were contracted for (as they were in the English counties), quite apart from the rent money. These obligations for improvement give special urgency to John Cotton's advice to the emigrants to "strive to attain the favor of your landlord [God], and be obedient to him" since he has provided shelter in a "foreine land." Again, Winthrop: "we deny that the Indians heere can have any title to more lands then they can improve. . . . God gave the earth to be subdued, ergo a man can have no more land than he can subdue."[28]

Statements like these are multiplied in Puritan writings and in part reflect man's very oldest aspiration to control nature, in this instance by transposing domestic animals and agricultural methods to a wilderness. But the issue is more complex here. Vitally important in the logic of Winthrop and his cohort is the tenet that improvement of the natural landscape constitutes civil right to it—and is prerequisite to a theological right. In other words, man evinces his dominion (and correlatively his stewardship over God's created world) by making a visible impress upon the natural world. He legitimates his claim to America by manifestly improving it. The Puritans' land claim was based literally upon their ability to make a mark upon America in the name of terrestrial enhancement. The Massachusetts Bay planters' theoretical justifications for claiming American land indicate not only that they came to plant a spiritual garden of churches in the wilderness but that they sailed with a heavy duty incumbent upon them, namely, an obligation to alter as much of the wilderness as they felt could earn them their right to live there.

To be sure, this beatified homesteading included concern for the civil amelioration of human life in New England. "Why should we stand striving heere for places of habitation etc," asked Winthrop about England, where a man spends "as muche labor and cost [for] an Acre or 2 of lande, as would procure him many hundred acres as good or better in another place?"[29] Joining the consensus of theorists of economics in seventeenth-century England, Winthrop speaks of "a lande over-burdened with people," a land grown "weary of her Inhabitants." He hates this cheapening of human life, the subversion of God's generic hierarchy that sinks man, the "most pretious of all creatures," to an economic valuation below that of domestic beasts. The confinement of a burgeoning population of despised poor in England while an entire fertile continent lies virtually empty of "the chiefest earthly blessinge" appalls Winthrop and forms a cornerstone of his argument in favor of colonization. Others agree. In language anticipating eighteenth-century attitudes, Thomas Thorowgood speaks of colonization as "advanc[ing] the good of mankinde in general." And John White suggests that horticulture itself be the model for civil settlement, since the principle "that *a large place best assures sufficiency*" holds for mankind as for plants, which "wither and decay, if . . . penned up in a little nursery," at best a few of the strongest surviving and starving the rest. In White's view, colonization promotes the common weal on two fronts: governmentally, "the setling of new States requireth justice and affection to the common good," while geophysically, "the taking in of large Countreys presents a naturall remedy against covetousnesse, fraud and violence."[30]

The Puritans expressed similar sentiments well after the initial New England colonization. Some fifteen years after the near-traumatic exodus of the Hooker party into Connecticut, John Eliot found in events of the Old Testament encouragement that the American dispersal enhanced civilization. He wrote, "The divided world [drew the sons of Noah] unto further and further spreadings, insomuch that men's minds being thus taken up, and their hands imployed, and now also living at great distances from each other, whereby all occasion of strife was taken away, hence the peace of all nations was not only continued, but grew stronger and stronger." Even the Indians were not excluded from life's felicities. "We shall come in with the good leave of the natives," says Winthrop, "who finde benefitt already by our Neighborhood and learne of us to improve it to more use then before they could doe the whole."[31] These are remarkably secular pronouncements, addressed as they are to economic and political life. The Hereafter, the state of regeneracy or unregeneracy, the question of purity of church membership—all such urgent questions are momentarily suspended as the most secular virtues of the New World are set forth. Central to these remarks is the belief that moral values inhere in a spacious life setting and that, regardless of the salient question of one's eternal salvation or damnation, earthly life can be civil and dignified if one but has ample space in which to work and breathe.

But because these Puritans had interpreted Scripture so as to invalidate "natural" land rights in favor of "civil" ones in the name of earthly improvement and subjugation, the fear of terrestrial philandering weighed heavily upon their conscience. Failure to make a civilizing impress upon the land they claimed could cancel their self-defined, biblically interpreted rights to those lands. There was the danger, in short, that the Puritans might defeat themselves in the trap of their own logic.

Thus, they worried about land greed long before Cotton Mather

uttered plaintive soul-searchings in the *Magnalia* about overextension
into the wilderness. In the early 1640s Nathanial Ward had complained about "the lavish liberality of the [General] Court in giving
away the Countrye." An essayist, endorsing Ward's view, deplored
the "unwarantable greate extente of Townes . . . beyonde all hope of
Subdoeing, or any Improvement."[32] The Indian War historian
William Hubbard was to impute the firing of Medfield during King
Philip's War to the folly of such overreaching. "The Inhabitants being
every where apt to engross more Land into their hands than they
were able to subdue," writes Hubbard, it was "as if they were seated
in the midst of a heap of bushes."[33] Increase Mather was vehement
on the point of land greed. While "first Planters" were satisfied with
"one Acre for each person . . . and after that with twenty Acres for a
Family, how Men have since coveted after the earth." Mere territory
had now taken precedence over Christian law and church, and both
were forsaken "for land and elbow-room."[34]

From these remarks we not only understand a Puritan tension
between ambition and ability in settlement but see how alien would
be the concept of an American Eden. For geophysically an American
Eden would be anathema to the Puritan commitment to transform
the natural environment, since an earthly paradise invites no reform
whatever. Mitigated toil in a more fertile river valley such as the
Connecticut or Hudson is one thing, but paradise quite another. The
Massachusetts marshlands are far better suited conceptually to the
improvement or subjugation of the earth than is the Virginia Eden of
the promotional tract. (In this regard the cessation of such effulgent
accounts of New England as those of the Puritan writers Francis
Higginson and William Wood probably was due as much to the
Puritan commitment to "improve" and "subdue" as it was to the
grudging soil and abusive winters.)[35]

The obligation to improve the New World manifestly may explain
why such writers as Johnson, Winthrop, and William Hubbard could,
with certain qualifications, approve of the geographic dispersal in the
northeastern part of the continent in a way that they could *not*
accept the departure of New Englanders for the Caribbean Islands,
for Virginia, or even for that "full-fed land," England itself. In contrast to the rustic Bay, England must have seemed in memory to be
what in *Richard II* Shakespeare's John of Gaunt describes as "this

other Eden, demi-paradise" (2.1.42). Something more than social
desertion seems at issue in these cases. For an escape to the West
Indies, the South, or to the comforts of England embodied the fantasy of a voyage to Eden in which improvement was inconceivable.
If, as the historical geographer Yi-Fu Tuan remarks, the desert has
traditionally in the Western imagination been a place inviting transformation for human use, then the Puritans' "desart wilderness,"
that ostensible tautology, may in fact have special meaning as the
unsown place that compels man to take dominion by reforming it in
a way that would be unthinkable in an earthly paradise.[36] In the
Puritan view, God deliberately imposed the onus of hardship,
"knowing that your heart would have beene taken off this worke,
which he must have done . . . had you met with a rich land filled
with all plenty."[37]

The New England Puritans who did not "abandon" the colonies
apparently had their fantasy, too, but it was one of advancing civilization, very clearly revealed in the first map cut in the new world,
the 1677 John Foster map of New England included in William
Hubbard's *Narrative of the Troubles with the Indians.* The book is
chiefly concerned with the events of the recent King Philip's War and
with the geographical extent of Indian affliction of the settlers. But
the graphic representation of New England in an American book led
the poet Benjamin Tompson to boast,

> *Moxon* who drew two Globes, or whosoere,
> Must make a third, or else the old ones tear,
> To find a Room for thy new Map, by which
> Thy friends and Country all thou dost enrich.[38]

On the map little, gabled figures of buildings represent settlement
which, south of the Merrimack River, appears to be very extensive.
The figures, which were conventional in European maps of the late
sixteenth century, look like tokens on a real-estate game board and
are for the most part of uniform size, as if the most remote settlement were as large and populous as those around Boston. According
with map conventions of the day, the formidably mountainous
Berkshires appear as hillocks, and the forest is reduced to a few
clusters of shrubs interspersed among the settlements. Only north of
the Merrimack in the Maine region (which was outside jurisdiction of

the Massachusetts-Connecticut-Plymouth Confederation) does the
map maker acknowledge the actual wilds. There the verdure is larger,
and wild animals (rabbit, bear, wolf) are drawn in, in addition to two
Indians, who more resemble sporting nymphs than the satanic agents
whose barbarities are set forth endlessly in the volume in which the
map is bound.

Scholars continue to debate the origins of the Foster map, which is
evidently a copy whose original is lost.[39]   Yet the depiction of such
pervasive English settlement graphically supports Puritan statements
about subduing and improving New World land. Indeed, binding *this*
map in a story essentially of colonial defeat and decimation makes a
bold, aggressive statement on Puritan prerogatives in the New World.
Both primitive and awry in its compass points, and badly scaled, the
map is nonetheless important for the vision it asserts in the midst of
documented death and ruin. In his text Hubbard complains of the
Machiavellianism of an Indian intertribal alliance proposed because
the natives were alarmed by English expansionism. He objects to this
tribal confederation intended to stop the settlers. But the map validates the basis of Indian fears in its representation of a New England
preponderantly subdued and "improved"—in short, reformed as a
kind of English suburb.

Taken together, all these Puritan remarks about land appropriation
in the New World constitute what some years ago Chester Eisinger
called a justification for taking the land, one which Alden Vaughan
finds to have been congruent with contemporary European
practice.[40]   In and of themselves, the Puritan statements do not comprise an ideology. The promised enclosure, subjugation, and improvement of forested lands is all but a civil preliminary to the
"theological right" by which man expands Christ's kingdom. As one
writer said, "I cannot yet se[e] that any man hath Theologicall Right
unto any possession without a practical care of the performance of
this principall Condicion . . . [that he] improve all his sayd
ground."[41]   Not surprisingly, after the initial few years of settlement,
theories about land appropriation cease in Puritan writings, since the
visibility of settlement canceled the need for theoretics. The directives of Genesis became an assumption, explicated anew only when
conflicting land claims arose.

There the issue might have rested, had not the Puritans been so mindful of the imminent Apocalypse. That is, without their expectations of the schedule of the final events of human history, the justifications for land appropriation in the New World might now be viewed only as one pre-Enlightenment point of American intellectual history concerned with the civil and natural rights of man. But this was not to be. For the final events prophesied in the Book of Revelation were so much in the Puritans' minds that we can call theirs an apocalyptic mentality. It was this consciousness of an apocalyptic—and especially millennial—future that elevated their theories of settlement into an ideology on the environment. From the Puritan belief that the Christian Millennium would originate in New England and that God intended Puritans to bear major responsibility for its site preparation came a literature fraught with millennial themes. Coupled with the directives of Genesis, that literature propounded an American ideology of environmental reform.

III

For the Puritans the emigration to America seemed not only to be economically and religiously propitious but cosmically momentous, essentially because of their conception of history founded in Christian typology. The messianic Jesus of the New Testament had enabled Christian exegetes from the Church Fathers onward to the Puritans to find a transcendent coherence in the Old and New Testaments. Their exegesis revealed a historic pattern which, in light of the prophecies in the books of Daniel, Isaiah, and Revelation, subsumed the past and present and pointed forward to the Apocalypse. In the seventeenth century the Puritans thought the Apocalypse to be imminent. Using Christian typology, they found an ascending pattern of specific events that proved the imminent redemption of Israel, itself figurally the true church or chosen people. Accordingly, eschatology, the study of the final events in human history, was a major Puritan preoccupation. Just as Puritans had deduced a formula for the individual's experience of salvation from his effectual calling to his ultimate sanctification in Christ, so did they discern an apposite, demonstrable pattern of events by which a communal Israel moved even closer toward redemption. In the cosmos each progressive step in the pattern was markedly closer to the ultimate redemption at the Day of Judgment. Events of the Apocalypse comprised the finale of this pattern, and Puritans believed them to be in motion.[42]

In particular, the Puritans in Old and New England believed that God's Johannine promises were coming due, that the prophecy in books 20 and 21 of Revelation was about to be realized. After a period of upheaval and persecution God would decree the suppression of evil on earth, the chaining up of Satan, and the onset of the New Heavens and New Earth of the Millennium. During that epoch of one thousand years Christ would dwell and reign among his chosen people before loosing Satan for the terrible final battle of the triumphantly righteous against the ultrademonic peoples of Gog and Magog. Their defeat would signal the very end of human history, and, for God's own Israel, the "chosen remnant" or "choice grain," there would be eternal heavenly bliss.

We now have abundant scholarship on the history of apocalyptic doctrine through the Christian millennia. In the first of his two books on the subject, Ernest Tuveson points out how attentive were the Protestant reformers to apocalyptic passages through the Old and New Testaments, and how for the Christian exegete the Book of Revelation became an apocalyptic schedule, virtually a timetable legible upon the conversion of its many symbols into sequential periods and events of human history. Tuveson, like other scholars, sees in Luther's commentary on Revelation a new model of the exegetical method, one that reinstated apocalyptic doctrine in a temporal framework.[43] For Luther understood historical events on earth as correlates to the symbols in Revelation. These symbols were therefore referential guides to history and to the future. Though he thought that the Christian Millennium had passed, Luther's method of correlation opened the way for others, notably for Thomas Brightman together with the German Johann Alsted and the Englishman Joseph Mede, to reinterpret the exact correlation so as to project the Millennium into the future.

Puritan New England shared these expectations, a point which Charles Sanford established and which others, principally Sacvan Bercovitch, have pursued in examining Puritan typology and eschatology and the rhetoric of their expression. Consequently we now understand Puritan literature to be rife with apocalyptic themes.

It does appear that in the course of one century of New England Puritanism there is a marked change in writings on the Apocalypse. The first, emigrant generation were concerned with "designing and constructing a grand model" and accordingly emphasized the idea of a national covenant, of a communal "Citty upon a hill" exemplary of reformed Christianity and, moreover, of the New Jerusalem. Closely allied in theology with English Puritans and eager to encourage emigration and to keep secure the royal charter in their possession, the first-generation leaders of Puritan New England wrote of their apocalyptic expectations with a strong community emphasis and with cis-Atlantic implications.

Later on, in the 1640s and 1650s, when the Civil War, the Commonwealth, and then the Protectorate made it appear that the vanguard of the Reformation had moved away to Old England, polemical American voices turned urgently to myth making, justifying the particular New England way with an apocalyptic emphasis that furthered the national epic, a point we shall see especially in the work of Edward Johnson. Later still, after 1660, amid "the crumbling of their design, the waning of their piety, and the waxing of their prosperity," the New England writers felt required "to remain loyal to a design that had failed."[44] In part they did so by making the jeremiad a celebratory genre, one that, as Bercovitch points out, continued to affirm the destined American New Jerusalem even as writers insulated that golden city from the vagaries of history by representing it in purely visionary modes of rhetoric.

Scholarship may continue to reveal subtle and important shiftings in the literary expression of apocalyptic doctrine against a changing social and political background. Suffice it to say here that apocalyptic concerns evidently pervaded New England Puritans' lives, not only as one article of faith but as a call to action. As J.F. Maclear says, "The cosmic struggles of the Apocalypse were not so much a matter of study as of participation." They invited "personal enlistment" and "activism." For Puritans the Apocalypse was a matter not only for surveillance but for engagement, since the "fervent millennial ideology in the English Puritan community" was held "in an especially vital form" by the immigrants to Massachusetts.[45]

Clearly, the New World landscape offered Puritan colonists an extraordinary opportunity for apocalyptic activism. Believing that the

Millennium was imminent, that one thousand years of Christian fraternity stretched before them, they could find their work of settlement to be an apocalyptic preparation. Having obligated themselves to subdue and to improve the New World lands, they could adduce from that work apocalyptic value. Especially in the writings of Edward Johnson (but not exclusive to him) we find that coupling of Genesis with Isaiah and Revelation which leads to the proclamation that God's chosen people were commissioned to subdue and improve the New World land in order to prepare the millennial New Earth. Some of the Puritans were convinced that God had called them to this task. Never did they view themselves as exploiters, but rather as blessed developers.

In this light the reform of the natural landscape of America was thus no mere colonial obligation but God's own imperative. It lay within the inexorable schedule of fixed events in the calendar of scriptural prophecy. To some colonists it became an incumbent and inescapable charge. Plausibly, the Holy Commonwealth of Massachusetts was not only a spiritual proving ground inhabited by a body of visible saints but the probable, palpable acreage of the Christian Millennium. In England the Puritan halberds felled Cavaliers, but those of New England, in action no less cosmically important, brought down the forest.

IV

The Bible offered the Puritans doctrines imparting cosmic meaning to their colonizing efforts; but representation of the endeavor in literature was complicated. In doctrine, the directives of Genesis and the promises especially of Isaiah and Revelation enabled New Englanders to feel that the exigencies of colonial life were compatible with the theological imperatives of the spirit. And, in brief, Puritan writings did represent colonial efforts as intrinsically apocalyptic. Roger Clap closed his *Memoirs* with an exhortation to his children "to build a millennial New England," and John Underhill, who lavished upon New England the descriptive phrases of a promotional tract, wrote of his certainty that colonial "outward troubles" were but afflictions sanctified by God. "Better in a fiery furnace," he wrote, "better in a lion's den in the midst of all the roaring lions with Christ."[46] Underhill's figure is apocalyptically apt, since the episode in the lions' den precedes Daniel's prophetic dream and causes King Darius to proclaim Daniel's as the living God whose kingdom is indestructible and whose "dominion shall be even unto the end" (Dan. 6:26). Scripture really made possible the connection between woodland hacking and hewing in Massachusetts and the purely spiritual life of New England Puritanism.

Difficult problems, however, existed for a writer attempting to represent both of these areas of the Puritan colonial experience in language not confined to biblical metaphor. Theirs was the problem of mimesis of the actual colonial experience within an apocalyptic framework. As Bercovitch writes, "In immediate geographical terms . . . America was consecrated from eternity for the New England way, [although] . . . to all appearances what [the Puritans] called America was just another plot of ground in a fallen world."[47] The mimetic problem lay in merging the geography with its apocalyptic meaning, that is, in finding a language both true to personal experience of colonial hardship and balanced with belief in an imminent Millennium. There was the task, too, of discovering a rhetoric of celebration and of validation, but one that stopped short of exaggeration. More difficult still, the available record of response to the New England landscape per se through the 1630s and early forties was categorically limited, dividing essentially into two modes, that of the familiar promotional tract and that reflecting the inevitable disappointments from life in the wilds.

For the former, we find one Edmund Browne scouting the "good places" of the New England terrain in 1638 in phrases that echo the edenic reports on Virginia and New England more than a half-century earlier: "lusty and fat" soil, an "abundance of strawberries, rasberries, gooseberries red and green," assorted melons and herbs, a "great store of fish," plentiful game and fowl. The Indians are "subdued" and mosquitoes exterminated.[48] Similar in tone is Underhill's *New and Experimentall Discoverie of New England* (1638), which extols the geographical virtues of Long Island, the Hudson Valley, and Maine's Casco Bay, but without allying those places with the millennial prophecy he cites in his reference to Daniel.[49] Less

rhapsodic but still celebratory, Philip Vincent's *True Relation* of the
Pequot War (1638) praises the fertility of the soil and the colonial
prosperity that results from mutual responsibility for the common
weal. Nowhere, however, does Vincent pursue themes of divine
meaning inherent to colonial life on New England soil.[50]

Meanwhile, on the other side there were inevitable voices of disil-
lusionment. In the eighteenth century these would crescendo as the
philosophes questioned the feasibility of civilized life in the new
continent. But some disaffected seventeenth-century New Englanders
wrote to correct earlier edenic reports. To one, the New England
agronomy had been celebrated from "affection, not judgment," and
he spoke in 1637 of sandy, "cold and barren" soil rapidly—and
frighteningly—depleted. "For the present we make a shrift to live,"
he says, looking desperately to the future, imagining Indian massacre
or "famine and misery . . . if God discover not means to enrich the
land." A less anxious but very blunt voice concurred a few years
later: "The air of the country is sharp, the rocks many, the trees
innumerable, the grass little, the winter cold, the summer hot, the
gnats in summer biting, the wolves at midnight howling."[51] Thomas
Dudley's "Letter to the Countess of Lincoln," a precursor to
Franklin's "Information to Those Who Would Remove to America,"
emphasized how arduous and painful was the work of
colonization.[52] Dudley was not the only Puritan to observe that
while he wrote the ink froze in his well.

The tonal range of negative reports on the geography of New
England is evident on one hand in Richard Mather's circumspect
comment that the land "looks not pleasant to the eye in many
places, being a rude and unsubdued wilderness yet with labor yields
sufficient sustenance for men of moderate means,"[53]   and on the
other in this spoof in doggerel at the New England Canaan of the
promotional tract:

> There twice a year all sorts of grain
> Doth down from heaven like hailstones rain;
> . . . .
> Wine sweet and wholesome drops from trees,
> As clear as crystal, without lees.[54]

The verse tweaks Puritans for striving after church purity, but the principal complaint is against the fraud of a New England Canaan.

In sum we have two opposing kinds of response to the New England geography, one celebrating fecundity (at least sufficiency) and the other announcing hardship or bare subsistence. But in none of these remarks are there apocalyptic overtones, let alone specific millennial citations. Through the seventeenth century Benjamin Tompson, William Hubbard, and Cotton Mather would refer to New England (without geographic elaboration) as utopian, but neither their writing nor these foregoing descriptions of the landscape contain corroborative hints of the Christian New Earth. In fact, Bercovitch finds that by itself eschatological theory "in history as in autobiography—could not altogether compensate for the palpable insecurities of day-by-day events: planting and reaping, suppressing schismatics, raising children, fighting Indians, maintaining order in an increasingly complex and heterogeneous society."[55] In literature he finds the biographical exemplary life embodying the self and the nation to be an aesthetically successful resolution of this disjunction in the early American experience.

Biography, however, was not the only means of resolution. From two major writers of Puritan New England we have an evocative, visionary New Earth presented without a literary fusion of actual colonial geography with the idea of the New Jerusalem. Both William Bradford and Cotton Mather avoided the mimetic problems of that fusion. Bracketing the Puritan epoch at its beginning and its closing, Bradford and Mather both espoused ideas of the New Earth in literary ways that enabled them to overarch problems and processes of actual environmental change in the New World. As purely visionary writers with millennial convictions, they had not to elide geographical change with spiritual reforms. For in the realm of vision alone—theologically the spiritual state or, in literary terms, ontology represented in metaphor or in symbol—there would exist no need to invest American geography per se with values of the consecrated New Earth of the Millennium. To visionary imaginations tangible acreage need not be mimetically important; no more the surveyor's measure or colonial demographics. That nexus of the actual geography of America with the prophesied New Earth instead absorbed the writer of a literal cast of mind. As we shall see, it was Edward Johnson who understood colonizing work literally as millennial site preparation. In American literature he initiated a programmatic view of the New Earth, a prescriptive, utilitarian approach amplified in the eighteenth century in the works of Joel Barlow and ramifying further in the nineteenth-century writings of Cooper and Bancroft and others.

Meanwhile, early and late in the Pilgrim-Puritan epoch, Bradford and Mather brought forth the purely prophetic vision of the New Earth. They embodied in their writings that qualitative, spiritually emphatic strain of millennialism which, by way of Thoreau, culminated two centuries later in the American New Earth of Whitman's own poetic vision. Bradford's, and especially Mather's, conceptions of the American New Earth interest us here because these writers suggest how in mimesis the visionary writer could transcend that actual and programmatic New Earth forever teetering on conditions and schedules to be met, its literary integrity often threatened by thematic contradiction as anticipated ideals collided with actuality in the present.

William Bradford is engaging here, first because his most extensive and inviting description of the New England landscape is to be found, not in his acknowledged masterpiece, *Of Plymouth Plantation,* but in the so-called *Mourt's Relation,* a Cape Cod explorer's and settler's diary coauthored with Edward Winslow. There we find a wealth of detail on the topography, the soils, the natural resources. "So goodly a land . . . caused us to rejoice," wrote Bradford, remarking on the "good harbour and pleasant bay . . wherein a thousand sail of ships may safely ride." He affirms "the greatest store of fowl," the air that "agreeth well with that in England," the "running brooks of very sweet fresh water," earth of "excellent black mould," and good ceramic clay. Intermittently Bradford acknowledges the "especial providence of God" pleased to deliver the settlers from Indians, then proceeds to catalog trees, streams, "champaigne and hills," at last to assert his disinterest, no doubt dreading to be thought a promoter.[56] But, significantly, Bradford's buoyant survey of the Cape Cod geography does not carry over to *Of Plymouth Plantation.* Contrarily, his history is memorable for the tableaux of vulnerable colonists beginning life in the forbidding land of "wild beasts and wild men." The contrast in landscaping cannot be explained sufficiently by the disparate genres of the two works or by the joint authorship of *Mourt's Relation*. Instead, it is in Bradford's eschatology that we may understand motives for the different landscapes.

Importantly, like the Massachusetts Bay planters, Bradford was preoccupied with millennial expectations, though for him they did not center geographically upon New England. As Jesper Rosenmeier points out, the Plymouth Separatists sought a country that was heavenly and not earthly. Their New Jerusalem would be *in* but not *of* this world, and they therefore were indifferent to the specific, physical site of their settlement as long as they left behind the "spiritual darkness and corruption" rampant in Europe.[57] Yet Bradford saw signs of that Millennium, filling his history with anticipations of the New Heavens and the New Earth. He recites "a great hope and inward zeal they had . . . for the propagating and advancing the gospel of the kingdom of Christ in these remote parts of the world." The conversion of the Indians would fulfill the prophecy of the marriage of Jew and Gentile, itself preliminary to the coming of Christ's kingdom. At several points Bradford connects the Plymouth emigrants typologically with the Israelites led by Moses, and he speaks of the advancing of the Gospel, of the coming harvests of the Lord, of the Light of the Reformation "breaking out" and glowing since with spiritually exponential brightness.[58] Several scholars have mentioned Bradford's apocalyptic assumptions, but Rosenmeier has looked further to the writings of the Plymouth group, including those of Robert Cushman and John Robinson, to enable readers to see the eschatological depth in *Of Plymouth Plantation*. Especially in the 1640s when Christ's kingdom seemed to be advancing elsewhere in the world, Bradford tried to "resurrect a bygone holiness" characterisitc of the Plymouth beginnings.[59]

In this context it is clear that *Of Plymouth Plantation* is what Rosenmeier calls it, "a deeply and deliberately prophetic book" and one which can sustain in theme an inverse relation between material and spiritual wealth. One of the very richest moments for the Plymouth settlers is that of their arrival on a wintry Cape Cod whose "weather-beaten face, and the whole country, full of woods and thickets, represented a wild and savage hue."[60] The starkness of this landscape suggests to us Bradford's reason to omit the felicitous

environmental information so abundant in *Mourt's Relation.*
Bradford's New Earth is not of palpable New England soil. It may be
the wonder of the world that Christ's churches flourish there, but
explicitly New England is only "a resting place for so many of the
Lord's people," "a roost" from which the unclean must be
banished.[61] Bradford's word choice conveys his sense of New
England space as a stopping place, decidedly not the site of the
chiliad. He can thus use the dreariness, even the repulsiveness, of the
New England environment as a strategy to emphasize the primacy of
the collective spiritual life. His New Earth is so centered in the communal spiritual vitality of the Pilgrims that he can fairly boast,
geographically speaking, that Cape Cod is no Canaan:

> Neither could they . . . go up to the top of Pigsah to view from
> this wilderness a more goodly country to feed their hopes; for
> which way soever they turned their eyes (save upward to the
> heavens) they could have little solace or content in respect of any
> outward objects.[62]

There is inward solace and content, of course, but in "the Spirit of
God and His grace." Bradford emphasizes its efficacy at the moment
when the Pilgrims "were ready to perish in this wilderness."[63] It is
but one of his repeated invocations of "wilderness," a term certain to
elicit in his intended audience a cluster of predictable responses
centered in Scripture. Replete with stories and themes based upon
the precariousness of human life in a hostile natural environment, the
Bible in part represented the wilderness as an indication of God's
attitude toward men, since it was self-evident that God could manipulate wilderness conditions so as to bless or to blast his creatures.

Bradford, as well as the Puritans of the Massachusetts Bay, understood not only the negative connotations of "wilderness," those pertinent to death, chaos, and punishment, but the existence of positive
values of contemplation, insight, self-testing, sanctuary, and the
promise of human fulfillment. George Williams's excellent study
delineates these varied meanings in their biblical sources, and Peter
Carroll documents their presence in the literature of Puritan New
England. From his work we see that contemporary readers of
Bradford, or for that matter of any Puritan writer, could understand
wilderness as "a place of redemptive, covenantal bliss" and of

"testing and tutelage," as well as a haven and place of purgation or consecration. From such figures as Elijah, John the Baptist, and the Seer of Revelation, the desert or wilderness takes on ascetic values of sanctuary, strengthened or purified faith, and special closeness to God—all meanings abundantly evident in Bradford and, as Carroll shows, present in the full range of Puritan writers.[64]

To encounter in *Of Plymouth Plantation* the terms "wilderness" or "desert" (or the contrary "garden") is to apprehend the great extent to which Bradford refers to the spiritual state of the settlers at Plymouth and not to the geography of Cape Cod. The grace of God extended to the Pilgrims in the wilderness anticipates the future attainment of paradise. It prefigures the spiritual state of the New Earth. Intermittently in his history Bradford writes in brief of the soils around the Massachusetts Bay, comparing them with those of Virginia without the investment of meanings either of the biblical wilderness or of Canaan. For New England agronomy is simply irrelevant to the imminent New Earth. Thus America can be "vast and unpeopled," at once "fruitful and fit" and "devoid of all civil inhabitants," being populated only by "savage and brutish men which range up and down."[65]

To emphasize spiritual solidarity in so unpromising a setting serves Bradford's purpose well, since he brings the spiritual community into sharp focus against the stark, savage background. (Later in his history he works in reverse, citing the seduction of a generous geography that spiritually impoverishes the colony. Those who "grow in their outward estates" and seek beyond Plymouth "a great deal of ground to keep them" threaten that Plymouth which is, in Rosenmeier's words, "a prophetic model of the heavenly city."[66] Virtually all critics have observed in Puritan literature the irony of material prosperity accompanying spiritual decline. It interests us here because Bradford never once is tempted to adduce the coming of Christ's kingdom from the prosperity of colonial New England. It is a spiritual coherence that concerns him, not that of geography. In the "prophetic" *Of Plymouth Plantation* Bradford keeps intact his themes of spiritual community by omitting the very phrases which in *Mourt's Relation* tend to evoke the pleasure and promise of an actual Canaan. Spatially Bradford thus keeps his vision of the New Earth clear of the actual geography of New England.

For Cotton Mather, however, the literary separation of space from spiritual life was not so easily accomplished. Sharing the eschatological faith of the Plymouth governor (while deferring the Millennium yet one more century into the future), Mather differed from Bradford on one crucial point in that he, Mather, believed in the geographic chiliad. He thought the New Earth would be not only a spiritual community but one situated in earthly space. This belief forced Mather to take upon himself literary problems that never burdened Bradford. Believing the New Earth to be imminent, Mather needed a plausible site for it, yet well understood how rotten with sin, savagery, and impiety was his contemporary New England. In his writings he needed a way to affirm the forthcoming New Earth though faced with the unremitting Indian scourge that kept so much of New England the province of those "vipers," "rattlesnakes," or "serpents" who kenneled in the "dark-places" of the country even as sectarian and civil strife fractured the towns from within. It is well documented that theologically Mather thought all this strife and Indian torment (in his words, the Wars of the Lord) indicated the nearness of the New Jerusalem. War and cataclysm, fire and earthquake all fit the prophesied apocalyptic schedule.

Yet mimetically Mather was obliged by his beliefs to suggest a fixed and bounded space appropriate to the New Earth and inclusive of that New World ground paradoxically desecrated in the impious present, yet consecrated by God eternally and hallowed by the work of his revered and illustrious Puritan forebears. Bercovitch points out that in Mather's view the Puritan effort to dislodge the Indians from their native habitat was not a territorial struggle but one "for a renovated earth," for a temporal Canaan mythically verifiable in figures of God's garden, and referent to the early flourishing of Puritan towns and to the symbolic fructification of Harvard College.[67] Of course Mather's *Magnalia Christi Americana* (1702) is filled with references to the wilderness journey of the New English Israel, to "little Israel now going into a wilderness," "carried into the wilderness," "journeying into the wilderness" (as well as "tempted" and "driven" into it)—all references certain to elicit the same responses to "wilderness" that Bradford called up repeatedly in his history.[68] Yet, even as he worked within the "mythico-historiography" of America, Mather needed to delineate fixed space for the New Jerusalem and to say how much of the fallen world beyond that space would be consumed in the conflagration. One strength of his imagination in the face of the Puritan declension was to "transform public defeat into private triumph by recourse to metaphor and myth."[69] As we are to see, it is really in metaphor that Mather found the solution to his mimetic problem of representing the American New Earth without riveting it to the actual geography of New England. To examine his representation of the New Earth in the *Magnalia* and elsewhere is to see how the visionary writer could be faithful to an ideographic America without attending to specific problems of a geographic utopia in-the-making.[70]

It is important to recognize Mather's own conscious separation of sacred from secular history in the *Magnalia*, since by it Mather dismisses as unimportant vast tracts of New World space. "Reader, I call these things prophesy . . . while writing history," he wrote amid his recital of abominations that signal the Apocalypse.[71] Such prophetic history did not admit of simple acreage, no matter how extensive or how promising its utilitarian potential. Thus, at the very beginning of the work, Mather carefully distinquished the realm of his church history from that of lesser narrations and chronicles of the exploration and settlement of America. Following a brief survey of the explorations of Columbus, whom he would elsewhere call "the Leader of our *American* colonies in the last two centuries," and of the Cabots and the Captains Gilbert and Gosnold, Mather abruptly closes this line of discussion and refers readers elsewhere for detailed accounts of exploration, commercial promise, and geography. Punning on "purchase" and Purchas, he sends to *Purchas His Pilgrimes* (1625) those readers interested in the terrestrial New World, rather than "endure any *stop* in our hastening voyage unto the HISTORY OF AN NEW ENGLISH ISRAEL."[72]

Thus Mather draws clear boundaries between the geographic and the visionary, or ideographic, America. The progress of the New English Israel is not pertinent to utilitarian geographic change in the New World. In fact, Mather categorically separates civil from Christian concerns in the context of complaint against Indians. "These abject creatures live in a country full of mines," he writes of the barbarous Indians, the doleful . . . *ruines of mankind"* who lack the wit and drive to exploit the metals and rely instead upon stone tools and shell and bead money. He complains, "They live in a country full of the best ship-timber under heaven," yet "never saw a ship till some came from Europe," instead crossing inland water in hollowed tree trunks. Worse, the Indians seemed unmoved by the civilized ways of those "who had *Houses full of Good Things* vastly out-shining their squalid and dark Wigwams." Mere onlookers to civilized life, they "did not seem touch'd in the least with any Ambition to come into such Desireable Circumstances" and remained instead "Miserable *Animals*" whose civilization—not to mention Chris-tianization—posed enormous difficulty. Thus, before the missionary John Eliot could even begin to Christianize the Indians, he had first the horrendous work of civilizing them.[73]

Mather's distinction between civil and Christian life is illuminating here because, once having established the need for civilization to precede Christianity, he dismisses as thematically unimportant the material progress of settlement. True, the New English Israel presup-poses a certain utilitarian development of the American environment. The Puritans are a people "Replenishing their *Fields* with *Trees* and with *Grains,* and useful Animals," a people who have "already made entrance upon iron" and plan the mining of copper, "besides other metals hereafter to be exposed." But this much said, Mather need have no further literary recourse to the utilization of the New World environment. In his view environmental change is integral to civilized life, which in turn precedes (and is requisite to) the spiritually vital New English Israel. But never does he understand the utilization of the New World environment as a correlate, let alone as an index, of the progress of God's elect toward the Millennium. His focus is solely upon "the work of *church-reformation* in America." As he says, *"Geography* must now find work for a *Christiano-graphy.*"[74]

As a metaphor central to the *Magnalia,* Christiano-graphy be-comes a seamless realm where the past joins the present, where Scrip-ture and secular history merge on a continuum toward the forth-coming Millennium.[75] What remains to be examined is how Mather represents the American New Earth of his Christiano-graphy, having severed it from the secular world of commerce, exploration, and geography and from the material progress of civil life in the New World. Scattered through many of his writings, especially in the 1710s and 1720s, he has left a desultory but evident pattern of his envisioned New Earth. Surrounded by holocaust, when "the Earth shall tremble and the Hills melt like wax," the Millennium will emerge not as "the *Destroying* of the Earth, so much as the Refining of it," a refinement that "shall make it a *New Earth.*" Because Mather expected all this to occur sometime in the eighteenth century, he urged repentance without delay, using analogies of the angel's warning to Sodom. (*"Immediately! Immediately!* Make Speed, Haste, stay not. . . . Escape to the Mountain, lest thou be consumed.") Yet he did set forth his vision, acknowledging that apocalyptic doctrine posed hard questions but asserting that "at the Beginning of the Millennium there will be not only *New Heavens,* and in your view the Holy City, possessed by our Saviour . . . but also a New Earth." Mather described it as "occupied by none but *Righteous* Ones, who yet shall *build Houses and Inhabit Them,* and plant Vine-yards and Eat the Fruit of them" (Isa. 65:21). [76]

Within these remarks on the chiliad, Mather's vision is unearthly, at least otherworldly. His *"Righteous* Ones" may build actual clapboard houses, but at the point of imaging what they will eat, Mather rests with the biblical metaphor of the vineyard, somewhere between the nutriment of viniculture and the nourishment of the spirit. [77] To the Massachusetts militia Mather asserts that in the Millennium the swords will be beaten literally into plowshares and pruning hooks, but he is silent on the agricultural results. He wrote that "the *Coming of the Son of Man in the Clouds of heaven* . . . will not be found a *Metaphor"* and so affirmed his literal interpretation of the prophesied events, including change to the earthly environment. The New Jerusalem is a "New World" reassuringly prefigured in that postdiluvian world of Noah. From the conflagration will come "a world in a little while hence to have a *New Face* upon it."[78] But Mather stops short of portraying that face with geographic explicitness. His imagination soars instead to the qualitative New Jerusalem. Uncertain whether the lion will actually lie down with the lamb, Mather is utterly confident of the qualitative change from discord to peace, love, and charity. Always it is spiritual change that absorbs him, and the symbolic possibilities that engage his imagination.

Thus we find in Mather's writings on the subject of the New Earth a movement in theme away from reality as the explicitly palpable or tangible and toward what is real in the imaginative realm of symbol,

metaphor, and allegory. Even after his careful geographical survey of
those parts of the earth susceptible to earthquake and volcano (a
survey employing the deductive method to predict the course of the
conflagration), his imagination moves into metaphor as he says that
in the Apocalypse the volcanoes, "which a *Metaphor* may call so, will
daily multiply" when, for instance, one's friends become "Vol-
canello's." Similarly, he introduces the figure of the rainbow with
remarks on prisms and light refraction before doing what he loves,
enlarging the rainbow to bind God's cosmography with a symbolic
arch forward from Noah to the covenant with Abraham and beyond,
all its colors an allegorical spectrum ("the Fiery Colour leads them to
think on that *Fire* which is e're long to consume the World").[79]

Accordingly, when in his Christiano-graphy Mather invokes geographical features, it is not for millennial site planning but as the
referential basis for spiritual lessons. *"Break up your fallow
Ground . . . ,* the *Heart* of Man," he instructs farmers in the outlying
towns, his message urging repentance as he works "to spiritualize the
common Actions of [farm] Life." He puts his lesson on the vanity of
earthly striving in the equations of allegory, the world as "Wretched,
Ragged, Boggy Hill," its summit a "deceitful Bog," and so on in this
Bunyanesque way. And though he seems to be thinking of an actual
New England Canaan when he writes of the *"Land* promised for, and
bestowed upon, the *Israelitish* Nation," Mather's is not a land of
palpable soil but the "Type of a Better Country, that is, an
Heavenly." His "Better Country" is Christ, and the promises of his
gospel are "so many Mountains." Consistently, then, we see the bib-
lical terms of landscape brought into the spiritual service of
Christiano-graphy.[80]

And yet Mather needs to suggest a plausible site for the New
Jerusalem. The affinities of his imagination were with metaphor and
symbol, with the spiritualism of allegory. But his article of faith
rested with the "New Face" of the actual earth, a geographic or
environmental refinement of some part of the world. The New Earth
is his fact. Having separated Christiano-graphy from the geography of
secular narratives, Mather yet must revert to the actual earth to
indicate just where in the Millennium God might locate the New
Earth.

Increasingly he focuses upon Boston, an emblem of the New England that is the elect New English Israel. With the eclipse of Puritan political power in the Massachusetts Bay and beyond, with the jeopardy and outright threat of Indian attacks, Mather finds in the boundaries of Boston a plausible (and perhaps comfortable) locus for the New Jerusalem. The *Magnalia* shows the pattern of Mather's constriction of space to a Bostonian New Earth even as it reveals Mather's evangelistic zeal to purify the town in order to hasten its apocalyptic moment. After the "Uproars, Horrours, and Slaughters" that signify the nearness of the Millennium, there will remain the holy remnant banded together in a Bostonian New Earth. It is there that the geographic and ideographic America can converge, in a Boston *"helped of the Lord,"* favored by God and, in turn, "THE MET-ROPOLIS OF THE WHOLE ENGLISH AMERICA." Historically, this is the town that survived fire, famine, pestilence, and military attack, that has been "wonderously" helped by—that is, favored by—the "one protector in heaven, and that is our Lord JESUS CHRIST." Mather exclaims, "O, helped and happy town!" and finds comfort in the protective wall of fire which God erected for Daniel as now he erects for Boston.[81]

Mather offers a program for the further purification of Boston. Chosen and blessed, it yet needs the correction of its errant ways and the purgation of its vices. To this end Mather urges the election of "pious and prudent" town officials, the closing of Boston's *"enormous number"* of taverns and ordinaries, a renewed "SANCTIFICATION OF THE LORD'S DAY," instatement of "EQUITY and CHARITY," an end to idleness. He pleads, in short, for a return to the "Utopia" that was New England in past days.[82] This is much more than nostalgia or a theological perspective on civic improvement. It is really Mather's effort to resolve the paradox which Bercovitch locates at the heart of the American experience. On the one side is the congregationalist America of the visible saints. This is a nation destined for redemption and transcendent of the vicissitudes of worldly events. As we know, Mather represents this destined Redeemer Nation in his metaphor of Christiano-graphy.

Yet, in urging the preparation of Boston as the site of the American New Earth, Mather draws from the other part of this American paradox. His program for the civic improvement and spiritual renewal of Boston shows Mather's indebtedness to the

Reformation tradition of the powerful, godly nation which is continuously on trial toward its fulfillment. This is the nation whose
mission is proven in the events of human history. In this sense,
Mather's America remains on trial, capable both of progression and
of regression. Importantly, it is dynamic and able repeatedly to
renew its spirit and thus its mission.

Mather really seizes the historical moment of the 1710s to find
possibilities for the conjunction of these two American nations. As
the plausible site of the New Jerusalem, Boston can embody in
geographic terms the America of Christiano-graphy. If it renews its
spiritual life at this bourn of the prophesied New Earth, Boston can
become the Redeemer Nation of the destined New Jerusalem. In this
way the paradox would be resolved. Boston, an emblem of America,
can actually become the Christiano-graphic New Earth. Thus Mather
scans "a knot of our enemies in those 'inaccessible thickets'" and
reads the imminent doom of the satanic Indians in prophecy. Avidly,
he charts which praying towns were providentially spared Indian
destruction. The example is encouraging for Boston, if only the town
would take heed and mend its ways, that is, renew the spirit of its
errand.

The renewal required more than ethics and philanthropy; it
demanded the imitation of angels, one of Mather's major preoccupations. "To *do good*" is the dispensation of a good angel, and such
"inventions to do good" as the compass and lodestone, both navigational aids for the spread of the gospel, also are angelical. By
implication, then, the Boston of the elect is potentially an angelic
city, and at the onset of the chiliad the New English Israel will join
Saint Botolph's town with that "unseen regiment of the world."
Spatially, Mather retrenches to the boundaries of Boston and draws
inside the visible saints, observing that God's *"elect"* are "brought
home unto himself" when Indians burn them out of their remote
settlements and they come into the vicinity of Boston.[83] In the ruins
of the outlying settlements the corpses of English settlers are those
of Puritan Christian martyrs. So saying, Mather turns inward to the
inspiration of Boston, to its reform into an angelic city. Unconcerned
with mercantile transactions per se, with plaster and lath, Mather
kept his Bostonian New Earth ideographic. Presupposing a civil
setting, Mather, like Bradford, represents the New Earth as a state of

mind referent to the space of Boston but of course not yet fused geographically with it. As a site, it is to be consecrated ultimately by the angelic presence of the New English Israel.

All these tendencies in Mather—to say without geographic precision what the Millennium will be like, to urge the angelicism of Boston in order to validate this site of the New Earth, and to write with greatest vitality of a world of conflated metaphor, allegory, and symbol (all the while presupposing the civil landscape)—converge in his *Theopolis Americana* (1710), a sermon directed to the merchants of Boston and containing the appropriate lesson in ethical business practices. Under the Golden Rule Boston's merchants are warned off the slave trade and liquor traffic and urged to settle debts and to give fair measure. Such is the lowest threshold of angelic do-good. But *Theopolis Americana* additionally compels attention for Mather's concerted evocation of the American New Earth. More than the *Magnalia,* this sermon for Boston's merchants reveals in American literature the visionary New Earth that would find successful amplification in the American vernacular of Whitman's *Song of the Broad-Axe* one and one-half centuries later.

From Mather's invocation we hear Boston exalted as the emblem of an ideal America. "Glorious things are Spoken of thee, O Thou City of God!" he writes. "The STREET be in thee, *O New England;* the Interpretation of it be unto you, *O American* Colonies." He calls the Millennium the "state of the Church on Earth ... a New Jerusalem ... when Jerusalem shall be literally Rebuilt." Here Mather is far more aggressive in locating the American New Earth than he had been, for instance, in the *Magnalia,* in which discursively he could only hope and trust that America would not be entirely excluded from the site of the New Jerusalem. In *Theopolis* he says outright that "there are many arguments to persuade us that our Glorious LORD will have an Holy City in AMERICA." And Mather is specifically geographical, resorting not only to Isaiah but to the landscape of New England to prosecute his theme. "We cannot imagine that the brave Countries and Gardens which fill the *American Hemisphere* were made for nothing but a Place for Dragons. ... Can you think that *America* shall be nothing but *Miery Places and Marshes, given to salt?* By no means."[84]

Despite his discourse on the New Jerusalem situated in America,

Mather does not work in any literal way. Every point of interpretation is an opportunity for metaphor. Each doctrinal explication of the prophesied New Earth is for Mather a moment of translation, really of transliteration as he moves into realms of symbol, embracing rhetoric of the Bible as he moves away from literal meanings. We see his method instanced in the figure of the golden street, "conceive[d] and so it may be translated, the Market-place; the place where the Affairs of Trade bring together a Concourse of People." Just when readers grasp the workaday reality, Mather departs into symbol as he writes, "The business transacted in the Market-Place of an *Holy City,* will have a *Golden,* that is to say a *Gracious* character upon it. *Golden* Proceedings, that is to say, *Godly* ones, will be found in the *Market-Place* of a CITY, which the Son of God has a favor for." So continuing, Mather at last contrasts Cortez's conquest with that of Christ's imminent kingdom on earth, at which point we understand history brought into the service of symbol, and not a connection of earthly events. When Mather writes that in the Millennium Christ will "Run down into, and through the World, and make the World become a *Watered Garden,* and an *Eden* for the *Lord from Heaven,"* we are in a purely spiritual realm to which the Charles and Merrimack rivers are irrelevant. Mather tries to return to the literal plane of being when he calls New England and America God's foremost possession in freehold, a *"Seisin in Fact,"* soon to be so in law, that is, in the divine unfolding of prophesied events.[85] But it is too brief, this assertion of literal meaning; it wants elaboration. As readers we remain overwhelmingly in the spiritually evocative realm of biblical metaphor.

In Mather's visionary environment of the New Earth there is this disjunction, of a New Earth announced but not imagined as it might come into being. We are asked to presuppose of it a civil environment that is essential yet fundamentally unimportant to the quality of its existence. It is revealing that while Mather speaks precisely of the refinement of the earth in the Millennium, and directs each living generation to make preparation for the next, the legacy he indicates is entirely spiritual, based solely upon piety and virtue. He offers no remark on hastening the Apocalypse by beginning the work of environmental change.[86] In *Theopolis* he urges New England to "Keep such a [Golden] Street; and *Sweep* it, where it wants to be better kept," but of course in this spiritualized passage the maintenance of Boston's pathways is not pertinent. It is true that Mather begins a kind of programmatic approach to the American New Earth. He offers steps of expedition as he tries to hasten the Apocalypse with mercantile ethics (or, in the "Bostonian Ebenezer," with civic improvements). His essay on the emulation of angels may be considered as one profound connection between the actual New Earth and the spiritual state of its inhabitants, since in that essay Mather really bridges the two realms of earth and spirit.

But the bridge allows just one passage, toward the "ecstasies of the spirit," to use Robert Middlekauff's term.[87] And while Mather affirms the forthcoming chiliad, he yet avoids in his writings a representation of it. Sociologically, we might call his a retreat into vision in the face of the social failure of Puritanism. Aesthetically, however, the strength of Mather's evocative, visionary New Earth lies in his freedom from entanglement in the temporal affairs that could make his Millennium provisional and tenuous. From John Davenport's removal to New Haven he well understood this kind of snare, for Davenport had done "all that was possible to render the renowned church of New-Haven like the New-Jerusalem; and yet after all . . . in this world it was impossible."[88] So instead Mather "builds a monument *against* realities," one founded upon myth.[89] Thematically, Mather takes up the matter of the environmental reform of the New World by presupposing that process, first in the civil life of the colony and at last in the holy refinement of the New Earth. To William Bradford the territory of the Millennium was irrelevant; to Cotton Mather it is a necessary premise of his myth of America.

It is not by coincidence that in the course of the seventeenth century the reformed American environment should move in literature from an irrelevance to a presupposition of the New Earth. In part, the very expansion of New England settlement and the evident conversion of forest into farms and villages made its due impress upon those writers who were witness to it. From the work of social historians in patterns of town development and social organization, we may readily grasp the social, political, and economic basis of Cotton Mather's presupposed civil setting.

There exists, however, a powerful literary basis for the change from Bradford to Mather, that is, from the dismissal of the New England environment as eschatologically unimportant to the premise of a civilized setting for the realm of Christiano-graphy. Here we must recognize not only palpable geographic change but the literary work that embodies that change. For Mather's premise of a civil setting for the American New Earth has its antecedent not only in the visible growth of towns and commerce but in literature that imparts transcendent value to the process of civilizing New England. It seems that the continuous impingement of the worlds of soil and spirit over the first thirty years of Pilgrim-Puritan colonial life had readied American literature for the imagination that could synthesize theology with colonial efforts, and do so in language drawn from both realms. For by the time Cotton Mather wrote the *Magnalia* and the cluster of sermons and tracts concerning the New Earth, he already had available an important literary work which joined ideas on environmental reform in New England with an apocalyptic ideology. At mid century (1653), when Bradford had stopped writing his *Of Plymouth Plantation,* the Puritan colonist Edward Johnson published *The Wonder-Working Providence of Sions Saviour in New England,* a book-length history informed with an American vision at once millennial and utopian. Utilitarian in his geographic outlook, Johnson understood the American New Earth as a colonial program from the mind of God. His work is the vital connection between Bradford and Mather. More than that, in the literary history of the American New Earth, Edward Johnson's *Wonder-Working Providence* stands as the benchmark of the Pilgrim-Puritan epoch.

2: *Edward Johnson's American New Earth*

> *A worship new I sing,*
> *You captains, voyagers, explorers, yours,*
> *You engineers, you architects, machinists, yours,*
> *You, not for trade or transportation only,*
> *But in God's name, and for thy sake O soul.*
>
> *Walt Whitman,* Passage to India

In the late 1640s the "Clerk of Writ" of Woburn, Massachusetts, settled down to compose *The Wonder-Working Providence of Sions Saviour in New England.* When he began to write, Edward Johnson—surveyor, fur trader, militia captain, delegate to the General Court—had roughly twelve years of experience in carving a livable colony from the North American space which the Puritan minister William Hubbard called "desert places, inaccessible Woods, and unknown Paths, which no Geographers had ever measured, scarce any Vultures eye had ever seen."[1] Not surprisingly, Edward Johnson used the writing of history to exalt to cosmic status those familiar, earthly, aspects of the New Jerusalem, an idea he had imbibed continually from the Puritan pulpit. For the Puritan view of history as "theology exemplified" led the ministers largely to scan theology manifest through time but moved an activist-colonizer like Johnson to ken the human part played in its exemplification.[2] As a book-length quasi-history of Puritan New England, *The Wonder-Working Providence* fused a double world of earth and spirit in a literary meld of scriptural authority, civil engineering, and technics. Writing became Johnson's ropewalk in which he braided together his convictions on the Millennium, the wilderness, and social purpose in America. The impetus for his ideas was evidently the memory of vigorous environmental change in England, especially in his native Kent, and a growing sense of the potential of technology to achieve those socially ameliorative aspects of the New Earth.

Little could Edward Johnson have seen himself as an antecedent of such writers as Joel Barlow, George Bancroft, James Fenimore Cooper, and even Whitman, let alone scores of others whose writings urge reformation of the American natural environment as a joint imperative with societal self-fulfillment. Yet in the mid-seventeenth century the Woburn Clerk of Writ, who in 1643 had taken leave of other duties in order to wage a holy war against Samuel Gorton, that skeptic of the imminent New Earth, settled down to write a chiliastic New England history that would ramify through the next two centuries of the national literature. As a writer Johnson was an activist out to use words in the same way he used his musket or surveyor's measure: as a means to bring about the New Heavens and New Earth in America. Among the many Puritan writers, he alone examined the material ramifications of the New Jerusalem. More than any of our early writers, Johnson fixed the ideology of environmental reform in American literature. He deserves full and separate discussion because *The Wonder-Working Providence* is our first major work to embody sustained themes of environmental reform. Johnson initiated in our literature a programmatic response to the American landscape, one complementary to Cotton Mather's visionary New Earth and antecedent to *The Columbiad* and to Cooper's fictional treatment of the American landscape. In fact, *The Wonder-Working Providence* would prove to be prophetic in literary ways its author never could have guessed or understood.

Over three centuries, it must be noted, neither Johnson's poesy nor his precocious vision of America has brought him a flourishing literary reputation. His unsigned verse narrative, *Good News from New-England,* has been confused with Edward Winslow's prose work of the same title. And since its first appearance in 1653, *The Wonder-Working Providence,* which has a quixotic publishing history, has been perennially unfashionable in American literature.[3] Doubly cursed, Johnson's book neither circulated widely (nor sold well) in his own day nor won him posthumously the literary honor belatedly come, for instance, to Anne Bradstreet. At best, he has survived three centuries as a somewhat eccentric favorite of a very few readers.

Intermittently there have been tepid praise and condemnation, and for varied reasons. Alongside the governors and great divines Edward Johnson has seemed a diminished figure, a town clerk instead of a governor, a leader of militia rather than a savior of souls. Some criticism of him rings of snobbery which Johnson himself abets, for instance in his apology for presuming to write a history more grand than Homer's while yet himself Clio's novice.

Too, internal evidence in *The Wonder-Working Providence* suggests that Johnson overcame a strong personal inhibition in order to write the book. He was riven with a sense of intellectual inferiority and perhaps because of it was even unwilling to have his name appear on the title page, just as he had left unsigned the verse *Good News,* which analysts of style indicate is surely his. Keenly aware of his ignorance of languages, of his deficiencies in scholarship, and of the literary ambitiousness that he feared outstripped his abilities, Edward Johnson nonetheless wrote his history, probably sustained by conviction that, whatever *his* failings, God's truth was evident in every line.[4] (Was not God's own scriptural language interspersed with his own?) Thus Johnson suffered title-page anonymity, perhaps gratified by the knowledge that his name was in the mental colophon of eminent Puritans, men like Judge Samuel Sewall among whom it was "a Thing familiarly known" that Capt. Edward Johnson was the author of *The Wonder-Working Providence.*[5]

We can speculate that, had Edward Johnson remained continuously in New England from the time of his landing with the Winthrop party from the *Arbella* in June 1630, his name might have come down to us as a genealogical avatar of the Massachusetts Bay. But after the year of Merrimack trade, he had returned to England and did not make the ultimate personal commitment, the transport of his family to New England, until 1636, by which time the socioreligious pecking order was well established and battle lines drawn for the Antinomian Controversy. Even then he might have achieved prominence had he truly rusticated himself in such a settlement of the New England outback as New Haven or Connecticut, where he could have risen to a position of high magisterial authority. His decision to help found Woburn virtually destined his stature to be that of his town, a yeomanly offshoot of the more prosperous and sizable Charlestown, roughly contiguous to it but always shadowed by the parent settlement and by Boston.

True, Johnson was a town father and tithingman, an avuncular

figure for the ten Woburn households whose spiritual, moral, and
financial lives he presumably supported by his counsel. As deputy to
the Massachusetts General Court (and for one week its Speaker),
surveyor general of the Commonwealth, and charter member of the
Massachusetts Ancient and Honourable Artillery Company, Johnson
was less parochial than his Woburn activities alone suggest. But
ineluctably, he was no figure of the first magnitude in the
Massachusetts Bay.

There is another reason why critics have given Johnson short shrift
over the years. The tendency to search into the past for the
parentage of values subsequently desirable or admirable has led
writers to bypass Johnson in their praise of seemingly modest,
mediating Bradford or Winthrop, who appear in tone more liberal, as
if suffused with an ineffably democratic spirit. Doctrinally, we well
know, Bradford and Winthrop are not less stringent than Johnson—
but they have long seemed so. For instance, Bradford's portrayal of
the spiritually errant Roger Williams rings with benevolence. Williams
is "a man godly and zealous," possessed of "many precious parts,"
and gifted in preaching. Bradford pointedly refuses to enumerate
Williams's offenses, and only when his reader looks beyond the
governor's modesty about Plymouth hospitality and his euphemisms
about Williams's "unsettled judgment" and "strange opinions" does
he find the doctrinal bedrock sealed against William's particular
pursuit of spiritual truth.[6]

Winthrop too shows in his rhetoric a liberal clothing. When the
heretic Gorton and his followers are brought to face him and the
other magistrates, as well as the public, Winthrop writes of the
miscreants' "contemptuous carriage" and their "obstinancy against
all the fair means and moderation we had used to reform them and
bring them to do right to those of ours whom they had wronged."[7]
Fair means, moderation, and then just deliverance—this is Winthrop's
vocabulary of reasonable liberality, and poles apart from Johnson to
whom religious deviance is "the sowre leven of unsound Doctrine."[8]
Of course, in a history constructed upon Christian militarism, a
vocabulary of moderation would be oddly flaccid. Johnson's personally humane sympathies do emerge throughout the work in such
portrayals as this of a paternal Christ, "with his own blessed hands
wiping away the teares that trickel downe [Indian-ravaged New Eng-

land] cheekes, drying her dankish eyes, and hushing her sorrowful sobs in his sweete bosome." This parental compassion by a man seven times a parent reminds us of Anne Bradstreet's *Contemplations*. But Gortonist or other heresies inimical to a saintly New England provoke Johnson's most vituperative, illiberal language. "Heale not lightly the wounds that Wolves make," warns his Christian herald, "lest from their festering Teeth a Gangrin grow."[9]

Quantitatively, too, Johnson's extant writings put him in the shade of other New Englanders compelled by the duties of magistracy or ministry to keep up a voluminous correspondence (along with careful historical records) and to produce a vast sermon literature in addition to the textual commentaries, tracts, gatherings of remarkable providences, and verses that issued from the presses and filled their manuscript books. But from Johnson we have remaining only the one long poem, two short ones (of which just one can be ascribed with certainty) and his history. All but the little verse prefacing the Woburn town records (1640–42) were written by a man in late midlife, one who afterward became too busy with the legislature, surveying duties, the militia, and the upkeep and increase on his own estate ever to write again (if even he wished to, which is uncertain). Once his experience as town clerk brought out the literary side of him and culminated in *The Wonder-Working Providence,* he evidently found insufficient time even to keep the Woburn records as accurately as he ought (as subsequent land claimants were to learn). From Johnson we have no diary, no journal, no sheaf of letters, no testimonial document of the kind that Cotton Mather was later to insert entirely in the *Magnalia Christi Americana.* There is no "Epistle Dedicatory," no tract clarifying his position in any grave controversy, nor, from any Puritan confrere of his, is there a biographical vignette. Nor is there a holograph of *The Wonder-Working Providence* against which divers editions could be collated to establish a definitive text. A few anecdotes in town records provide scant evidence of literary development, and thus Johnson has deprived literary scholars of such favorite work as plotting intellectual and aesthetic development, establishing biographical-literary relationships, or graphing creative processes. In return they have generally ignored him until very recently.

He was both the most probable and improbable of writers. He had an engineer's mind, pragmatic and literal, one more deeply engaged by mechanics than by metaphysics. He seems to have come to literature through the back door of his Woburn clerkship, for the town records show him to have become impatient of the verbal constrictions of a clerk *qua* clerk. Quantifying by names and numbers could fix events in time and place, but Johnson sensed early on that statistics alone could not evoke the quality of them. Within four months of assuming the clerkship in 1640 we find him interspersing anecdotes among the records, venturing modestly into narrative and into verse as well.[10] By 1648 he had published his verse essay, *Good News from New-England*, an ambitious exposition of New England history combining Puritan orthodoxy with the economic prospects of the region, all in some six hundred lines of varying verse forms.[11]

What finally galvanized the writer Johnson was the dire cultural moment of the late 1640s, when ironically the very triumph of Puritanism in England eclipsed its American counterpart. Not only had emigration to New England virtually stopped and an economic depression ensued, but there emerged colonial fears of godly abandonment, which found expression in internecine feuds about church-state relations and in ambivalent attitudes toward those departing from New England for Cromwelliam home shores. Ever underlying the New England Puritan bravura about being God's "choice grain" and "chosen remnant" had been an undercurrent of fear that they were really more banished *from* England than led *to* Canaan. In the 1600s Cotton Mather said it outright: the Church of England, "misemploying their heavy church-keys, banished them into his plantation."[12]   At midcentury Edward Johnson was more circumspect in his phrase, "—forced to retreat to a place of greater safety."[13] But the Cromwellian hegemony forced into focus the question of the meaning of New England, whose erstwhile "specialness" and "metaphysical necessity" Johnson worked to reinstate in his polemical history.[14]

Strategically, he invites his audience to a continuous participation in the events of colonization.[15] The book begins in an England plagued by popish idolators, and from which Christ musters an army and commands their departure for New England. Through the commissioning of that army Johnson sustains a sense of immediacy and contemporaneity by using the present tense instead of the historian's customary preterit. The military commissioning takes up the first six chapters, whose very titles—"Of the Demeanor of their Church Officers," "How the People are to behave themselves," "What Civill Government the People of Christ ought to set up," "How the People of Christ ought to behave themselves in War-like Discipline"—indicate a New England Puritan conduct book (though it is one of course derived deductively from twenty years of prior New England colonial experience). The Christian army's "voluntary banishment" from England culminates in a wrenching departure from friends and family and a dreadful sea voyage in which Christ mercifully preserves his chosen people. Once landed, they pitch "some Tents of Cloath" and "small Huts, in which they lodge their Wifes and Children," and begin to enlarge Christ's kingdom church by church and town by town.

Johnson devotes single chapters to the churches and towns, indicates the reason for their founding, describes topography and prospects for economic development, and names principal magistrates, usually "tendring" verses on each minister whose godly qualities often portend spiritual success for the church and town itself. Interspersed among these town-church chapters are others dealing with such momentous events as the Antinomian Crisis and with remarkable providences interpreted through Johnson's own caveats and Isaiahan praises for the divine phenomenon of the nation born in a day. Throughout the work he renders a sense of horrendous Puritan midwifery, as instanced in his account of the founding of Concord.

Having bought land from the Indians, the settlers began to explore the "unknowne woods" and "watery scrampes [swamps]," sometimes in thickets "where their hands are forced to make way for their bodies passage." From poor footing they sink "into an uncertaine bottome in water, and wade up to the knees" before, weary, they reach "a scorching plaine" where "ragged Bushes scratch their legs fouly," shredding stockings and lacerating unprotected skin. Some "have had the bloud trickle downe at every step," and in summer others constantly felt faint from the odor of close, rank fern.

Johnson deduces from this God's own strategy, initially to conceal the horrors while luring on the curious. He tenders a memorial verse on the Concord minister, Mr. Jones, and observes how meager the diet of the colonists and how exasperating the search for woodland direction without sunlight, a reliable compass, or available Indian paths. Instancing the ease and mortal danger of becoming lost in the forest, he goes on to detail the misery of encampment and the colonists' efforts to keep up their courage. "Lying in the open aire, while the watery Clouds poure down all the night season, and sometimes driving Snow dissolving on their backs, they keep their wet cloathes warme with a continued fire, till the renewed morning." At last they locate a town site and "burrow themselves in the Earth" and make a "smoaky fire" to shelter "themselves, their Wives and little ones." Still, "the long raines penetrate through, to their great disturbance in the night season." Nevertheless, "in these poore Wigwames they sing psalmes, pray and praise their God, till they can provide them houses," customarily after "the Earth, by the Lords blessing, brought forth Bread to feed them."

Johnson then writes of the pains of groundbreaking and of the unforeseen problems of agriculture and of animal husbandry which of necessity made the colonists vegetarians. "They have been forced to cut their bread very thin for a long season." Worse, this was bread of Indian maize. Ample water, springtime supplies of fish, and occasional "Venison or Rockoons" traded from the Indians (along with the garden crops of "Pomkins and Squashes") hardly alleviate the miseries of colonization in this account of a Puritan democracy of hardship. Thus, Johnson concludes, "this poore people populate this howling Desart, marching manfully on (the Lord assisting) through the greatest difficulties, and forest labours."[16]

This account of the swamp trek is among the oft-reprinted passages from *The Wonder-Working Providence* and is in part significant here because it implies a symbiotic relation between Puritan minister and bushwhacker. The two categories are crude, given the likelihood that no early New England minister escaped manual labor any more than the saintly woodsman avoided doctrinal hard questions. But the distinction between the ideologue and the activist is a valid one. Principally from the ministers came the theological watch and ward over the Puritan enterprise and the sustaining ideas about the meaning of the New Jerusalem. And from colonizers of Johnson's ilk came the land surveys and forest clearance that supported the ministers' ideas and images in which those ideas were conveyed. Before Cotton Mather could write metaphorically of "brave Countries and Gardens which fill the American Hemisphere," he needed some reference for the figure.[17] Even chimeras revert to real beasts.

Conversely, it was from the spiritual guardians that Johnson found courage to advance by inches into the unending wilderness. In a task psychologically so appalling, Johnson is sustained—in fact, inspired— by the idea that the New Earth would be wrought from the onerous labors of colonization.

Johnson's idea, however, needed validation in his mimesis. Believing colonization to be site preparation for the New Earth, he needed a mode of rhetoric that could make of this motley band of amateur explorers plausible agents of the Christian Millennium. To the glory of God, the weak Concord settlers survive, but unlike William Bradford's Plymouth Pilgrims who are fed spiritual manna in the wilderness, Johnson's characters must turn the wilds of the New World to nutritive account. They are very much "in" *and* "of" this world. As initiators of the New Earth, they must be made powerful, and in his rhetoric Johnson needed a way in which to make them so.

Like Cotton Mather, he chose metaphor—though aptly one of means rather than of place. For Mather found in his "Golden Street," his *Theopolis Americana* and Christiano-graphy a reality unto itself, an ideographic place of America existing solely in the imagination. Johnson, however, had fixed the site of the New Jerusalem on this same swampy, thorny, thicketed, rank, labyrinthine, and agriculturally defiant land he describes in the Concord episode. Of the Massachusetts Bay he wrote, "this is the place where the Lord will create a new Heaven, and a new Earth in, new Churches, and a new Common-wealth together."[18] Johnson therefore needed a metaphor of power and of expedition of the American New Earth, a metaphor of the means of that millennial work. Thus, throughout *The Wonder-Working Providence* he exploits the military metaphor which is typologically true and polemically plausible in his story. It is the one with which he opens his book:

Oh yes! Oh yes! Oh yes! All you people of Christ... answer to your severall Names as you shall be shipped for his service, in the Westerne World, and more especially for planting the united Collonies of new England; Where you are to attend the service of the King of Kings.[19]

This muster and commissioning begins the Christian militarism that forms the structural spine of *The Wonder-Working Providence*. Most obviously the figure comes from Johnson's biography, since he was a charter member of the still-surviving Ancient and Honourable Artillery Company of Massachusetts and had been early accorded the captaincy by which he continued to be addressed. But the figure is less self-generated than referent to 2 Timothy and to Samuel, in whose theocratic monarchy lies a representation of God's rule over both Israel and the heathen, clearly an auspicious and reassuring sign to settlers about to dwell among heathen Indians. Lacking numerical strength, the New England soldiers are as David before Goliath, and Johnson is further comforted by the smiting of Philistines and Syrians and by the military figures in which lessons of deliverance are cast. Shielded and girded by God, David is invincible, a point Johnson warms to as he writes, "Take up your Armes, and march manfully on till all opposers of Christs Kingly power be abolished... for the Armies of the great Jehovah are at hand."[20]

In his metaphor of Christian militarism Johnson is so absorbed with power that his words ring of the overcompensation of someone deeply suspicious of weakness. These suspicions, however, do not surface into ambivalence in his text. For him the destined and the provisional America were one and the same. It is true that he prods, persuades, and drills his army to its millennial mission, but his mind is not divided on the subject of America's destiny. He drives on and on the point that Christ is "Captaine of our salvation" and "crusheth with a rod of Iron." "Could Caesar so suddenly fetch over fresh forces from Europe to Asia, Pompy to foyle?" he asks. "How much more shall Christ who createth all power, call over this 900 league Ocean at his pleasure, such instruments as he thinks meete to make use of in this place?"[21] Rhetorically this strategy assures divine protection by a commander transcending Roman legend to be fixed in mythic godhead. The eminent English Puritan Richard Baxter could scorn "the Narratives of the great Victorys of ... Caesar" as mere "portraiture of Phantasms" and "Dreams of Vagrant Imaginations," but Johnson's quantum leap of power from the pagan to the divine is meant to quell notions that the Puritan emigrants were but a weak and vulnerable band.[22] Johnson's Caesar is meant to catapult the

Puritan colonists into a position of unimaginable power. Justly could they be made invincible since the outcome of their mission—the New Earth itself—was never in doubt. And *that* was the real stanchion of Johnson's faith, the certainty of events moving inexorably toward the Apocalypse which will elevate the "city" or "nation" into paradise at last.[23]

II

The literalness of his mind enabled Johnson to espouse an ideology of environmental reform as a correlate to the reformation of church polity. God's garden was a constellation of New England churches gathered and governed in the congregational way, but so was it correlatively in Johnson a palpable garden and farm village carved from the forest. Purposively, his phrases do ring with spiritual meanings, since, like other Puritans, Johnson used the "allusive shorthand" of spiritualizing, a technique by which objects, persons, and situations from life and from the Bible carried certain predictable connotations comfortable in their reinforcement of Christian unity of experience.[24] Johnson's "Souldiers of Christ," for instance, echo from David to Constantine to the Woburn militia and point toward the New Jerusalem and to the final battle of the righteous against the fabulous peoples of Gog and Magog, after which God would destroy the world and the chosen would dwell with him eternally. But for Johnson these meaningful texts in life and Scripture were not spiritual concerns separate from New England geography. *Literal* and *symbolic* were not intellectually, imaginatively, or mimetically separable to him, with the result that *The Wonder-Working Providence* affirms a real and necessary relation between scriptural metaphor and New England hardscrabble.

A useful point of mimetic contrast is that between *Wonder-Working Providence* and the *Magnalia*. Putting aside the particular cultural conditions that help to account for differences between the two works, we can nonetheless find in Mather some passages at first view much like Johnson's. "Never was any plantation brought unto such a considerableness, in a space of time so inconsiderable!" says

Mather, "an *howling wilderness* in a few years become a *pleasant land.*" Subtracting Johnson's statistics of horticultural yield, we can find such phrases in *The Wonder-Working Providence*. For Mather, too, the "desert" is metamorphosed into paradise, a change evinced in figures of *"great farms . . .* protected by a guard of angels" and of the "vine" that took "deep root and filled the land."[25] As is now well understood, however, Mather's arguments are not theology couched in metaphor but metaphor itself, as the *Magnalia* appropriates the Puritan colonial experience entirely for myth. In Mather the actual woods of Concord or Cambridge are not converted into paradise; instead, the *"wilderness*-condition," a mental-spiritual testing and purification, transforms the soul's desert into paradise. Mather's transformed desert is thus a spiritual state, and his Garden of God radiant as a "mythical-green glow." As Bercovitch says of Mather, "When, sporadically, he turns in the *Magnalia* to the world around him, it is to reject it for the world of his creation.[26]

Thus Mather's *"Plough-shares* and *Pruning hooks"* are "MAXIMS of the Everlasting Gospel . . . for the Cultivation of the New Earth,"[27] whereas those of Johnson are actual New England farm tools sanctified in an agrarian New Earth. As we have seen, Mather's New England, mythically powerful, is a state of mind, a realm of being in the imagination. God's garden in the *Magnalia* has no geographic locus but exists in that symbolic realm of Christianography.

This is not to make Johnson the foil of Cotton Mather. It is to say that *The Wonder-Working Providence* is the work of a programmatic imagination. Its cosmos is at once mythic *and* literal, even though one is well reminded that a literary definition of myth as a controlling, supernatural image embodying universal meaning through time is surely one Johnson would reject. Instead, he would favor the traditional definition of myth as essentially a religious and cosmic formulation to be regarded not as a representation of the truth but as truth itself. From this belief, supported in Isaiah and Revelation (and implicitly in Genesis), Johnson could infuse *The Wonder-Working Providence* with themes predicating the New Earth upon its colonial construction by the "Souldiers of Christ." They were God's elect reforming their churches and at the same time reforming the satanic and chaotic virgin land as well.

Stylistically, Johnson's beliefs open *The Wonder-Working Provi-*

dence to language reciprocal from Scripture and from colonial life, with no compunction that they be kept separate. Johnson laminates figures from Scripture and from social realms of his own participation. Neither in literature nor in life does he seem to have been a private person. There is no meditative strain in his work and no singular vocabulary of the individuated writer.

Johnson's language consistently suggests the intellectual reciprocity between the biblical wilderness and the New England forest. That they should merge was perhaps inevitable because, as William Hubbard said, ancient Israel had but to pass through the wilderness, not to plant it as did Puritans in New England.[28] Thus, twenty years after the Winthrop "planting," we see the spiritual inscape and physical landscape drawn close together in such of Johnson's phrases as "western wast," "wilderness of rocks," and "wild-woody wilderness."[29] The geographical locus of the West, the rockiness of land irrespective of scriptural stones of Jacob or Samuel, the semantic and alliterative link between virgin forest and spiritual wilderness—all these work toward connection of the palpable and spiritual. They reveal the great extent to which American topographical and geophysical properties were making incursions upon the a priori scriptural wilderness the Puritans thought themselves in before ever they arrived on New World shores.

III

The work ethic manifest in *The Wonder-Working Providence* is crucial to Johnson's imperative of environmental reform. For, by emphasizing the importance of human labor in expediting the Christian Millennium, Johnson can see in the dreariest of colonial toil certain apocalyptic value and reserve for man an active role in bringing about the prophesied New Earth. Two of Johnson's own notions about the Apocalypse evidently led him to regard colonial labor not only as a godly vocation but as a social catalyst for the New Earth.

As we know, he was convinced that the millennial epoch would begin in New England itself. Johnson's lodestone of history and prophecy pointed unerringly to the Massachusetts Bay, literally to be the site of the New Jerusalem, which would radiate outward from

New England in the Fifth Monarchy. Moreover, Johnson characterized this epoch as Christian in aura rather than in the Nazarene's
actual residence among the saints. He regarded the thousand years of
peace as a period of Christ's second advent and scorned dissenters
expecting a palpable Christ as those who "vainly imagine."[30]

The clear thrust of these views on the geographic location and
communal Christian harmony is to make the saints responsible for
developing the New Earth. Focusing attention upon the human role
in millennial preparation, Johnson adduces apocalyptic value in
colonizing work. In this way he removes from the Millennium such
hints of human passivity as are implicit in other Puritans' visions of
Christ and angels suddenly descending to earth.[31] *Their* Paradise
would be regained by godly fiat, but the cost would be the nullification of value in the active husbandry and gardening and technics so
vital to Johnson's chiliad. The actual work of colonization would be
negligible or at best reduced to the presupposed civil site we find in
Mather's apocalyptic writings. It is not at all surprising that Johnson
should find inadequate that Millennium inaugurated by God in a
context solely of spiritual preparation and ethical dealings. On the
contrary, he exalts the place of labor in millennial preparation and,
in his apocalyptic work ethic, reveals his ideology of environmental
reform.

That seemingly bumptious title—*The Wonder-Working Providence
of Sions Saviour in New England*—emphasizes Sion's (Zion's) savior
as Christ who, having redeemed man by his death, works awesome
wonders by guiding and directing Puritan New England, which is the
true Zion, the New English Israel. But just as "providence" indicates
godly direction, so it also implies foresight or preparation for the
future, in which sense it is vitally important in Johnson's scheme.

Semantically, "working" shows two meanings crucial to Johnson's
story of a New World transformed. First, God's "working" providence is operational; it brings about the awesome wonders. Johnson
had written in *Good News from New-England* of "the great *Jehova's
working word* [my italics] effecting wondrously/This earths vast
globe, those parts unknown."[32] But the title of his history additionally carries the idea of work as labor, which is the key to his
story of a wilderness transformed and to his idea of the appropriate
relationship of Puritan to Christ in New England. In his opening

chapters, when Christ's army is commissioned and empowered, Johnson cautions that continuous energy can flow only from Christ, whose power, imparted to the Puritan troops, will be wondrously operational *through man's labor.* "All men that expect the day, must attend the means."[33]

The great virtue of Johnson's work ethic lies, then, in its millennial expedience. The New Earth is to be man-made. Possibilities of this theme had engaged him even in *Good News,* in which Indians are naked men "whom labour did not tame" and the colonists initially in straits "till labour blesse the earths encrease." In that verse we see "the Husband-man rejoycing" and a panoply of grains brought to exportive surplus by the "Plough-man." The marvelous oysters are not enjoyed for succulence (or even for comparison to the then-famous oyster beds of Johnson's native Kent) but for conversion of their shells for lime "to lay fast stone and brick." Prefacing a eulogy to twenty Puritan ministers, Johnson had written of "work and workman" as God's blessed creations, and in *The Wonder-Working Providence* he relentlessly pursued his theme of spiritual ana manual labor on behalf of the New Earth. Even at the conclusion his gauntlet is down: "You that long so much for it, come forth and fight; who can expect a victory without a battel?"[34]

Not that Johnson alone among Puritan writers gave witness to the visible transformation of the landscape through hard work. Benjamin Lynde extols the beauties of a Boston intrinsically satisfying as a cityscape:

> Enrang'd street under street, she forms below
> A beauteous crescent, or Heaven's painted Bow
> Of various hewes.[35]

He goes on to celebrate Boston's spires and its window glass and to sing the aesthetic pleasures of pier and warehouse full of merchandise. As his fellow Puritan versifier Grindall Rawson put it, "Cittizens of the New Jerusalem . . . Rightly improve their towne."[36]

Other Puritan writers use the obvious transformation of the New England landscape as a caveat against worldliness or ingratitude to God. William Bradford is one:

O Boston, though thou are now grown
To be a great and wealthy town,
Yet I have seen thee a void place,
Shrubs and bushes covering thy face.[37]

Bradford scorns the gold, silk, and hosiery signifying material lust, and he warns Bostonians—or, those in a too-urbane "Boston condition"—to recall their humbler origins and the great moral leadership of their founders. He warns them not to defile the land in materialistic trafficking: "The trade is all in your own hand,/Take heed ye doe not wrong the land." Like Bradford, John Higginson uses the visible metamorphosing of wilderness into prosperous settlement to remind the Puritan burghers that thanks go to God alone. "Many earthly comforts," "small beginnings to great estates," "townes & fields," "shops and ships"—all visible signs of civilization invite a resounding *No!* to the rhetorical question from Jeremiah 2:32, "O generation see the word of the Lord, have I been a wilderness to you?"[38]

Apart from his literal-mindedness, one major difference in mimesis between Johnson and these others is that they portray the reformed new world landscape as a fait accompli, whether for good or ill, depending upon their rhetorical purposes. But theirs is a static view, a kind of "before" and "after" diptych. Johnson, on the other hand, is vitally concerned to portray the process of transformation, the dynamic movement through which the new earth emerges—the Wonders Work*ing*. True, at several points he hearkens to that "instant" nation of Isaiah 66:8. But Johnson validates his Isaiahan bravura with accounts of the labor involved. *The Wonder-Working Providence* is very much a story of America earned through the toil of settlers.

All these emigrants had relinquished well-plenished tables and coin-filled coffers, as well as beautifully built and richly appointed houses, in exchange for a "dolorous" beginning in the New World. Though scurvied, they begin in "steddy resolution . . . to plant the yet untilled Earth, having as yet no other meanes to teare up the bushy lands, but their hands and howes." Men unaccustomed to manual labor "fall to tearing up the Roots and Bushes." "Cutting down of the Woods, they inclose Corne fields." Forced to go barefooted at first, there are yet none "so barbarously bent" that they do not gather churches, even though "the toile of a new Plantation, being like the labours of Hercules, [is] never at an end." Ever strengthened by Christ, singing psalms and praising God "in these poore Wigwames," the colonists nonetheless are at times grievously in a "lonesome condition," though in Christian "love and unity," the settlers "translat[e] the close, clouded woods into goodly corn fields."[39]

Twenty triumphant years from those beginnings, Johnson lauds the environmental reform of New England. "In ten or twelve years planting, there [is] such wonderful alteration, a Nation born in a day, a Commonwealth orderly brought forth from a few Fugitives." Even century-old "Forraign plantations" based in staple commodities, gems, or precious metals and sponsored by kings and leagues of merchants pall in comparison:

> [T]his remote, rocky, barren, bushy, wild-woody wilderness, a receptacle for Lions, Wolves, Bears, Foxes, Rockoones, [game] Bags, Bevers, Otters, and all kind of wild creatures, a place that never afforded the Natives better than the flesh of a few wild creatures and parch't Indian corn incht out with Chestnuts and bitter Acorns, now through the mercy of Christ becom a second England for fertilness. In so short a space, that it is indeed the wonder of the world.[40]

Having declared the present New English "demi-paradise," Johnson celebrates the environmental metamorphosis. The original Puritan "wigwams, huts, and hovels" have given way to "orderly fair, and well-built houses, well furnished many of them, together with Orchards filled with godly fruit trees, and gardens with variety of flowers." Then Johnson moves to the statistics he loves to cite, the "neer a thousand acres of land planted for Orchards and Gardens" in Massachusetts, besides "fields filled with garden fruit." Now there is "supposed in this Colony, about fifteen thousand acres in tillage, and of cattel about twelve thousand neat, and about three thousand sheep." He is delighted to announce that "whereas at their first coming it was a rare matter for a man to have foure or five Acres of Corne, now many have four or five score."[41] Johnson has been criticized for his statistical errors, but to know that in his native Kent a farm of five to ten acres often supported an entire family, and that orchards and gardens ran to less than one acre, is to recognize the propagandistic value of the New Earth affirmed in statistics proving fantastic abundance realized through man's labor with God's blessing.[42]

We notice that Johnson's validation of the New Earth is in these statistics, in the quantification that proves the existence of the New Earth not in spiritual realms alone but in the palpable New England soil under intensive cultivation. Wrested from its primeval state, the erstwhile "wild-woody wilderness" is metamorphosed into a kind of godly bonanza farm of the sort America would see in the 1870s when journalists, significantly, would again invoke military figures to suggest efficiency and precision. In 1650 Johnson expected no less from the "souldiers of Christ" franchised by God in whose mind *The Wonder-Working Providence* begins. Ever palpable, Johnson's New Earth could be affirmed in statistics and thus quantified in the very process of its development. In writing his program for the American New Earth, Johnson established a pattern of symbolic demographics that was not to be used successfully until Whitman. Materially, Johnson's New Jerusalem was a civil engineering project in the wilds, one motivated by God and validated in irrefutable numbers. Its success was not judgmentally vulnerable to the disposition of one or a few but was proven and verified for all to read in unbiased numbers. It was, in short, a fact.

IV

There is an important technological side to the making of the American New Earth, although this area of the Puritan imagination—one based upon English assumption and precedent—has remained obscure, largely because scholars investigating the English origins of Puritanism have been engaged elsewhere. William Haller, Perry Miller, Alan Simpson, and Sacvan Bercovitch (to name but a few) have worked to disclose both the English religious background of Puritanism and its theological legacy in New England. At the same time, complementary studies in Puritan demography and politics by the social historians Sumner Powell, Michael Zuckerman, Kenneth

Lockridge, and Richard Bushman have revealed sociopolitical differences between Puritans before and after emigration and have showed the gradual metamorphosis (in Bushman's term) from Puritan to Yankee.[43]

Nevertheless, in his work on the interrelation between society and technology, Lewis Mumford long ago alerted us to the kinds of social attitudes and dispositions that predetermine technical development well before the creation of actual mechanical artifacts makes technological development verifiable. Mumford offers no systematic discussion of this point in regard to American culture, but his *Technics and Civilization* and *The Myth of the Machine* both imply a necessary acceptance of the power and potential uses of machinery in America long before the so-called Industrial Age.[44] Of course, Leo Marx has revealed the intellectual dialectic of technology and the pastoral ideal of American thought, principally in the nineteenth century when the machine encroached upon the garden in pervasive and palpable ways. Marx sees the lines of contention as drawn clearly only in a post-Revolutionary America when economic feasibility of manufacturing became a point debated publicly. By then the machine and the garden did stand opposed in many quarters.[45]

But they had not in the mid-seventeenth century when English Puritans came to America prepared to use both an available and an anticipated technology for their own purposes. *The Wonder-Working Providence* and other writings by New England Puritans reveal a readiness to use technics for the amelioration of society and, in Johnson's case, to bring about the New Earth. Technology is one servant of his millennial vision.

In its civil engineering, the "forest labour" of environmental reform in *The Wonder-Working Providence* is markedly English. Just as the Puritans transported to America their a priori notions about land appropriation, about the wilderness and the Apocalypse, so does Johnson reveal that his models for landscape reform are English ones. For instance the swamp trekking seems based upon similar efforts in England. The social and economic historian of seventeenth-century Kent, C. W. Chalklin, writes that "the principal means [of forest clearance] seem to have been the building of farmsteads in the forest, and the gradual clearance of the surrounding land." One is well reminded that Johnson was born at the very turn of the sixteenth century and was thirty years old when he sailed on the *Arbella*—just five years short of the average life expectancy in Kent. When we read his boasts about American trees felled and vast acreage planted in orchards, we are listening to amplified echoes of contemporary English (and particularly Kentish) life. Throughout England in the sixteenth and early seventeenth centuries, a rising population "led to the clearance of woods, the enclosure of moorland, and the drainage of marshes and fens on a scale unknown for at least two hundred years."[46] In an agricultural economy the arability of land determines value, and the potential for reclamation is a touchstone of worth. When William Hubbard wrote bitterly of the English blood spilled in the cause of Indian suppression in the Maine region, his complaint was based on the worthlessness of the Maine land, "a barren and Rocky Country . . . being of little worth, unless it were for the Borders upon the Seacoast and some spots and Skirts of more desirable Land upon the banks of some Rivers."[47]

This same attitude surfaces in other Puritan writings. An anonymous essayist proposed that each New England colonist allotted land for home and farm ought also to be burdened with an equal proportion of "Swampes and such Rubbish waest grounds . . . which harbor Wolves and such noyesome beasts and serpents," which the settler would be obliged to clear, in order that such ground "may be suppressed."[48] In *The Wonder-Working Providence* the triumphant thrust of roads and bridges in the wilds is New England's successful emulation of the dynamic landscape alteration which Johnson had witnessed since his boyhood in Kent. It is environmental reform for the amelioration of life in New England. Winthrop felt the Indian land claims were invalid because the natives had "no artes, cattle, or other menes to subdue or improve any more of those lands then they plant with Corne," but Johnson's is the imagination rife with possibilities for America's technocracy.[49] Specifically, Johnson's New Earth is attainable not only through tillage but through mechanization and invention.

One reason why the technological side of the New England Puritan imagination has been obscure is that discussions of the Puritan tribal society have invited close attention to Puritans' organic metaphors of community but not to those suggesting the uniform discipline and synchronized movement of machinery. For instance, we recall

Cotton Mather's "vine here planted" which God has "Caus[ed] to take deep Root, and fill the land, so that it sent its boughs unto the Atlantic Sea Eastward, and its Branches unto the Connecticut Westward, and the Hills covered with the shadow thereof." Though Edward Johnson draws from the scriptural font of botanical images, his preference for military figures from the Bible permits him meanings that cannot be conveyed in organic figures of vines and trees. Even an army commissioned for Christ is disciplined and synchronized in movement, its strength concentrated, and its power an exponential multiple of one individual's capability. Two centuries later Melville spoke of the "mechanical magic of discipline," meaning collectively the superhuman machine into which the individual submerges (or integrates) personal identity for the greater identity of the whole, be it the military or the manufactory.[50] John Winthrop's often cited warning aboard the *Arbella* that society must maintain its fixity of interlocking classes has been viewed as reflecting a medieval socioeconomic structure soon to disappear in entrepreneurial America; but it also suggests the Puritan conviction about the virtue of a disciplined social machine whose components submit to the common work goal. As John Eliot wrote, "Grounds and ends are secret things from the sight of other men . . . and therefore the best way to prove unto men that our grounds and ends are Religious, is to let it appear to be so, by our [outwardly] religious waies and workes."[51]

It is important to recognize that the particularly Christian themes in *The Wonder-Working Providence,* especially those of Christ's parental mercies and the oft-evoked apocalyptic destiny of New England, prevent Johnson's soldiers from becoming automatons in a huge colonizing machine. But the attainment of Johnson's New Earth, as well as the final battle against Gog and Magog, demands a military preparedness. On New England's side is the orderly, controlled, powerful social machine of an army, while the forces of antichrist are comprised of the human disorder and the dissipated strength of a "whole rabble."[52]

From the seventeenth century onward in America, the amelioration of society has been regarded largely as a moral problem which, nonetheless, has its materialistic side pertinent to human mastery—or at least management—of nature through technology and its handmaidens, the crafts. It seems that, as Perry Miller and Thomas Johnson say, natural science had not in the seventeenth century "demonstrated its utility by the intervention of time- and labor-saving devices."[53] Too, Puritans suspected that scientific absorptions would lead men away from God, that meteorology, for instance, might become engaging per se rather than opening the ways of God to men who were better off striving to understand such of his messages as Samuel Sewall perceived when he called the darkening sky "metaphoric." Still, the use of God's world for the improvement of life remained an unchallenged human prerogative. Accordingly, socially ameliorative devices were very much in the imagination of certain Puritans committing their colonial visions to paper.

From seventeenth-century England we have a clearer view of the New England Puritan penchant for technology and science. Despite recent revision, Robert Merton's study remains very useful in its correlation of the ascendance of Puritanism with that of science and technology. He points out that it was incumbent on the Calvinist "to conquer the temptations of this world by *remaking it* through ceaseless, unflinching toil."[54] With ample statistical verification of increased technology in such areas as marine transport, munitions, and mining, Merton has frequent ideological recourse to Richard Baxter's writings from which he asserts a strong utilitarian strain in Puritan culture. It is one which, bolstered by diligence and industry, fostered scientific study and technological activity. Baxter, whose respect in the New England colonies is proven by the importation of his treatises (which we may suppose to have been circulated among the intelligentsia), had written in his *Christian Directory* (1664–65) that "If a man were to take the comfort of his learning and wisdom, one way is by . . . making discoveries . . . in arts and sciences, which delight him . . . by the very acting."[55] Baxter goes on to speculate on the "delight" of the inventors of the sea chart and magnetic attraction, and of printing, and of guns, in their inventions. That delight may have been shared by contemporaries witnessing the new inventions and thoughtful about their future potential.

Historians continue to debate the relationship between pure science and technology in seventeenth-century England, and to be sure, Edward Johnson was long settled in Woburn and had largely completed *The Wonder-Working Providence* in the years in which the German émigré Samuel Hartlib published in London a spate of technological pamphlets under the encouragement of Robert Boyle's sister, Lady Ranelagh, and with the blessing of the Commonwealth and then the Protectorate. And the early Restoration years when the Fellows of the Royal Society were in committee drafting a preamble asserting the "business of the Royal Society: to improve the knowledge of natural things, and all useful arts, Manufactures, Mechanic practice, Engynes and Inventions by experiment"—those were the years in which Edward Johnson was absorbed by quite different committee work relating to New England's "Patent, laws, privileges," suddenly frightfully negotiable as the restored monarch sent royal commissioners to investigate colonial waywardness long rumored in England.[56]

Yet fully one-half of Edward Johnson's long life was spent in his native England, of which a historian of science has recently written that "the idea of studying nature to glorify God and benefit mankind through inventions and discoveries was something of a commonplace by the time Francis Bacon made it the dominant theme of his reformation of all learning."[57] Johnson, we recall, was the man called upon repeatedly to survey land, to plan repairs of the fort at Castle Island, to take charge of the inventory of fire-powered colonial armaments. His were the similes drawn from technics, as when he wrote that it was "as unnatural for a right N. E. man to live without an able Ministery, as for a Smith to work his iron without a fire." It was Johnson who, in order to flee England without attracting notice of Laud's agents, listed himself as a "joiner," a technical occupation his editor believes to have been more an evasion than an untruth, since Johnson may have been a shipbuilder in Herne Bay, just as his son was to become one in New England.[58]

This is not to suggest that but for his emigration Johnson would have been welcomed to fellowship in the Royal Society, or even that he would have been on the fringes of the Hartlib group whom the younger Winthrop evidently met and encouraged to establish a scientific college in the colonies. The point is, rather, that Edward Johnson's Puritanism was practiced with an engineering bias formed in England where cultural conditions nurtured it. Once in New England, he evidently saw technology (both in machines he knew and those he dreamed of in metaphors of military power) as an important means by which to expedite the New Earth.

America's technological potential is a theme muted and desultory in Puritan colonial writings, but it is one ineluctably in evidence and spurred by yearnings to render the intractable New World subservient to human needs and desires. Johnson observed that in 1641 "the Lord was pleased to send a very sharp Winter, insomuch that the Harbor where Ships ordinarily Anchor, was frozen over of such a thickness, that it became passeable, both for horse, carts, and oxen, for the space of five weeks."[59] Johnson's haste to assert God's more recent moderation of New England winters suggests his ambivalence, for the severe cold was a high price for the natural bridge. Contrarily, Samuel Danforth, Sr.'s little almanac verse for 1647 speaks wistfully about the ease of winter's engineering.

> Great bridges shall be made alone
> Without ax, timber, earth or stone,
> Of crystall metall, like to glasse.[60]

The contrasting sobriety of Edward Johnson's Woburn Town Record entry for 26 June 1641 is immediately apparent: "A bridge was made across Horne pond River; though the place was so boggy that it swallowed up much wood before it could be made passable; yet it was finished, and called Longe Bridg." Johnson's terse entry takes on deeper emotional value in light of his record of the previous day: "Things going heavily on, and many blocks in the way, especially some of their own company disheartening, this day was set apart for humble seeking the Lord by fasting and prayer, whom they found gracious in keeping up the spirit of some to the work."[61] Such glimpses of discouragement and of resolute confrontation with the new land impart particular significance to Johnson's later boast in *The Wonder-Working Providence* about "wild and uncouth woods fil'd with frequented wayes, and large rivers over-laid with Bridges passeable both for horse and foot."[62]

Along with other Puritans, Johnson also shows strong interest in mechanics and the possibilities of invention, other harbingers of the technocracy. John White had said in 1639 that the "shifting into empty lands, enforceth men to frugality, and quickeneth invention." The Puritans' pursuit of physical science was intermittent, but they were interested in mechanical devices and in engineering feats likely to improve New England life. John Eliot remarked that Noah's age had no doubt mastered enology, since "they had inventions of far greater consideration and difficulty."[64] Such inventions were exactly what the Puritans needed to exploit the resources of New England. In *Good News* Edward Johnson had depicted the region as rich in natural resources. "With mineralls the earth is fraught, though Alcumists are wanting." There are trees potentially sawable into clapboards, there is clay for brick and tile and ores that but want discovery and smelting. Puritan appreciation for inventive ingenuity is revealed in Johnson's remark that

> Monopolies is by their lawed forbid,
> Unlesse invention rare from others hid.[65]

Johnson is pleased later in his verse to say that New England's resources are being exploited, though not until he wrote *The Wonder-Working Providence* did he reveal the mechanical means of it, principally milling. A quarter-century later William Hubbard was to appreciate the power of sawmills in the Maine settlements by waterways. "Those late Inventions," as Hubbard calls the "Saw-Mills," "[are] so useful for the destruction of Wood and Timber, specially of Firr-Trees, which no doubt so abound in those Coasts, that there is scarce a River or Creek in those parts that hath not some of those Engines erected upon them."[66]

Edward Johnson had been delighted to present mechanics as indices of sophisticated improvement in New England life. He boasts of the "iron mill in constant use," "the Corn mill," "the saw mill[s]," the "fulling-mill" that enabled Rowley's citizens to be "first that set upon making of Cloth in this Western World." He proves how modern the colony is in his catalog of artisans liberated from the plow:

Carpenters, Joyners, Glaziers, Painters, follow their trades only; Gun-smiths, Lock-smiths, Naylers, Cutlers, have left the husbandman to follow the Plow and Cart, and they their trades; Weavers, Brewers, Bakers, Coster-mongers, Feltmakers, Braziers, Pewterers, and Tinkers, Ropemakers, Masons, Lime, Brick, and Tilemakers, Cardmakers to work, and not to play, Turners, Pumpmakers, and Wheelers, Glovers, Fellmongers, and Furriers, are orderly turn'd to their trades, besides divers sorts of Shopkeepers, and some who have a mystery beyond others, as have the Vintners.[67]

This colonial division of labor, so different from conditions in Kent where the farmer typically doubled as compleat artisan, enables Johnson to conclude that "the Lord has been pleased to turn one of the most hideous, boundless, and unknown wildernesses in the world in an instant, as 'twere ... to a well-ordered Commonwealth."[68]

The technics and disciplined social structure are, then, Johnson's instruments of earthly reform. They are the "artes" and the "menes" that Winthrop found wanting among the Indians. They have transformed thickets of suckling wolves and bears into "streets full of Girles and Boys sporting up and down" in a Boston whose "continuall inlargement presages some sumptuous City," even if the royal commissioners in 1666–67 sniffed at crooked streets "with little decency and no uniformity" and belittled the "wooden college" which Johnson cherished for its conversion of wilderness into parietal "bowling green."[69] Johnson's recourse to a variety of machines and crafts and his boast that in New England a large group of mechanics "follow their trades only," having "left the husbandman to follow the Plow and Cart," bespeak a New Earth in which machine and garden coexist amicably, conjoint with reformed (or, in Johnson's term, purified) religious and political institutions.

It is true that Johnson's was not a mind prone to envision fantastic futuristic possibilities for machines. It was Edward Taylor, not Edward Johnson, who mentioned in verse "Archimedes Engins made for war," even though Johnson's awe of Archimedean power emerges in his metaphor of Christ's "dazeling brightnesse . . . to be contracted in the burning-Glasse of these his peoples Zeale."[70] Still, Johnson thinks of God as an omnipotent engineer before whom the most advanced contemporary technics is mere gadgetry. (God has "caused to fall before your eyes . . . cunning Engenires, men skilful to destroy with all the terrible engins of war.") New England's success is the godly phenomenon of such magnitude that mechanic dreams alone would be a perverse, small-minded, and sinful waste of imagination. In Johnson there is no desperate Connecticut Yankee meddling in the Massachusetts General Court. But if he is no Puritan Leonardo, he avails himself nonetheless of existing technics in order to prove progress in New England life. Johnson's New Earth may be scented acridly with the gunpowder of Christ's artillery, but its godly engineering is just one function of the dynamic conversion of amorphous New World space into the utopian demesne of the American New Earth.

Aesthetically, Johnson's achievement in American literature is yet unclear. To be sure, his work is flawed, though not necessarily in ways the genteel critics of the past have thought. The "roughness" and "shocking" images that so long banished the metaphysical poets from the canon of approved English literature had also banished Johnson, and doubly so in American literary circles to whom the militance of the Puritan ancestry had become embarrassing. Despite his meandering sentences, Johnson's readers can enjoy the freshness and energy of his prose which, for literary purposes, bears lengthy excerpting more easily than does that of his theological mentor, John Cotton, who often must be paraphrased, his style requiring a twentieth-century suspension of disbelief in the aural dreariness of his endless Ramist dichotomies. Yet while Johnson survives with vibrancy on the page as Cotton does not, there are serious structural flaws in *The Wonder-Working Providence*. For, ironically, the very mind that saw environmental reform as a joint imperative with church reform was finally trapped, aesthetically, by the literalness that had opened and shaped his vision of a millennial America.

Early on, Johnson's "Herrald at Armes" had warned the Christian troops, "Fayle not to ship lusty Mares," since in the wilderness would be "Troopes of stout Horsemen marshalled." Soon we learn why; the ultimate battle of the righteous against Gog and Magog requires cavalry:

> You shall see great smoake and flames ascending up on high. . . . Then oh! you People of Israel gather together as one Man. . . . For Christ and the great King of all the Earth is now going forth in his great Wrath and terrible Indignation to avenge the bloud of his Saints, . . . and now for the great and bloudy Battell of Gog and Magog, Rivers of bloud, and up to the Horse-bridles, even the bloud of those [who] have drunke bloud so long. Oh! dreadfull day, when the patience and long-suffering of Christ, that hath lasted so many hundred of yeares, shall end.[71]

So we have it, spirited mares swimming in blood in this War To End All Wars. Only in the meantime are the "wondrous workes now suddenly to be wrought for the accomplishment of these things!" In short, the millennial America is but an interlude, spatially a staging area for the final holocaust. And the American New Jerusalem with its gardens and orchards, its technology and social harmony, is but an interim. Theologically, Johnson is fixed to his calendar, hastening this watch to Apocalypse.

But, aesthetically, *The Wonder-Working Providence* suffers from contradiction between its internal literary themes and its external theological assumptions. Within the work there is no abrasion between machine and garden, which cohabit harmoniously in New England. Thematic focus is upon the contention between wilderness chaos and a civilized order both agrarian and mechanical. But since the primeval forest has no value in the work, being chaotic, satanic, at best irksome, all reader sympathies lie with the settlers' efforts at conversion of thickets and bogs to the New Earth. The literary engagement is all with the millennial effort. Even the artillery train in a "Garden" which, though but the conventional name for such training ground, reinforces themes of wilderness reform. The "Souldiers of Christ" are not guerrillas. And, theologically, man's and God's time are approaching the apocalyptic hour, which is splendid for Johnson's contemporary readers for whom biblical values swirl about the text. For them the notion that any human garden should in kind approach God's was preposterous. That the hard-wrought New Earth should warrant perpetual preservation was unthinkable. Theological truth simply relegates New England (and outward from it, the world) to its proper temporal interlude of one thousand years before The End. It is both paradigm and specimen as the New Earth. Therein lies its glory and triumph, to be superseded by the greater glory of Eternity.

Not so, however, for non-Puritan readers neither able nor willing to follow *The Wonder-Working Providence* beyond its own pages. For them the values intrinsic to the work are those of the saints' struggles to survive, to maintain orthodox purity against insidious and powerful heresies, to conform precisely to an inflexible godly commission, and to transform the "desart wilderness" into a utopian civil landscape. An apocalyptic transcendence of the chosen remnant is indeed the expected climax toward which *The Wonder-Working Providence* builds by way of the saintly, soldierly action here on earth. But Johnson offers no vision of transcendence except the holocaust that will obliterate the very New Earth on whose behalf the sympathies of the reader have been enlisted. He builds the bridge from God's time to man's but does not within the work reconnect events of human history with the ultimate unity of God's eternity. The horrendous *rite de passage is imminent* and deliverance assured, but Johnson makes no structural preparation for it other than a lustful yearning for the Doomsday Battle.

Thus the "goodly fields," once "close clouded woods," are in due time to become a battleground. But while the dynamic process of wilderness transformation is valuably rendered in *The Wonder-Working Providence,* the forthcoming metamorphosis of orchards and gardens to battleground is only asserted. Theologically, the apocalyptic calendar shows the battlefield to be closer to Eternity than is the New Earth. From a purely temporal perspective it is therefore advantageous, since the battle against Gog and Magog is the passageway to eternal heavenly bliss. Yet within *The Wonder-Working Providence* Johnson does not establish priorities stucturally. His reader is thus urged to accept truth asserted, even when it contradicts truth rendered in the literature. We are asked to anticipate the final bloodletting with terrific joy, though it means the obliteration of the New Earth whose construction we have sympathized with and participated in vicariously. Unlike Edward Taylor, Johnson does not really try to evoke the transcendent bliss of a Christian Heaven through such figures as perfumes and jewels and flowers. Instead, his Christ glows like burnished armor, searing as light beamed through a convex lens. Johnson's imagination stops short of transcendence and lingers instead with the far prospect of holy carnage.

The horrific Gog and Magog are, however, latent. Temporally they portend but narratively do not importune to destroy *The Wonder-Working Providence,* which for the most part remains geographically focused upon New England, itself an emblem of America. No precursor of democracy, Johnson reveals instead his paternity of other, environmental, American ideas just nascent at the time he wrote. In the long run his importance may be unrelated to his "middlebrow" corroboration of Puritan doctrine expounded by those intellectually more subtle than he. Certainly, for purposes here, Johnson's mythopoeic shortcomings in mimesis are offset by the coherent vision in which he elevates seventeenth-century American environmental attitudes into imperatives for action under a theological rubric sanctifying reform of the natural landscape. We read Johnson closely and seriously not to resuscitate yet one more minor figure in American literature but rather to see what parts of the peculiarly American puzzle of experience are available in *The Wonder-Working Providence.*

It is a singular book but not, as we see from complementary Puritan writings, an eccentric one. Above all, it suggests a special American version of the Judeo-Christian tradition authorizing human mastery (and implicitly exploitation) of the natural world. To endow the New England settlement effort with cosmic meaning, Johnson goes beyond the historicism of the Creation with its assertion of man's dominion over all the earth. He reaches moreover to the imminence of the prophesied Millennium, thereby obliging immigrant Americans not only to custodial charge of the earth but indeed to its second creation as the New Earth. Johnson is no propagandist for plunder of the New World, no advocate of geographic profligacy. On the contrary, his terrestrial imperatives—utopian, messianic, martial—are as rigorous and close ruled as the orthodox Puritanism to which they are alloyed. They commend Johnson, not as an intellectual patriarch, but certainly as an ideological paterfamilias of American environmental reform. As subsequent American literature would prove, *The Wonder-Working Providence* is no thematic mutant but the cultural initiate of ramifying, reformist visions of an American New Earth.

3: The Revolution Begins
the World Anew

> *Year of the purpose accomplish'd!*
> *Year of the marriage of continents, climates and oceans!*
> *(No mere doge of Venice now wedding the Adriatic),*
> *I see O year in you the vast terraqueous globe given and*
>   *giving all,*
> *Europe to Asia, Africa join'd, and they to the New World,*
> *The lands, geographies, dancing before you, holding a*
>   *festival garland,*
> *As brides and bridegrooms hand in hand.*
>
> *Walt Whitman,* Passage to India

In the autumn of 1812 John Adams told Jefferson that his "curiousity had been stimulated by an event of singular Oddity," namely his son's, John Quincy's, purchase at a Berlin auction of "three Pamphlets bound together" and sent on to Adams *père* in New England. One of these was the "Wonder working Providence of Zions Saviour in New England."[1]

His correspondence with Jefferson shows John Adams to have been interested chiefly in another of the "pamphlets," specifically in Thomas Morton's *New English Canaan* with its Maypole of Merrymount episode perennially irresistible to American writers. As for the author of *The Wonder-Working Providence,* Adams neither guessed at nor puzzled over his identity, nor did he remark upon the contents of that work. We can suppose him uninterested in it—or we can surmise a likely alternative, namely, that for John Adams, as for numerous of his contemporaries, the doctrinaire Puritanism of *The Wonder-Working Providence* seemed as archaic as the values of conjoint spiritual and environmental reform in that work were timely and true. For these latter values had in one and one-half centuries of American life become culturally so pervasive, so entrenched, that Edward Johnson's once radical polemic on the American New Earth was now a warranted assumption and thus thought unremarkable.

Like other heirs of Johnson's Puritan America, John Adams had in fact already done his eighteenth-century exercises in affirming the New American Earth, and in phrases typical of the American Enlightenment. In 1765 Adams wrote in his *Diary,*

> I always considered the settlement of America with Reverence and Wonder—as the Opening of a grand scene and design in Providence, for the Illumination of the Ignorant and the Emancipation of the slavish part of Mankind over all the Earth.[2]

Nine years earlier and, again, in the *Diary,* Adams had described with satisfaction the American environmental reform incorporated in that millennial "grand scene and Design in Providence." Then he paused to consider two centuries of change from an American "dismall Wilderness." "Now," writes Adams, "the Forests are removed, the Land covered with fields of Corn, orchards bending with fruit, and magnificent Habitations of rational and civilized People." He goes on to praise "rich Countries fraught with every delightful Object, and Meadows painted with the most beautyful scenery of Nature, and of Art." Instead of Indian huts there are "fair and lofty Edificies, large and well compacted Cities.[3]

From the parochial security of Quincy, Massachusetts, the young schoolmaster Adams considered American environmental reform as accomplished fact. It is as if the settlement proceeding in Puritan writings were now completed, as if aspiration could be enshrined as achievement. Were this the only point to be drawn from literature on this subject in Adams's time, then the American Enlightenment would but offer a corroborative, if secular, footnote to those seventeenth-century Puritan writings concerned with spiritual and topographical reform of the New World to the utopian state of the prophesied New Earth.

Yet Adams's very diction suggests other possibilities. Nowhere in his remarks is there the familiar and customary Puritan tone of contention between Americans and the landscape. Edward Johnson's seventeenth-century Puritan phrases on toil, torn flesh, and hard forest labors yield in Adams to language of easeful removal of forests, deserts, and "offensive Swamps" from land artfully covered or painted into "magnificent Habitations of rational and civilized People." Over one century, vis à vis the American and his landscape, the artist has replaced the bushwhacking colonist. In Adams we see, in short, the suggestion of a new, eighteenth-century environmental attitude. It is one that gained special prestige—in fact, validation— from the American Revolution.

Persistent themes in praise and encouragement of environmental reform in American literature of the Revolutionary and Early National period suggest how important the idea of an engineered New Earth had become in some one and one-half centuries of colonial American life. Through the Enlightenment, which Adrienne Koch dates from 1765 to 1815, including the advent and institution of republican government (and, of course, the war itself), American writers, especially those of the Northeast, continued to incorporate paired themes of imperative spiritual and environmental reform in such diverse offerings as history, travel narrative, poetry, diary, geography, and the informal essay.

More telling than generic variety, however, is the survival of the theme in quite new modes of thought. The strength of cultural conviction is of course best measured not by mere endurance over decades but by adaptation to new ways of thought within a changed sensibility. By the time of the Enlightenment, Cotton Mather's yearned-for and intellectually respectable "Theopolis Americana" had become, in the very strictest Puritan reading, but the self-delusion of the ranting field orator—at least according to Philip Freneau, the Revolutionary War poet who felt that millennial peace could be attained only through gradual change in human nature "by reason's aid . . . in the slow advance of things."[4] The implication of Freneau's view is clear: if the Puritans' messianic, doctrinaire New Earth were to survive otherwise than as a butt of generation-gap satire or as the cherished doctrine of the millenarian reactionary, then it had to be ideologically revivified, modified, assimilated anew in American thought.

And it was.

In fact, writers of the late eighteenth century gave even greater emphasis to the idea of an engineered New Earth than had their

Puritan predecessors. In part they did so from growing belief not only in social and earthly *improvement* (the word Puritans so often invoked) but in human *progress* in both spiritual and material realms. Belief in progress was bolstered by assumptions of plenitude in nature which, as we shall see, alleviated fears of human exhaustion of the world's resources and tended to encourage their exploitation for the betterment of the human condition. Moreover, strong convictions of man's power to effect environmental change coupled with English aesthetic models provided a new vocabulary which lent belletristic prestige to landscape change and in turn gave impetus to themes of environmental reform in the American Enlightenment.

Such factors, however, were subordinate to the one transcendent idea that sanctioned environmental reform in America by placing it in a new epochal context. As influential as were attitudes toward progress and plenitude, one powerful idea surpassed these others and brought about radical change in the way American writers regarded the environment. That idea—for so it was—was that of the American Revolution. Whether one saw it (as Mercy Warren did) principally as a military event or viewed it (in John Adams's terms) as a revolution within Americans' minds in the fifteen years before muskets fired on the Battle Green, the Revolution held one meaning central to American thought of the post-Revolutionary and Early National period. By consensus writers affirmed that, as of the Revolution, the Golden Age of Liberty had begun. It was no longer in the future, or even near at hand, but was vibrant in the actual present. (The sudden spate of Rising-Glory-of-America hymns in verse and prose marked and verified the Age of Liberty as an article of literary faith.) The Revolution was thus no mere *sign* of the beginning of the millennial Age of Liberty; for many writers it *was* the beginning.

This is not to say that on the subject of the American environment post-Revolutionary writers unanimously greet the new Golden Age with mellifluous rhythms in a dulcet vocabulary. In the late eighteenth century and beyond we continue to find passages evocative of harsh colonizing work. Despite Benjamin Franklin's 1743 proclamation that "the first drudgery of settling new colonies which confines the attention of people to mere necessaries is now pretty well over," there remains a literary record concerned with those "mere necessaries." For instance, in 1817 a contributor to the

Portico spoke of the "unbounded forests of our country, where now the wily Indian lies in ambush for his prey, . . . where the panther and wolf howl fearfully through the dark foilage, or where the malignant and ferocious buffaloe with uncouth and hideous roar, disturbs the awful reign of silence and of darkness."[5] Substitute, say, bear for "buffaloe," and the feeling might be that of the insomniac Winthrop recording in his *Journal* one memorable night when he was lost in the woods.

Moreover, eighteenth-century writers in their secular way justified colonial settlement and expansion with the same reasons Puritans offered:

> When the colonist beheld desolate yet fertile plains, hundreds of miles in extent, unfrequented by a single human being, . . . he would naturally imagine that he had a right to make it his dwelling. He would conceive it a sort of breach of duty to leave to wild beasts and to a few scores of savages, fields that were capable of supporting cities and villages where thousands might enjoy all the blessings of civilization, freedom, and religion.[6]

Echoes of John White are unmistakable.

Yet, despite a continuing tone and logic from the seventeenth century, the predominant environmental attitude in the American Enlightenment is a marked contrast to that which we have examined in Puritan New England. This new attitude, not itself of American origin, is based on belief not only in authority but in human *power* to bring about change in the environment. At length the Revolution would give it epic validation in the literature of late eighteenth-century America, but its origins were European, inclusively English, and its suppositions cis-Atlantic.

We have evidence that in Western thought the concept of man as a geologic agent emerges strongly in the late seventeenth and eighteenth centuries in the bold syntheses of the philosophes. Such writers as Linnaeus, Volney, Montesquieu, Hume, William Robertson, and especially Count Buffon go beyond discussion of the kinds of desultory environmental changes easily accomplished in a preindustrial culture (sporadic forest clearance, swamp drainage, stream damming, etc.). They reach to divers and intensifying discussions of climatic causality, a subject which in the eighteenth century

achieved secular independence of religion and which ramified to
related matters of natural history, national character, health, and
independent invention. Natural histories like Buffon's, Clarence
Glacken writes, inevitably considered man's place in nature and
focused upon "the contrasts between environments long settled by
man and those remote from his influence."[7]

Not surprisingly, as Glacken remarks, "the most dramatic comparison was that between long-settled Europe . . . and the relatively
virgin areas of the colonies of North America." European travelers to
America were especially mindful of the contrast and generally agreed
that here, too, in the New World nature must submit to changes
imposed upon it by its new inhabitants.[8] These changes would be
sponsored philosophically by such ideas on aesthetics, economics,
biology, and health as were put forward by Jefferson and his friend
the Marquis de Chastellux. Additionally, American writers
emphasized their singular motivation for environmental change,
namely, the conviction that there the New World would be reformed
into the millennial New Earth.

In these new and various eighteenth-century syntheses there is one
point of agreement, that man is empowered by himself to bring
about environmental change. In part this conviction grew deductively
as the natural philosophers surveyed the globe and began to understand just how much of it had been altered already over the centuries
by human effort. As the Scotsman William Robertson wrote, "When
we survey the face of the habitable globe, no small part of that
fertility and beauty which we ascribe to the hand of Nature is the
work of man," whose efforts "change the appearance and improve
the qualities of the earth."[9]

In part, too, the conviction of human power over the environment
was bolstered by what Peter Gay calls "the interplay of the Enlightenment among ideas and events, inventions and expectations"
whose "raw materials were the triumph of Newtonian science" and
"striking improvements in industrial and agricultural techniques."[10]
These improvements are described in detail by Brooke Hindle, who
remarks in his study of science in Revolutionary America that "it
was one of the articles of faith of the Enlightenment that science
could be applied to the improvement of the material conditions of
life," and that "this utilitarian emphasis was particularly welcome in

America where youth and necessity gave added prestige to all that was useful."[11] As we have seen, the Puritan colonists had from the beginning technologically utilitarian aspirations—even fantasies—but ones which their heirs in the Enlightenment were able at least to realize. As the Connecticut Wit David Humphreys put it, "Ingenious engines wondrous works perform,/The hungry nourish and the naked warm."[12] In his extensive discussion of technology and republican values in this period, John Kasson points out how republicanism became "a dynamic ideology consonant with rapid technological innovation and expansion," how such values as thrift, moral purity, and economic independence came to be seen as manifest in technological power within capitalistic economics. Thus can Mercy Warren express pleasure in the "industry and enterprise . . . in the numerous canals, turnpikes, elegant buildings, and well constructed bridges, over lengths and depths of water that open, and render the communication easy and agreeable, throughout a country almost without bounds. In short," she adds, "the arts and agriculture are pursued with avidity, civilization spreads, and science in full research is investigating all the sources of human knowledge."[13]

Thus, the sanctioning in Genesis of human *authority* to take dominion over the earth now in the eighteenth century becomes additionally a conviction of achieved human *power* to remake the environment. And it is power seen as independent of the providential disposition of an intervening deity. There is now a quantum leap from environmental yeomanry to that of creativity itself. As the New Englander Jared Eliot said of his Puritan colonial forebears, "It may be said, That in a Sort, *they began the World a New.*"[14] Eliot's remark, however, is purely of the eighteenth century, for no Puritan colonist ever uttered such blasphemy. In this human appropriation of genesis in the New World there is environmental God-play. The human role changes from agency, with its implicit subordination, to that of causation. Now, not only can man clear some acres to welcome warming sunlight for the first time to a field or garden plot, but with massive deforestation he can plan to alter the very climate itself. Late in the seventeenth century the Puritan Samuel Sewall had watched the darkening New England sky and called the weather "metaphoric," since he knew it to be rich with divine meaning. Roughly one hundred years later, imaginations like Sewall's concentrated, not on divination of cloud masses, but on planning how to manipulate and govern weather themselves.

This new confidence in man's power radically to change the environment emerges not only in European writings but in those of Americans. Here in his *Diary* the young John Adams exemplifies the new attitude when in 1756 he writes that despite the "small and contemptable" power of the human body, man can "invent Engines and Instruments, to take advantage of the Powers in Nature," that he can "rear the Valley into a lofty mountain, and reduce the mountain to a humble Vale," and can "rend the Rocks and level the proudest Trees. At his pleasure the forest is cleared and Palaces rise." Approvingly Adams cites technologies in agriculture and in water transport, and those that forestall disaster and enable "Enjoyments and Pleasures."[15]

Noteworthy is Adams's tone of wonder and pride that stops just short of arrogance. Clearly, the power for environmental change is no license for profligate manipulation of the environment. Man's "pleasure" is tempered by his reason, a faculty of invention and of judgment. As engineer and horticulturist, Adams's "Man" is an enlightened custodian responsible to the world he is empowered to change.

English belles lettres as well as European science provided American writers of the Enlightenment with models for environmental change. Particularly, the Augustan and pre-Romantic writers exemplified in literature the power and aesthetic prerogatives of landscape alteration. Edward Malins has revealed how intimately connected to belles lettres were the works of the English landscape designers.[16] For instance, the designs of Lancelot Brown and Humphrey Repton, realized in the small Garrick estate or on the South Front of Harlestone Park, evoked literary responses both appreciative and critical—but always assumptive of human rights and abilities to change the landscape. In his play, *The Clandestine Marriage* (1766), coauthored with George Colman, Garrick satirized Brown's methods of landscape "improvement" through his character Mr. Sterling, a merchant parvenu who boasts of his improved estate now denuded of trees and wound intricately with a mockery of the serpentine curve, "worm-like" walkways. Contrarily, in appreciation of Brown as a Merlin of the English landscape, Cowper calls him an "omnipotent magician":

> He speaks. The lake in front becomes a lawn;
> Woods vanish, hills subside, and vallies rise:
> And streams, as if created for his use,
> Pursue the track of his directing wand.[17]

In full context it is clear that Cowper enjoys the power of landscape alteration as much as he values the aesthetic of the results. It is really beside the point here to recite the theories of aesthetics which in the eighteenth century shaped perceptions of the natural world and governed landscape design. Among others, Malins traces the lines of argument on the oft-discussed sublime, beautiful, and picturesque through Addison's series on the imagination in the *Spectator,* especially nos. 411 and 412; through Burke's *Enquiry into the Origin of Our Ideas of the Sublime and Beautiful;* through Kames's *Elements of Criticism;* and many others. Landscape so designed to be perceived in thrilling sublimity or in calming picturesque beauty not only exemplifies these writers' theories of aesthetics but demonstrated the fundamentals of human psychology as they understood it. It seems that by the end of the eighteenth century crucial questions of taste were degenerating into those of mere fashion, instanced satirically in Jane Austen's *Mansfield Park,* in which the obtuse and monied Rushworth plans chic changes to his estate. Primarily, however, the motivation for landscaping in eighteenth-century England made the estate parks, gardens, grottoes, and so forth, not only pastoral respites or little worlds made cunningly but laboratories for demonstration of the psychology of perception.[18]

Among those aspects of English landscape and literature relevant to eighteenth-century America—and there are many—one is especially significant here. For Americans, the interplay between British writers and bold landscape projects in England elicited a new language of artful enhancement of the natural world, just as it made environmental change a subject demonstrably worthy of high literary art. When Pope or Hogarth engaged in the subject of landscape alteration, the subject itself gained prestige. Pope urged those contemplating landscaping, "Let Nature never be forgot" and "Consult the Genius

of the Place in all." The Poet's concern is for the aesthetic achievement, yet he presupposes man's power

> To build, to plant, whatever you intend,
> To rear the Column, or the Arch to bend;
> To swell the Terras, or to sink the Grot.[19]

This assumption of power, coupled with a mandate for aesthetic
standards in landscaping and incorporated in the heroic couplets that
were themselves an achievement in art, had important consequences
for eighteenth-century American writings on the land. Now,
American writers could relinquish as outworn their former attitudes
of contentiousness toward a diabolical or intractable New World.
They could adopt instead the perspective of the pleased or the anticipatory artist. English Augustans and pre-Romantics had shown the
way. Therefore do we find the young John Adams portraying
American "Meadows painted with the most beautifyl scenery of
Nature" or John Wilson writing of "enameled pastures."[20]

Americans were apt to give special utilitarian emphasis to the subject of "improved" landscapes. This is evident when, for instance, we
hear the New Englander Jared Eliot at mid-eighteenth century compare the primeval New England landscape with that enhanced by the
"needful Culture" of man. First, Eliot offers "a View of a Swamp in
its original Estate." He lists "Bogs, poisonous Weeds and Vines," and a
"miry Bottom" harboring "Turtles, Toads, Ests, Snakes, and other
Creeping Verm'n." He cites "baleful Thickets of Brambles, the
dreary Shades of larger Growth, and a Cage of every unclean and
hateful bird." Then. in contrast, Eliot describes the same area transformed to agrarian splendor in "a Resemblance of Creation." His
subject is entirely utilitarian as he catalogs food and fiber crops; his
vocabulary is that of the aesthete:

> Behold it now cloathed with sweet verdant Grass adorned with
> the lofty wide spreading well-set Indian-Corn; the yellow Barley;
> the Silver coloured Flax; the ramping Hemp, beautified with fine
> Ranges of Cabbage; the delicate Melon, and the best of Turnips,
> all pleasing to the eye, and, many, agreeable to the Taste. [21]

Declaring it a "wonderful Change," Eliot tries to dissemble into
humility, but his sop of "impotent Beings" cannot hide his obvious

pride. His New Englanders are themselves the *genius loci,* and he the approving critic whose judgment is pictorial.

The environmental emphasis in eighteenth-century American literature was shifting from bread to beauty, or perhaps from bread to manna. But neither the new confidence in man's power to make geophysical changes nor the emulation of English poetic models can account, alone or together, for the new ways in which American writers were speaking about landscape changes. For Americans of the Enlightenment had not abandoned the millennial vision inherited from their forebears and present in American literature since the 1600s. They continued to think of landscape change as reform that must proceed together with the reform of the human spirit. On this point writers like Timothy Dwight, David Humphreys, and especially Joel Barlow parted company ideologically from their Augustan models. For English belles lettres offered an aesthetic but not a socially inclusive (much less millennial) vision of the reconstructed landscape. Were the extant American literary record on the environment confined to the "improved" estate, say, to Monticello, to Joel Barlow's Georgetown Kalorama, or even to John Adams's Mount Wollaston farm which in old age he spoofed as "Montezillo" to Jefferson, then we could accede to the long-held notion that on this point as on others the Americans were but Augustans-come-lately. Even Timothy Dwight could be forced into the mold, had he not in addition to *Greenfield Hill* also written the four-volume work of travels into unsettled New York and New England where "the eye perceives a prevalence of forest . . . in so vast an expansion."

The fact is that American writers could not allow the nation to be represented geographically by estates or plantations, those oases of self-sufficiency, or to be encompassed mimetically by the narrow strip of the civil eastern seaboard. For the idea of nationality—the ideographic America that descended directly from Winthrop's "Citty upon a hill"—now assumed specific geographic definition on a continental scale. Thomas Paine, more than any other writer, was responsible for that definition. In the times that tried men's souls, Paine equated American independence with "independency of this continent" and spoke of the Revolutionary era as "the seedtime of continental union, faith and honor." (In the first section of *Common Sense* Paine invokes the word "continent" thirteen times in lieu of "united colonies" or even "country.") In the more than 100,000 copies of *Common Sense* which were dispersed through the colonies in the weeks following its January 1776 publication, Paine's readers saw the cause of the Revolution focused in this geographic way: " 'Tis not the affair of a city, a country, a province, or a kingdom; but of a continent—of at least one-eighth part of the habitable globe."[22] Thus writers of the American Enlightenment reached beyond parochial political geography and beyond national emblems of the enclosed garden. As of 1776 they really had to. Yet, in order to feel free enough not only to confront a seemingly illimitable and troublesome landscape but to impose upon it a thoroughgoing vision of utilitarian *and* aesthetic reform, American writers needed a tremendous new center of belief. They needed in the Enlightenment some phenomenon of cosmic moment which could encourage their geographic outreaching and validate the environmental attitude on a continental (or even bicontinental) scale. These needs were fulfilled by the American Revolution.

II

Susceptible to varied interpretation, the American Revolution meant one thing to those impelled to divine its meaning in the years following the Treaty of Paris. Then, in a remarkable consensus, American writers celebrated it as the fulfillment of the seventeenth-century idea that America would be the world's redeemer nation. Significantly, the colonial expression of what Bernard Bailyn calls "a world regenerative creed" based in incantations of liberty marked not an anticipation but the *fulfillment* of the "ancient idea, deeply embedded in the colonists' awareness, that America had from the start been destined to play a special role in history."[23] More than a symbol, the American Revolution was regarded in fact as the inauguration of moral, political, libertarian renewal throughout the world. As such, its significance surpassed that of the transatlantic exodus of Puritans in 1630, for the Puritans had been poised between prophecy and its fulfillment in the future. But the Revolution was that future arrived, or so it seemed to many prepared to interpret its meaning. Thus Timothy Dwight, struck by the ordinariness of Concord, a village he saw endlessly replicated through New England, was moved to mark the epochal significance: "from the plains of Concord will henceforth be dated a change in human affairs; an alteration in the balance of human power; and a new direction to the course of human improvement. Man, from the events which have occurred here, will in some respects assume a new character, and experience a new destiny."[24]

Dwight's remark sounds like conviction and not bravura, but what enabled him and his countrymen to understand the Revolution as the start of worldwide redemption was the typological tradition of historical interpretation. For in the American Enlightenment we find historical events and personages once again interpreted within the context of Christian eschatology, especially typology, which presupposed a unity between the Old and New Testaments and made of history an ultimately redemptive process. As we have seen, the Puritan progenitors of the Founding Fathers had believed the Bible to be the map of redemption, its two testaments constituting *the* book of history, God's final authority on the course of human events in his cosmos. Following an eschatological tradition that traced back to the Middle Ages, Puritans had believed persons and events in the Old Testament to be prefiguring types whose fulfilling antitypes could be found in the New Testament, thus assuring astute readers of Scripture that events of world history were occurring as prophesied.

The comfort of typology was in knowing that historically the redemption of God's chosen people was moving apace toward the Apocalypse, although the nettlesome process of coupling type with antitype required the skills of a theologian able to interpret arcane biblical symbols that baffled laymen. Of course, by the post-Revolutionary period American intellectuals were no longer absorbed, strictly speaking, in finding time-space coherence by matching Old Testament types with their antitypes in the New Testament. Yet, as Ursula Brumm reminds us, it would be a mistake to regard the typological idea of history in this period as a "mere curiosity or outmoded way of thought." As she says, "After independence and the founding of the nation this kind of history was written in the conviction that all human events were developing toward the fulfillment of man's aspirations in America."[25]

Although the American Enlightenment provided a largely secular contrast to the Puritan era, writers of the post-Revolutionary and

Early National period continued to use methods of typology in their version of America's spiritual biography. Their civil religion kept the typological method but changed its spiritual culmination. That is, instead of anticipating redemption with the second coming of Christ, they regarded redemptive Liberty to be the culmination of the American Revolution. As Michael Bell has observed of the American historians Palfrey and Prescott early in the nineteenth century, they "were seeking types, not of the coming of Christ, but of the triumph of 'Liberty.' Each instance of the struggle between liberty and tyranny, . . . could be regarded as a type of the great culminating example of the victory of liberty over tyranny—the American Revolution."[26]

Since the Revolution was thought to surpass in its importance all prior events of American and even world history, its principal players not only were hailed as the first truly national heroes but were elevated as redemptive antitypes whose lineage was prophetic and biblical. The Puritan patriarchs—Moses and Aaron in the presence of John Winthrop and John Cotton—were now parochial and superannuated in the New Age. The intercolonial Founding Fathers easily supplanted them. Thus the writings of Jefferson and Adams would "enlighten Europe and posterity in the great science of social and political happiness" as "we now view the whole human race as members of one great and extensive family." Further, "While we have a Franklin, a Washington, a Morris, the Adamses, a Dickinson, . . . we cannot despair of the republic." And from a third writer: "in later times the *supreme* has appeared on our behalf as formerly on behalf of the Jews. He has raised up a Hancock, an Adams, a Franklin. By the hand of Washington he has saved united America from bondage and destruction." While John Adams confided to Abigail the possibility that *he* was the antitype of Moses, the minister-geographer Jedidiah Morse looked elsewhere and claimed Washington as "the Moses of our nation," a man whose "prudence, sagacity, and paternal care, vigilance and solicitude for the safety, peace and happiness of the people, and his possessing their entire confidence and esteem, may with singular propriety be compared to Moses." Still another writer democratically invites all his American audience to "come forth, like the patriarch Abraham, and contemplate the stars of heaven, or the sand upon the sea shore; for such shall be the number

of your posterity." He counsels adoration of "the supreme goodness" and neighborly love ("then will divine providence make of you
a great and mighty nation, and a blessing to all families upon
earth!").[27]

Understandably, writers of the late eighteenth century were eager
to transcend the confines of New England history and to include
other regions, especially the South, in their affirmations of America
reborn to national redemption in liberty. Perhaps for this reason
America really discovered Columbus in the Enlightenment. As an
instrument of destiny, Columbus was not associated with any specific
region and so could attach to all. In the seventeenth century both
Samuel Sewall and Cotton Mather had recognized Columbus's significance as an early leader of American development. Now, however,
the literati saw his importance as a national symbol. Thus, the
Genoese was "directed by that Sovereign Finger, which can trace in
one moment, not only terrestrial, but celestial creation."[28] As David
Humphreys, the aide-de-camp of Washington, saw it, America was but
"vast wilds which human foot ne'er trod/ . . . 'Till great Columbus
rose and lead by heaven,/Call'd world to view hid in the skirt of
even."[29] Americans were the "sons and daughters of Columbia," and
Joel Barlow could call his American epic *The Columbiad,* just as a
prominent magazine was named the *Columbian.*

With emphasis upon the millennial Age of Liberty, numerous
writers hailed the rising glory in America or worldwide. Jedidiah
Morse scanned the nations of Europe, Asia, Africa, and the Indian
subcontinent to declare them all defective by reason of wars, fixed
social caste, immorality, and subjugation of their populations. Only
America withstood his scrutiny with its "blessings of PEACE,"
including "internal tranquility," "individual rights," and "educational institutions." Morse concluded, "If the Governor of the
Universe has thus distinguished us with his favours—then surely we
ought to be the best people in the world."[30] Others equally
rhapsodic take a more generous world view, adducing global regeneration from the French Revolution, the "regeneration" of Poland, a
less prejudiced and less bigoted Germany, a tottering Spanish
monarchy, and England itself on the brink of insurrection. "The
emerging of thirty millions of people from vassalage to freedom,"
writes one, "forms one of the sublimest spectacles in nature—and

presages the final overthrow of despotism in every corner of the globe." "Propitious era!" cries another essayist, "happy event! which has softened the rigours of tyranny, and taught even kings to revere the great laws of justice and equity." One equally fervid writer urged praise for Washington, "for he has rescued you from the bonds of British tyranny and usurpation, and exalted you unto the stars of heaven." Another echoed, "May a *Washington* never be wanting to conduct *the human race* to glory and honor."[31]

These expostulations are nationalistic, yet go beyond chauvinism. Whether one believed that liberty was imminent worldwide or that the American continent alone was *"once more* destined to become the asylum of oppressed humanity, exiled from the shores of Europe," still America's role as redeemer nation was assured. Morse chose to have it both ways, on one hand urging that "as God hath made of one blood all nations, . . . it is part of a good man to possess the feelings of a *brother* towards the whole human race," and yet on the other asserting chauvinistically that "we have a healthful, extensive, and fruitful country, equal to the support of the largest Empire that ever existed on earth."[32]

Regardless, however, of whether writers thought the libertarian New Earth would be achieved by a chain of overseas insurrections or by an ineffable softening of tyranny worldwide, or whether they felt that the New Earth would be truly global or confined to the American continent, or whether they, like Morse, entertained both possibilities, still it is clear that their preoccupations were with possibilities for the millennial future. "The history of the world is before them," wrote one. And from another, "The commencement of our government has been *eminently glorious:* let our progress in every excellence be *proprotionately great.* It will—it must be so. What an enrapturing prospect opens on the UNITED STATES. . . . HAPPY COUNTRY! MAY THY HAPPINESS BE PERPETUAL."[33] As Thomas Paine wrote in *Common Sense,* "We have it in our power to begin the world over again. A situation, similar to the present, hath not happened since the days of Noah until now. The birthday of a new world is at hand."[34] These hosannas ring with millennial fervor. The past, with its burden of superstition, tyranny, military oppression, enslavement, and the rest is gone, as if washed away in the post-Revolutionary dawn of the Age of Liberty.

These rhapsodic utterances did not come only from anonymous contributors to American periodicals. As Peter Gay points out, "the American *philosophes* were not slow to celebrate their political sagacity," and he cites in particular James Madison's retrospective description of the American "experiment," a "great Political Machine" that would prove to be "more of a Pilot to a good Port, than a Beacon warning from a bad one." Because of America, the entire "Civilized World" has become the beneficiary of "Representative Government." Madison called the United States the "workshop of liberty" and said that its people "enjoy the great merit of having established a system of Government on the basis of human rights, and of giving to it a form without example." Even John Adams, less inclined to praising paragons, wrote in 1815 that "the last twenty-five years of the last century and the first fifteen of this, may be called the age of revolutions and constitutions. We began the dance."[35]

In phraseology of environmental reform, the "dance" might have been an American dithyramb at threshing time. For in belief that the Revolution realized apocalyptic prophecy, writers chorused and echoed Isaiah. Of course they delighted to change the verb tense from future expectation to present fact. Timothy Dwight witnessed the transformation of "an absolute wilderness" into orchards and farms and remarked, "Considerable tracts I have traced through the whole progress from a desert to a garden; and have literally beheld the wilderness blossom as the rose. Such sights," he said, "when seen only in prophetic vision, enraptured the mind even of Isaiah; and when realized, can hardly fail to delight that of a spectator." David Humphreys hearkened to the same prophecy, emphasizing power of industry that "changest nature's face—thy force is such,/Ev'n desarts blossom at thy genial touch."[36]

Magazine contributors took up the same theme:

Part of yonder western wilderness is now budding like the rose—and her barren wastes are turned into fruitful fields. . . . We may anticipate the period, when the yet uncultivated desert will become the center of this rising Empire, and exhibit to mankind the splendid monuments of art and labour; when civilization will tame the untutored mind, and savage cruelty be no more a terror to the human race.

One writer exhorts his audience to "remember that the invincible industry of our ancestors caused the desart to change its original unwelcome aspect" and reminds them that the "extended fields" that supplanted sites of Indians' war councils "declared the first dawn of civilization." Still another: "America three hundred years ago was a howling wilderness. Ferocious beasts and unnumbered tribes of savages were its tenants." Now, "The beast and barbarian have fled before the sons of Europe as the dew before the sun. America has risen to the zenith of celebrity. The arts and sciences, philosophy and religion here flourish with immortal vigour." Moreover, the American "sons of freedom" with their example of "virtue and liberty" have transformed the "howling wilderness" into a "paradise of nature in America."[37]

III

But what of the actual environment on which this international, millennial "dance" began? In the inaugural Age of Liberty, what obtains in a landscape that not only has been the setting for moral regeneration but, as we know, has been itself an object of reformist imperatives for some one and one-half centuries? To put the case from the viewpoint of the American writer: the prophetic, visionary moment had arrived; the literary task ahead was to enmesh the idea of the New Earth with reportorial images of the American topography. Within the purview of the New Earth, an intractable, forbidding landscape filled with topographical obstacles would be conceptually abrasive—worse, contradictory to the very spirit of the new age. One simply could not quarrel with the New Earth. By definition it compelled acceptance. It prompted celebration and hope.

Moreover, it required some proof. By themselves, borrowings from scriptural rhetoric would not do. Supernal visions would not do. (Nor, it goes without saying, would propaganda or cant.) Specifically, since the American Revolution was thought to initiate the millennial New Earth, writers were pressed to substantiate their conviction by citing those parts of the American topography that were, if not blatantly paradisal, at least hospitable to man. Some good evidence was needed to prove that the North American continent

had been all along a proper, destined site for the redeemer nation. If
for the most part the country had still to be earned by its people, the
beginnings of the New Earth compelled proof of ultimate environmental felicity. In this regard the wilderness, howling or benign, was
limited in value. Now gardens were called for—though with the
proviso that they be inhabited by regenerate Americans. By definition the New Earth must manifest hospitable features, and for the
first time, in a manner of speaking, geography was summoned to
prove destiny. Now Yankees needed features of the southern pastoral
Eden to verify their own ideas on America.

The spiritual election of America thus was asserted in a certain
predestination of geography itself. "Have not God and nature done
wonderful things for us?" one writer exclaims. And another boasts,
"Thus situated, the United States appear formed by nature for a
great, permanent, and independent government." In much the same
way a third writer urges us to trace the network of western rivers and
to "examine the luxuriant soil which those rivers traverse":

> Then we ask, can the God of wisdom and nature have created
> that vast country in vain? Was it for nothing that he blessed it
> with a fertility almost incredible? . . . View the country, and you
> will answer for yourselves.[38]

This idea of geography as destiny became, not surprisingly, a favorite
of proponents of the Louisiana Purchase, and one which fit nicely
the concept of manifest destiny. Expressed in phrases resonant of the
promotional tracts of an earlier era, the idea differed essentially in its
emphasis on national destiny vivified by the Revolution.

Because it was thought to be the inauguration of the millennial
New Earth, the American Revolution really made possible for the
first time in American culture a reconciliation between two deeply
rooted and opposed conceptions of the American environment: that
of the New England howling wilderness and that of the Virginian
pastoral Eden. As we have seen, Puritans of the seventeenth century
repudiated the conception of an edenic South, thought Virginia a
fleshpot, and, to prove it, chronicled dire providential judgments
upon southerners. For themselves, incumbent duty lay in improving
"this sayd ground" in preparation for the imminent Millennium.
Thus the Puritan Edward Johnson deduced apocalyptic value from

the colonizing work that carved from the "howling wilderness" the plausible site of the prophesied New Earth.

Virginians, meanwhile, gradually developed a sense of their own "errand into paradise," to use Lewis Simpson's term. From that first promotional vision of paradise as it appears in the days of the Virginia Company, particularly from its leading exponent, Capt. John Smith, there at last emerged a century later the work which both Simpson and Leo Marx recognize as a new development in those paradisal accounts of Virginia. Robert Beverley's *History and Present State of Virginia* (1705) and, later on, the correspondence of William Byrd of Westover contain what Simpson calls a blend of "the delights of the natural garden and the plantation garden." Byrd was to understand that paradise "exclusively in terms of the plantation society of Virginia," a society subverted by slavery even as it reached its apotheosis at Monticello. Those literary Virginians, however, consistently portrayed their region as "a paradise improved."[39]

Improvement notwithstanding, the Virginian base line was paradise, its conceptual framework the pastoral, a genre subject to extensive attention by Henry Nash Smith, Leo Marx, and more recently Annette Kolodny. Not that New England hadn't its own cherished tradition of the pastoral. As we have seen, the figure of God's garden was a favorite of Puritans who read it as a metaphor for the spiritual community of saints comprising the church. But appetites for actual newfound Edens in America has struck them as idolatrous and blasphemous from the beginning of their settlement, and by repute Virginia continued to be obnoxious and thus to provoke from New England a battery of unsolicited preachment. Whittier's title, "Massachusetts to Virginia," only named a long didactic tradition. Environmentally as well as theologically, Roundheads stood ever righteously aloof from Cavaliers, and so through the eighteenth century landscape reform remained the imperative principally of Yankees who continued to regard it as inseparable from necessary reforms of the spirit. It was the New England mind that kenned the future to imagine not some primitivist Virginian garden but the New Jerusalem. Nathaniel Ames, a popular almanac writer from Dedham, Massachusetts, put it this way in 1758, when he imagined the "Coelestial Light of the Gospel" at last banishing the "night of Heathenish Darkness from America":

Arts and Sciences will change the Face of Nature in their
Tour . . . over the Appalachian Mountains to the Western Ocean;
and as they march thro' the vast Desert, the Residence of Wild
Beasts will be broken up, and their obscene Howl cease for
ever;—Instead of which the Stones and Trees will dance together
at the Music of Orpheus.

Ames envisions the discovery of gems and precious metals. More, he
foresees a utilitarian Millennium under the law that " 'all fit Matter
shall be improved to its best Purposes.' " His mines and quarries in
turn presage "an Infinity of Utensils improved in the Exercise of
Art" and point toward great and elegant cities. Indirectly Ames asks
readers of his millennial prophecy not to destroy their almanacs at
the end of the calendar year but instead to let posterity know "that
in Anno Domini 1758, we dream'd of your Times."[40]
The Revolution, of course, changes such anticipation as Ames's
into conviction that the millennial epoch has begun. Therefore the
howling wilderness is no more. In New England we hear Dwight, that
grandson of Jonathan Edwards, speak instead of forests, whose disappearance he anticipates with pleasure. He is "transported in imagination to that period in which . . . the hills, and plains, and vallies
around me will be stripped of the forests, which now majestically,
and even gloomily, overshadow them; and be measured out into
farms, enlivened with all the beauties of cultivation."[41] He is irked
by endless treetops in one green blur, but the Dwight who saw post-
Revolutionary America as "Canaan's promis'd shores" has long abandoned the howling wilderness rhetorically so fraught for his ancestors.
It must be recognized that this post-Revolutionary reconciliation
of the South with the North was the work principally of northern
writers, especially those with connection to Harvard or Yale, institutions rooted traditionally in Calvinist theology. In the Enlightenment
the Millennium of the Book of Revelation became secular within a
civil religion. As for the South, its writers had not the apocalyptic
tradition from which ideas on the New Earth could evolve. Yet this
does not mean necessarily that southern writers were indifferent to
ideas on American environmental reform. From the colonial Maryland belles lettres examined closely by Leo Lemay, we can infer

particular reasons why, on matters of landscape change, the southern silence may signify a hushed acquiescence and not indifference.

First of all, well into the eighteenth century we find continuing the edenic images prevalent in promotional literature on the South from the Renaissance. James Ralph celebrated the richness of American nature, while the Marylander Richard Lewis praised "th' extensive Land,/Adorn'd by Nature with a lib'ral hand."[42] Not surprisingly, there exists as well a concurrent lament for an American Eden—a floral respite—threatened or damaged by greedy men for trivial reasons. In this context the South, this "uncultured Paradise," is implicitly an ephemeral Eden. Should it pass, its best hope lay in the creativity of men who would not destroy it but convert it to agrarian and pastoral splendor.

Yet, ominously in the future is the question of foreign imperial domination, especially the "ambitious Schemes of France," as the Maryland writer James Sterling put it. His projected defense against this threat was the cultivation and improvement of *"our large and fertile Empire on the Continent."*[43] His plan for continental empire includes the unification of the colonies and, in due course, the expansion westward to the Ohio and the Wabash whenever those midwestern lands should become necessary for an expanding population. In Sterling's proposals we recognize a secular version of the schemes incorporated in the millennial visions of writers of the North. In both regions we find incumbent ideas on manifest destiny.

Perhaps more important for the South, the idea of a millennial New Earth could give transcendent meaning to a region whose writers were sensitive to the meagerness of cultural life. At mid-eighteenth century Dr. Alexander Hamilton wrote pejoratively of "our Woodland Country," and some twenty-five years before that, Richard Lewis had complained that problems of *"bare Subsistence"* preoccupied men in a landscape where the *"Buildings"* were yet "mean" and "rough Woods embrown the Hills and Plains."[44] In part the future could redeem this culturally rude South, since, as Lemay shows, Maryland writers believed in the idea of the inevitable westward movement of the arts and sciences. Lewis spoke of the arts flourishing on "Columbus shore," and Sterling wrote of "Western climes soon to be enriched by poetry" and of the progress of a planter (albeit a slaveholder), who fells the forest and becomes "Free and contented in his own Estate," thereafter finding pleasure in his racing stable and in hunting and fishing.[45]

Omitting the recreation, these southern views on the westward progress of civilization form a motif consonant with the millennial notions of New England writers. It seems that for southern deists and philosophical skeptics the post-Revolutionary period became a time of "bleak stoical resignation," one without a mythos and lacking too a vital literary center and a vigorous church. As Henry May says, the "southern upper class [was] part of an old-regime world, a world whose intellectual spokesmen indulged in few Utopian hopes for humanity."[46] Utopianism, however, was not wanting in northern advocacy of the American New Earth. If southern writers shied away from subscription to an idea rooted in Puritanism, they did not on the other hand scorn it in satire or invective. Silent on the subject, they appear to have let New England writers advance ideologically the themes incipient in their own literature since the late seventeenth century.

The specific image which permitted convergence of the forested North with the Eden of the South was, of course, that of the farmer. Leo Marx is correct in saying that only at the end of the eighteenth century did a fully articulated pastoral idea of America emerge, and then in a turn from literary artifice to a plausible ideology for the country at large. Marx's splendid documentation of the growth of the political pastoral in America, together with Chester Eisinger's collocation of late-eighteenth-century almanac verse (most of it published in New England), reveals how compatible—even apposite—was that figure of the yeoman farmer North and South. It is true that the Northern hymns to the farmer include special tributes to one who keeps starvation and winter's menacing cold at bay. But songs to rural virtue, whether those of Jefferson or of Timothy Dwight, converge in a unified moral geography that supersedes regional convention.[47]

What we do find in writings of the post-Revolutionary and Early National period is the assumption that in the new Age of Liberty the conversion of rustic forest to rural landscape depends solely upon energetic work, which the farmer symbolizes. "The *industrious village,* the *busy city,* the *crowded port*—all these are the gifts of liberty." The New England writers, including contributors to the periodicals, speak endlessly of "industry," "perseverence," and "enterprise" as the catalysts of landscape reform. Exemplary is the settler who "brought under improvement a tract of land which almost bounded the eye." Promethean is he who with "the torch of adventurous enterprise has penetrated the glooms of this wilderness." Summarily, "our forests fall before the hand of labor." The axe is a metronome of civilization as the new race of hearty, enlightened Americans (chiefly yeoman farmers) relentlessly push back the forest wilds. But the erstwhile "howling wilderness" of the Puritans—that belongs to another era entirely.[48]

It is not only by disarming the wilds of their menacing howl and supplanting them with farmsteads and virtuous husbandmen that writers of the American Enlightenment enabled reconciliation of South and North. The single quality that readily brought together an edenic South with a reformist North in the New Earth was that of abundance or plenitude in nature, a concept that formed one part of the Great Chain of Being. In the Enlightenment the Jeffersonians modified the traditional metaphor to read "chain of beings," meaning "the absolute fullness of nature," which Daniel Boorstin interprets in Jeffersonian theology as "an expression of personal faith and a description of the material universe." Importantly, Jeffersonians believed the chain had remained intact throughout time, since "it was axiomatic that no divine energy had been wasted." If the philosopher could not comprehend the whole design, "he was nonetheless sure there had been no errata in the book of Creation," since the entire chain remained intact from the beginning to the contemporary moment.[49] This assumption did not, it must be said again, free Americans of the eighteenth century from responsibility for their environment any more than faith in the providence of God released the Puritans from fears of squandering their land. Throughout his *Travels* Timothy Dwight is appalled at indiscriminate deforestation and worried about the effects on animals of human meddling with the landscape. He is troubled, for instance, about possible connections between damming of streams and the disappearance of the salmon once plentiful in them. Yet Dwight is heartened to see trees mulch their own seedlings, and from this concludes that "forests are furnished by the Author of Nature with the means of perpetual restoration" in "a process totally superior to any contrived by the human mind."[50]

Dwight and the others of his time were reassured by this belief. Typical in his sense of delight and wonder is the young John Adams who wrote in his *Diary* of the world's endless "Variety of Substances, mutually connected with and dependent on Each other." Adams celebrates the "amazing profusion of vegetables, which afford Sustenance and covering to the wild Beasts," while the "cultivated plains and Meadows produce grass for Cattle, and Herbs for the service of man." Adams then describes the food chain and man's place in it and confesses awe at the "Stupendous Plan of operation projected by him who rules the universe," itself a "great and complicated Drama."[51]

The idea of nature's plenitude surfaced often in remarks upon other subjects. At the much reported Independence Day procession in Boston, 1788, James Wilson's oration included this geographical panorama of the nation:

What an enrapturing prospect opens on the UNITED STATES! Placid HUSBANDRY walks in front, attended by the *venerable plough.* Lowing herds adorn our vallies: bleating flocks spread over our hills: verdant meadows, enameled pastures, yellow harvests, bending orchards, rise in rapid succession from East to West. PLENTY, with her *copious horn,* sits easy-smiling, and in *conscious complacency,* enjoys and presides over the scenes.[54]

Before Wilson had finished, allowing his audience its "plentiful repast, and TEN toasts," he went on to describe a nation commercially bustling, its waterways crowded with ships, and its shores lined with populous cities whose inhabitants have all "necessities, decencies, and ornaments of life." Like all Early National allegorists he crowned the scene with the usual statuary: INDUSTRY, PEACE, LIBERTY, VIRTUE, and RELIGION. But PLENTY is the key figure who partakes of the two worlds of earthly environment and spiritual value. Wilson's American landscape is strategically idealized to pastoral, agrarian perfection. But plenitude is vital to his vision.

Plenitude or abundance became in time an important bond of the South to the North in American literature, since as a fact it was both inarguable and innocent of regional prejudice. For inspirational purposes it counterbalanced figures of icy expanses elsewhere, of mortal cold and barren mountains. "Picture to yourselves," reads the typical description, "that immense territory from the St. Lawrence to the

Mississippi, covered with lofty forests, traversed only by ferocious beasts, and not less savage men, now the seat of a mighty empire!"[53]
It is true that North and South would not fully reconcile in American literature until Whitman, but the aesthetic resolution of the two was first made possible by an epochal interpretation of the American Revolution and by ramifying ideas on industriousness and on plenitude in the natural world.

There remained ineluctably the same kinds of geophysical features that earlier generations had loathed and felt impelled to reform, and which were no more welcome to those of the post-Revolutionary era. Fens, floods, and unrelieved vistas of treetops were no more appealing to writers of the American Enlightenment than they had been to Puritans more than one century earlier. If anything, the problems inherent in such features loomed larger now as explorers and travelers revealed their presence in the seemingly endless North and West. Moreover, writers of the Enlightenment could not honestly avoid the apparent contradiction between the utopian concept of the American New Earth and the intermittently irksome—worse, perilous—topography. Millennial vision and topographical sight were at odds with one another, not only in tension but in apparent contradiction. Optics and imagination had somehow to be reconciled. We find writers doing so in two ways: they portrayed the landscape in willing collusion with its human reformers, and they displaced the geophysical troubles of the present into the past.

For the latter, we find that the Timothy Dwight who traveled so much in the New York and New England outback at the turn of the nineteenth century could not really bring himself to say how discouraging contemporary travel was, and instead he displaced his feelings into historical sympathy for the first settlers of New England. "A reflecting traveller passing over these roads is naturally induced to . . . realize some of the hardships those intrepid people endured in settling this country," he writes. Then, listing dense forests, bad roads, dangerous streams, swamps, mires, and a bestiary of wolves, bears, and catamounts (in addition to Indians), Dwight regrets most of all the early colonists' helplessness before it all: "the forests they could not cut down; the rocks they could not remove: the swamps they could not causey, and over the streams they could not erect bridges." Nevertheless, "Men, women, and children ventured through this combination of evils; penetrated the recesses of the wilderness;

climbed the hills; wound their way among the rocks; struggled through the mires; and swam on horseback through deep and rapid rivers."[54] The early colonists may be indomitable, but they are forced to accommodate to natural conditions because they are impotent adversaries of an intractable and overwhelming environment. Readily could such attitudes as Dwight's be channeled toward the past. As Joel Barlow said, ostensibly of the early colonists, "Their enemies were the elements of nature yet unsubdued."

More frequent—and more important—than the displacement of environmental difficulties from present to past is the literary alternative of representing Americans in creative harmony and partnership with their environment. Anthropomorphic as it is, this mode is the more important of the two because it truly reconciles the visionary moment with the optical report contradictory to it. It does not require displacement of present to past and can allow topographical enormity into the millennial epoch. The American continent, sanctified by the Revolution, becomes the manifest site of the New Earth. And its inhabitants (Indians excluded) are the chosen people whose reforms, welcomed by the earth, complement and bring to perfection the original work of genesis. As is, the New Earth is viewed as complete but yet rude, unfinished. As artist-engineers, those Americans newly born into liberty are called to their apparent task. As David Humphreys put it, human industry would "mend ... rude nature's works." Since human industriousness can "turn Nature's wilder growth to human use," Humphreys begs

> Give me the music of the sounding axe—
> Let the keen adze the stubborn live-oak wound—*
> And anvills shrill, with stronger strokes resound.

*Humphrey's line is best explicated by Dwight's remarks on the girdling of trees: "I have mentioned above *girdled trees*.... When a planter, in this country designs to cutivate a piece of forested ground, his first business, as you will readily conceive, is to get rid of the trees, This is a work of no small labour; and to fell them is often beyond his power. . . . Therefore, he makes a circular incision with his axe through the bark of the tree. This process is called girdling. All the trees . . . die; and thus leave the ground sufficiently open for the purposes of cultivation. . . . Still the process is attended with many inconveniences. Beside the uncouth, and disgusting, aspect of the fields, left with many dry trees standing, and others blown down, and lying in every direction; whenever the trees fall, they tear up considerable parcels of ground with their roots, and . . . leave the earth totally bare of its soil. . . . The practice of girdling has gone much into disuse . . . [but] there is a sufficient number of girdled trees standing in many places to give the new settlements a disagreeable appearance" (*Travels,* 2: 126-27).

In all this there is no expression of contention between the natural world and colonial efforts. On the contrary, a "grateful nature, cloath'd in harvests, smil'd" at its transformation. Should that process be viewed as a military conquest of the "hardy cultivator" over "savage NATURE" (and Colonel Humphreys was often disposed to think in such terms), still the impact of conquest is softened as the environment plays the part of a coy Cinderella: "NATURE herself, once rustic and rude, now embellished and adorned, appears the lovliest captive that ever fell to the lot of a conqueror."[55]

Using the same sexual figures whose meaning Kolodny has recently brought to our attention, Dwight too describes the harmonious partnership of Americans with their land. "In a word," he writes, "whatever is rude, broken, and unsightly on the surface will, within a moderate period, be levelled, smoothed, and beautified by the hand of man. Where nature, stripped of her fringe and her foilage, is now naked and deformed, she will suddenly exchange the dishabille; and be ornamented by culture with her richest attire." Then, says Dwight, "The meadow will glow with verdure, and sparkle with the enamel of flowers. Flocks and herds will frolic over the pasture; and fields will wave with harvests of gold."[56]

Presently we shall see how in the *Columbiad* Joel Barlow rewrites Genesis so as to emphasize this reformist partnership between Americans and their continent. For Barlow and Humphreys and others so to render that relationship indicates how the redemptive ideology of the Revolution accommodated the eighteenth-century confidence in man's power to alter his environment and the English aesthetic models for artful reshaping of the landscape. More than that, it proves on what basis Americans of the post-Revolutionary and Early National period were able to confront and accept the vastness of a new land, to praise grandeur, and to celebrate size and scale that had appalled their seventeenth-century counterparts.

"Parson" (Mason L.) Weems provides in his *Life of Washington* (1800) an excellent example of the new environmental acceptance made possible by the Revolution. He intends to portray the Father of the Country as the pastoral-agrarian Patriarch at Mount Vernon (and thus no militarist at heart). But Weems additionally proves in his landscape description how the Revolution, symbolized in Washington, changed Americans' environmental sensibilities to make the man-land relationship a harmonious one. Thinking back into 1753, to the beginnings of the French-Indian War when young George Washington was about to travel inland to the unexplored Ohio, Weems's description of the Alleghenies is a baleful catalog: "immeasurable forest," "gloomy haunts of ravening beasts and murderous savages," "awful silence," "dreary woods," "hiss of rattlesnakes," "shrieks of panthers," "yells of Indians," "howling tempests." Of course the passage is wrought for propagandistic advantage, to show the bravery or "firmer nerves" of young Washington.[57]

Yet this passage shows something else when contrasted with Weems's vision of the post-Revolutionary American continent. Not only is the continent now replete with idealized bucolic scenes, but at the same time it boasts those of fearful sublimity. This mythic Washington, who explores inland, sires his nation, and is virtually assumed into heaven, so sanctifies the American environment that Weems can now celebrate its geomorphology. The same terrain which in the pre-Revolutionary dark ages had prompted fear and loathing now, in Early National America, becomes "that greatest Continent," rising "from beneath the frozen pole" and stretching "far and wide to the south, running almost 'whole the length of this vast terrene'" to sustain "on her ample sides the roaring shock of half the watery globe." Now, "in a style of the *sublime*," the "Almighty has reared his cloud-capt mountains, and spread his sea-like lakes, and poured his mighty rivers, and hurled down his thundering cataracts." This geography is so far "superior to anything of the kind in other continents that we may fairly conclude that great men and deeds are designed for America." In chauvinistic pantheism Weems cries, "Where shall we look for Washington, the greatest among men, but in America?"[58] It is an America imagined to be repulsive in pre-Revolutionary America, but now, in a messianic Early National period, it inspires celebration and optimism for the future.

We notice that in this passage Weems leaves the woods and goes to the mountaintop, not only in time but in space. He leaves the gloom and rattlesnakes in the Alleghenies and climbs, if not to Patmos, certainly to dazzling heights from which particulars of the terrain disappear into broadest outlines of God's geophysical "furniture." The grand aerial panorama of America is intentionally inspirational. But

while Weems easily makes the sweeping visual transition from a pre-
and post-Washingtonian American landscape, other writers could not.
To think seriously about reform of the American environment meant
engagement in the utilitarian details of its engineering. If the
visionary, millennial America were to correspond with actual environmental conditions (and literature on the subject both activates
and celebrates the process of reform and enhancement), then serious
writers had to expedite reform. They had not only to lift (or avert)
their gaze from the pedestrian to the sublime but to attempt comprehension of the two. One writer who approached these problems of
comprehension was Philip Freneau.

At about the turn of the eighteenth century (1797), Freneau suggested in his verse, "To a Field Orator," that the Puritan forebears'
cherished millennial doctrine was really the self-delusion typical of
the ranting field orator blind to leonine human nature actually so
discordant, angry, murderous. In Freneau's view, human nature, captive to emotions, had only one frail hope of attaining millennial
peace, hope of "reason's aid . . . in the slow advance of things." Yet
back in 1775 Freneau had seen America's future inscribed in the
Book of Revelation. Less skeptical, at that time, about the compati-
bility of the millennial lamb and lion, Freneau (together with Hugh
Henry Brackenridge) used his *Rising Glory of America* to envision
human progress destined to occur within the Christian schedule of
the Apocalypse, when America should become "perhaps . . . a new
Jerusalem,"

> Whose ample bosom shall receive, though late
> Myriads of saints, with their immortal king,
> To live and reign on earth a thousand years,
> Thence called Millennium. Paradise anew
> Shall flourish . . . [59]

Paradise regained, then, on "this land"—perhaps. But Freneau had
been more certain earlier in the poem, when his speaker had assumed
the powers of the Old Testament prophets Isaiah, Jeremiah, and
Amos to foretell Glory burgeoning in the civilization of the North
American continent, with populous towns growing by the rural Ohio
and Mississippi rivers.

> I see, I see
> Freedom's established reign; cities, and men
> Numerous as sands upon the ocean shore,
> And empires rising where the sun descends!—[60]

The rising glory of America seems, in fact, to be a millennial preparatory rite.

Even in his verse in which the frame of reference is not biblical, like "On the Emigration to America and Peopling the Western Country" (1788), Freneau poses the ideal relationship between the settler and the virgin land. The country is bucolic ("fair plains," "rural seats") and majestic (Nature's "wildest genius reigns" over it)—two qualities the New American, unlike the retreating and benighted Indian, is able to appreciate. On this site unsullied historically by despots, the New Man is charged to "tame the soil and plant the arts" so that the pristine Western Country with its incomparable waterways will no longer be useless. The heavens decree an age of commerce to justify the very existence of North America.

Freneau rests easiest with the generality of this theme. His American Palaemon, a pastoral figure, is both an aesthete in Nature's gallery and an explorer and spiritual Worthy. Sparing himself and his reader all details of settlement, Freneau simply asserts that *Palemon* can tame the soil and inaugurate "a future age/. . . whose genius may the world engage/. . . and happier systems bring to view,/Than all the eastern sages knew."[61]

Elsewhere, however, Freneau does confront and describe the means òf reforming a rude American topography to a second Eden. For he understood that paradise regained meant, first, reclamation of the American "drear wastes." In his ode "To Crispin O'Connor, a Backwoodsman," Freneau examines the process of reform by reclamation.[62] His Crispin is no Palemon but an augury of the immigrant "wretched refuse." He is a peasant bold enough to leave the "ungrateful soil" of England's political stepchild, Ireland, whose people subsist "like famished crows." In a sense, Crispin is Freneau's answer to Brackenridge's Teague O'Regan, the bog-trotter whose ambition and egocentrism pose in *Modern Chivalry* a very real threat to the delicate balance of American democracy. Not that Freneau has notions about the nobility of the Irish peasant; the poem makes clear that he does not, for an ignorant Crispin moves westward to an unenviable, though unclaimed, "paltry spot of land/. . . a woody hill beside a dismal bog/[where,] . . . responsive to the croaking frog,/[he] grubbed and stubbed." Freneau had difficulties with the tone of the poem because, as his mock-heroic betrays, he is at once contemptuous of Crispin but grateful for this dim being whose value to America in his brawn and energy uncomplicated by sensibilities of a high order. Freneau masks his own ambivalence with praises for Crispin's newfound liberty in a land free of the royal dragnet of taxation. But he is careful to show the important results of Crispin's New World toil:

> Now times are changed—and labour's nervous hand
> Bids harvests rise where briars and bushes grew;
> The dismal bog, by lengthy sluices drained,
> Supports no more hoarse captain Bull Frog's crew.

Timothy Dwight wrote succinctly of those "Crispins" best suited to convert the wilds. He called them "Men, accustomed to patient labour, of persevering firmness, and superior even to the real ills of life; men, influenced by some great and commanding motive, connected with a settlement on the soil, such as the hope of civil or religious freedom, or the necessity of providing for an increasing family." These, says Dwight, are "the only persons fitted to subdue forests, encounter frost and hunger, and resolutely survey the prospect of Savage incursions." As Mercy Warren wrote, only "in the anticipation of better prospects in future . . . does the laborious exercise of felling trees and erecting log-huts for themselves yield much satisfaction to those of a rougher class."[63] Freneau's rough Crispin achieved his future reward, and Freneau has him acknowledge that fact ("The axe has well repaid my toil"). But for the poet, the Irish peasant is a necessary link in the evolution of drear waste to millennial America. He is the same isolated borderer whose fraternity with livestock had repelled Edward Johnson (and, after him, Crèvecoeur), a type of the Irish coolie who lost all spiritual life, in Thoreau's view, to support the inexorable railroad. Freneau avoids in his hymns to freedom, that keystone of a millennial America, the darker implications of these issues. But praises to liberty cannot conceal Freneau's ambivalence and the dilemma it presents. He despises Crispin as much as he acknowledges America's need of him. Symbolically, Palemon may "tame the soil," but Crispin's is the real onus of briar clearance and bog drainage. Crispin, in fact, makes possible Palemon's America, though the two figures exist in separate worlds, virtually as different species.

Poetically, of course, Crispin and Palemon survive in different verses as well. No poem of Freneau includes them both. They remain divided in his poetic consciousness, comprehended only ideologically in realms of freedom or liberty. Freneau could not generically reconcile them, either as symbols or types, and he did not try, unlike Whitman who both tried and succeeded. Freneau was doubtful of human progress and skeptical about the virtue of democratic leveling. But Freneau did recognize that the aesthetics and the exigencies of environmental reform in America were parts of the same problem. Offering no solutions, he at least reveals the contours of the dilemma.

Not every writer conceived of the problems of environmental change as Freneau did—though in seeking solutions Hector St. John de Crèvecoeur also looked to the emigrant from the British Isles. Not to the Irish, whom he thought alcoholic, quarrelsome, litigious, and violent, but to the typically faithful, honest, industrious, and frugal Scot. In the *Letters from an American Farmer* (1782) Crèvecoeur's figure of Andrew the Hebridean solved symbolically a problem which Crèvecoeur thought central to the reform of the American environment. Unlike Freneau, whose New Earth meant transforming an intractable landscape in an enervating climate, Crèvecoeur worried about the character of those doing the work of transformation. He was dubious about the integrity of settlers converting the "howling swamp" and "rough ridge" into "pleasing meadow" and "fine field."[64]

All readers of the *Letters* are struck by its agrarian aesthetic, that is, by the material, emotional, and intellectual sufficiency of the American "race of cultivators" flourishing without restraint throughout America. Crèvecoeur's is a moral aesthetic, emphasizing the well-being of these cultivators who are made by (and in turn give shape and character to) America. The pleasing geography of orderly and prosperous settlement reflects the American mind, that of the New Man. His "regeneration," "resurrection," and "metamorphosis" from the servility and prejudice of Europe is the achievement of Americanization, itself the outcome of settlement.[65] Crèvecoeur's agrarian aesthetic is really indigenous to the cultivation of American soil.

But, importantly, it is a hospitable soil in a friendly geography, a point on which Crèvecoeur differs from Freneau. Strategically the *Letters* were directed toward a European audience.[66] In part, Crèvecoeur's trenchant criticism of Europe comes from the contrast of Old World decadence to New World felicity, to its ease, peace, bounty, fine rivers, endless game birds. "There is room for everybody in America." "He becomes an American by being received in the broad lap of *Alma Mater,*" itself a "smiling country." For every taste and proclivity there is an apt soil, climate, local government, and produce; therefore "we know, properly speaking, no strangers." The emphasis in all of this is upon environmental welcome. The poor or middling folk of Europe, "cyphers" in their native countries, can here become freeholders, citizens, residents. "From nothing," from a state of vegetation they can "start into being."[67]

But Crèvecoeur presupposes a hospitable geography. His is the middle landscape not only in its agrarian midpoint between forest wilderness and decadent metropolis but in its inherent hospice to settlers. Anthropomorphically, Crèvecoeur evokes America as a broad and maternal lap welcoming to all. This is an important point because by it Crèvecoeur avoids Freneau's anxiety about the rigors of environmental reform. Crèvecoeur's America is "our great parent" who says in convocation, "Welcome to my shores," to "my verdant fields, my fair navigable rivers, and my green mountains." Here "alma mater" offers "bread" and "greater rewards" of "ease and independence," in addition to "a comfortable fireside" and "a decent bed." Perhaps most attractive of all, this American mother country promises the beginning of a new history, an assured perpetuation of these same gifts "for thy progeny." There are no real limits upon time or space, since Americans will not populate the "unknown bounds of North America" for an indeterminate "many ages" to come.[68]

The cost for all of this is citizenship: to be "honest, sober, and industrious" in character and to manifest these qualities in work, in the education of children, and in reverence for the prevailing "philanthropic government." America is no Eden; neither is it in Crèvecoeur an environment so demanding that brute Irishmen must make it livable and pleasing. Just as the putative author of the *Letters*, Farmer James, embodies the agrarian ideal, so the geography of America forms a part of that idea as Crèvecoeur presupposes inherent geographic felicity. In passing he mentions the "huge forests," the "formerly rude soil," and the "wild, woody, and uncultivated" landscape of a hundred years ago. Yet these are but reminders of the past, brought forward now in contrast to but not in representation of Crèvecoeur's contemporary America, itself a place of "fair cities, substantial villages, extensive fields, an immense country filled with decent houses, good roads, orchards, meadows, and bridges."[69]   The yelling Indians, screeching owls, and hissing snakes are a part of the American past, since what was rude is now the rural.   Crèvecoeur's America has long achieved the middle distance between wilderness and city, and given that position, Crèvecoeur need see no significant disjunction between the primeval America and its transformation into civil setting. Unlike Freneau, Crèvecoeur need not straddle the gulf between what is and what will be and try bridging it with Gaelic brawn and a pastoral aesthete. Like Mather before him and somewhat like Thoreau afterward, Crèvecoeur presupposes a civil American environment which is both hospitable and responsive to human enterprise.

Thus, the crux of the American environmental problem, in Crèvecoeur's view, lies elsewhere than in the landscape itself. It lies, rather, with the nature of the borderers and frontiersmen at the vanguard of civilization, really at the point where the primeval American past becomes the agrarian present. Crèvecoeur describes these outlying settlers in the letter-essay, "What Is an American?" Quite simply, they are the pariahs of American culture. In theme echoing the Puritans, Crèvecoeur laments the lack of government, social influence, and morality on the frontier, whose inhabitants go there from land greed or to escape earlier misfortunes or bad debts. Drunk, discordant, idle, and contentious, these men "appear to be no better than carnivorous animals." They form the "most hideous parts of our society," yet represent "a kind of forlorn hope" in the future of the landscape they inhabit, since in ten or twelve years they will recede deeper into the "great woods" as respectable and industrious folk come to "finish their improvements," to convert log houses into the "convenient habitations" of permanent settlement.

These vicious frontiersmen so preoccupy Crèvecoeur that he

returns repeatedly to them, in part to make them the caveat of the corrupt emigrant, since they represent his destiny in a country that demands unremitting honesty and industry. Unregenerate European emigrants have "moldered away their time in inactivity, misinformed husbandry, and ineffectual endeavors."[70] Not everyone becomes a true American.

For Crèvecoeur, then, the vulnerability of American cultural and environmental progress lies not in an intractable or even discouraging landscape but in that failure of human will exemplified in the barbarous frontiersmen. Significantly, these borderers have not refused outright the work of settlement; they accomplish the "heavy labours" of clearance and begin rudimentary farming. But their energies flag; their motivation lessens. Living as hunters they do not show the economy and skillful survival with which Cooper later endowed Natty Bumppo. Instead they instance the failure of the human will and the breakdown of society. Continuous industry is requisite to the vitality of American civilization, and Crèvecoeur's frontiersmen symbolize the loss of the will to progress and the consequent dissolution of society. It appears significant that the settlers who at last supplant this dissolute lot are a "respectable army of veterans," the military figure suggesting the disciplined and dependable energy necessary (as the Puritan Edward Johnson knew it to be) for civilization.

It is precisely here that Andrew the Hebridean becomes useful as Crèvecoeur's political symbol for the continuation of American civilization. "All I wish to delineate," writes Crèvecoeur of Andrew, is "the progressive steps of a poor man, advancing from indigence to ease; from oppression to freedom; from obscurity and contumely to some degree of consequence," all by the "gradual operation of sobriety, honesty, and emigration."[71] And he offers a biographical sketch of this best emigrant, a man already long practiced in thrift and hard work when he arrives in America in the "full vigour" of life from a Scotland of "no wheat, no kine, no apples," a land cold, thin, and overpopulated. Disembarking in Philadelphia in 1775 with his wife and son, eleven guineas, a character reference, and, naively, a little hand plow, Andrew gets good advice and guidance toward American farming practices as a hired man, while his wife elsewhere learns domestic arts. Symbolically, this is the moment he is apprenticed to America. Accomplished after a few years with the axe and plow and livestock management (and proving loyalty to his master in a comic scene in which Andrew mistakes the intentions of fur-trading Indians), he is ready for independent frontier life. Now he is offered an excellent lease on good but unreclaimed frontier acreage. Told that he can sell the lease or dispose of it in his will, Andrew feels an "inarticulate joy" as well as "astonishment and confusion" that mark the beginning of his initiation into full American identity as "a freeholder, possessed of a vote, of a place of residence, a citizen of the province of Pennsylvania."

So he sets out for the frontier, dwelling at first in the house of the settler whose holdings abut his. "His first work was to clear some acres of swamp," and from the beginning he is "indefatigable." His honesty wins him friends, and his industry earns him the respect of his neighbors. He learns quickly: "and thus the spade man of the island of Barra has become the tiller of American soil." His story progresses through a house raising, the clearance of fields, and Andrew's own employment of a carpenter to finish the house. Within a few years the pattern of outreaching settlement has extended beyond his land, so that Andrew is no longer a frontiersman.

Crèvecoeur concludes the biography with an appended inventory of Andrew's possessions four years after his frontier settlement. Like the symbolic demographics of Edward Johnson, Crèvecoeur's list of the dollar value of Andrew's land improvements, livestock, grain, stores of food and fiber, tools, and debts owed him has a spiritual significance. It proves "the happy effects which constantly flow in this country from sobriety and industry, when united with good land and freedom." These crops and durable goods reveal the life of the spirit in the world of matter. Crèvecoeur's Andrew is thus the answer (and antidote) to the vicious, dissolute frontiersmen. More, he is Crèvecoeur's symbol for the meritorious character, the unflagging energy, and the libertarian ideals of American civilization. In this sense Crèvecoeur needs him as deeply as Freneau needs his Crispin. Andrew is indispensable to the processes of environmental reform in a vital America.

Significantly, Crèvecoeur looks beyond the agrarian America. It is true that Andrew and Farmer James represent America's present and future agrarian equipoise. Yet Crèvecoeur relishes the promise of social change when he writes approvingly of the "embryos of societies spreading everywhere" in America, of the "fair cities" and the prospects for technology. He sees a future in which "mankind here will have leisure and abilities to ... search ... for subterranean riches" and to initate systematic research rather than rely upon serendipitous discovery in chemistry. His farmer invents simple machines for domestic life, and Crèvecoeur frankly admires the German emigrants for their "mechanical knowledge" that has produced the "finest mills in all America."[72]

Crèvecoeur's vision of a postagrarian America comes clearer in an unpublished essay, "The Rock of Lisbon" (1770), in which he contrasts two prospects, one from a high peak in the Catskills a few miles from the Hudson and the other recollected from a convent site atop the rock of Lisbon, from which the entire city and the ocean spread before him.[73] The American scene presents "a hughe Roughe Continent, a wide waste of Trees, a perpetual Forest." It offers none "of those pleasing sensations which Richer Landscapes usually afford in Europa." But though it is "an half Tilled Continent ... Inferior in the Splendor of appearance to what may be Seen in Europa," Crèvecoeur's America of the future quickens in his imagination. This "Embrio of Nations" anticipates the "labour of thousands and the Toyl of ages" that will in time bring forth all the accoutrements of a sophisticated civilization. The libertarian (if not the aesthetic) consolation in the meantime is America's freedom from "imperious Masters" and "Greedy Landlords" as Americans instead sweat and toil "in removing those trees & clearing those vast swamps ... for themselves." When his thoughts then turn to Lisbon, it is with derision for a nation of "Lands not Tilled ... by the Strong hands of Liberty but by the Enervated Sinews of wretches whom [he] then Pitied more than slaves."

We recognize here as in the *Letters* the cultural split between decadent Europe and libertarian America. The additional dimension in the "Rock of Lisbon" essay is Crèvecoeur's deep appreciation for the refinements, the sophistication, the high art of the Old World. Its ruins suggest the ingenuity of ancient cultures, its "Multitude of spires, castles, Dwellings present to the eyes some of the fairest work of Man," and in the continuing recovery from the earthquake of 1755, Lisbon "exibit[s] a Singular medly of New Edifices intermixed with old ones." Crèvecoeur's complaint centers solely upon the injustices of its government. He abhors the broad base of wretched toil that enables "300 Fat Men," monks, to live in sybaritic splendor, having abandoned the vital pursuit of arts and sciences. All of Lisbon in fact, evinces the loss of will, the failure of industry that signals its stagnation. The richest groves, tended by "the oppressed Portugese," are a sham, since "balefull Tyranny poysons the seeds which he commits to the ground." Crèvecoeur concludes that, in Portugal, "the fair Race of Man is dwarfed into Pigmies" and that "the only durable strength of Nations [is] . . . refined Ideas of Civil Liberty." These ideas, however, are not inconsistent with taste, elegance, and even luxury. The structure of the essay suggests Crèvecoeur's assumption that one day the view from a Catskill mountaintop will feast the eye with a "luxury of objects" and "diversity of Imagery," all the while the virtues of agrarian America remain intact, in effect to make possible the advanced civilization he proclaimed in the *Letters* when he wrote that Americans are the "western pilgrims, who are carrying along with them that great mass of arts, sciences, vigour, and industry which began long since in the east," and concluded, "They will finish the great circle."[74]

It appears that for Crèvecoeur the nexus of civil liberty and social change is to be made possible by the likes of Andrew the Hebridean and Farmer James, since they represent for Crèvecoeur the foundation of a just civilization. It is true, as Leo Marx recognizes, that there is an implicit contradiction in the *Letters* as Crèvecoeur endorses the achieved pastoral-agrarian ideal at the same time he advocates social change. Within Crèvecoeur's own undetected contradiction, however, lies the reassurance that America can have it both ways, that it can keep the spiritual balance of agrarianism even as it ushers in exciting changes in its material culture. That middle landscape is not the end of environmental change in America.

Throughout the *Letters* Crèvecoeur is remarkably free of anxiety about cultural and religious plurality in America. The diverse geography and climate please him, and the variety of religious sects causes him no alarm. Rhetorically he asks, so long as the farmer "works in his fields, embellishes the earth, clears swamps, etc., what has the world to do with his Lutheran principles?"[75] Without regret Crèvecoeur anticipates a religious melding in America and pleads for

religious toleration. His heart of American culture is good citizenship, including secular virtues of which industry is the most important. As a writer outside the New England tradition, Crèvecoeur did
not understand the processes of environmental change as the
hastening of God's apocalyptic schedule. His New Earth is less millennial than it is a pastoral alternative to the degradation of Europe.
Thus in the Enlightenment Crèvecoeur largely avoided the apparent
contradiction of an American Israel—soon, in a civil sense, to be the
United States—growing ethnically diverse over an appallingly varied
continent. *That* problem belonged to New England, and Jedidiah
Morse took it up.

IV

In the successive and best-selling editions of Jedidiah Morse's
American Universal Geography there is a permutation of the
reformed environment so important to Crèvecoeur, Timothy Dwight,
John Adams, Mercy Otis Warren, Freneau, and (as we shall see,
preeminent among these) Joel Barlow. In Morse it appears under a
different rubric, one of systematized observation rather than of lofty
inspiration couched in history, verse, travel narrative, and so on.
Morse, a Charlestown, Massachusetts, minister, promised in his first
preface (1789) to publish the geography in editions that would
"grow and improve as the nation advances toward maturity."[76] He
saw the last substantive new edition through the press in 1812.

Morse began his work with nationalistic biases, as did those of his
contemporaries who understood the power of geography to influence
American development. For instance, in his novel *Modern Chivalry*
(1792), Brackenridge has the authoritative Captain Farrago rebuke
the upstart O'Regan, the ignorant peasant who aspires to elective
office in America. The captain's objections go like this: "Teague, . . .
Do you know what it is to be a member of a deliberative body?
What qualifications are necessary? Do you understand any thing of
geography? If a question should be, to make a law to dig a canal in
some part of the state, can you describe the bearing of the mountains, and the course of the rivers? Or if commerce is to be pushed to
some new quarter, by the force of regulations, are you competent to
decide in such a case?" At the other end of the spectrum is

Brackenridge's German professor who knows "more of the classics than of the geography of these United States." In the new nation his "Academic knowledge" is as useless as Teague's naked ambition is dangerous. But both lack vital expertise in geography.[77]

That was expertise which Charles Brockden Brown worked to acquire and to disseminate for purposes of national expansion and development. At the time of his death Brown had published his prospectus, *A System of General Geography* (1809), which announced his plan to compile a global geography with special emphasis on North America, and in particular on the United States. America's foremost novelist had abandoned fiction some eight years earlier to devote literary energies to what he considered to be more practical, utilitarian, and above all efficacious literary ways to influence settlement patterns. He meant to unite Americans who were scattered in the various regions and to incite the growth of an American empire westward to the Louisiana Territory and beyond. Geography was evidently Brown's "favorite science," for which he had an "early and constant passion." Preparing to make that passion serve his nationalism, Brown paused to praise the work of Jedidiah Morse, who he thought gave Americans "that knowledge of their country which they would seek in vain in any foreign publication."[78]

By design Morse intended his *American Geography* to refute the disparaging European view of America by such outspoken critics as the Abbe Raynal, Buffon, and later on, Count Volney, all of them skeptical about the healthfulness of American soil, climate, and weather. Having already written an elementary schoolbook, *Geography Made Easy* (1784), Morse was eager to go on to lessen American dependence upon foreign-made geographies whose British or Continental focus led America to be slighted. "Europeans," wrote Morse, "have too often suffered fancy to supply the place of facts, and have thus led their readers into errors."[79] America had been neglected and misunderstood; Morse would rectify that. In the process he earned the title, Father of American Geography, which is somewhat misleading because Morse depended heavily on others' work. The first edition of the *American Geography* is replete with lengthy excerpts from leading American periodicals, from pamphlets, and from the quasi-geographical writings of Jefferson and others. In addition he rendered others' maps into prose. With "utility" as his touchstone, Morse filled half of his book with these available sources and swelled the remaining half with information he solicited from correspondents, some of them men of science and others ordinary citizens who replied to his questionnaire soliciting information about the America that lay beyond the ministerial study in Charlestown.

We see in Morse's geographies an America "methodiz'd" in a combination of textbook and vademecum for the future, and an America symbolically unified in an orderly representation of its space. Washington himself wrote to Morse to express his expectation that the geography would bring about "a better understanding between the remote citizens of our States." When Morse appeared to some southern readers to have scanted the South, one reader wrote his regrets, since the "Geog'y, being a national work and much circulated, may be extremely serviceable in cementing the Union of the states, by making them not only acquainted but pleased with one another." Sales figures indicate that Americans were indeed eager to become acquainted with each other, for when Morse split the *American Universal* into two volumes (the second concerned with the non-American parts of the world), the public still bought four copies of the first, American, volume to every three of the other.[80]

Throughout his geographies Morse returns compulsively to themes of America's moral and environmental reform. Like Joel Barlow and others of the Enlightenment, Morse regarded moral and material changes as conjoint, interdependent, and mutually indicative. He finds America's spiritual ascendance manifest in its environmental improvement—and vice versa. His geographies are above all moralistic works.

Not surprisingly, Morse's exemplar of the national character is New England. (In fact, other states and territories are valued according to the number of New Englanders filtering into them and gaining influence.) A true Federalist, Morse feared the effects of popular democracy. On the positive side it inspired "a high sense of personal independence, and a jealous care of national freedom," and checked "pride of place and the insolence of office." But Morse believed it also led to "calumny, flattery, trimming, and falsehood," to destruction of necessary social distinctions, to reverence for mere human numbers at the expense of individual intelligence and worth, and to a general coarsening of society. The exception to all this, Morse implies, is New England (profligate Rhode Island aside). Because New Englanders labor without slaves, live in communities neither too dense nor too dispersed, and are religious and literate, they represent for Morse a kind of national golden mean, a model for the American national character and a reproach to other regions that fall short.

His New Englanders are "tall, stout, and well-built," educationally inspired with "high notions of liberty," and so committed to economy and industry that they are as removed from vices of luxury as they are from want. "It may in truth be said," Morse writes, "that in no part of the world are the people happier, better furnished with the necessaries and conveniences of life, or more independent than the farmers in New England." Its future is assured as the children, "those imitative creatures . . . imbibe the manners and habits" of their elders. Singing highest praises, Morse even compliments New England women, ever his "geographical" test-by-gender of the cultural ascendance or degeneracy of a region.[81]

Because Morse's America entered a new, millennial epoch with the Revolution, he is watchful for national illumination that transcends regional boundaries. Thus, since the Treaty of Paris, New Yorkers have "experienced [a] great elevation of mind, as of circumstances; a spirit of liberality diffused among the Dutch, the clouds of ignorance and national prejudice dispelled." Moreover, the South, whose slavery and sloth endlessly vex Morse, shows marked signs of improvement. Since the peace, no state has made better progress in the arts of civilized life than North Carolina," where the citizenry are now orderly and industrious, thanks "to the great immigration of farmers and artizans from the northern states, who have roused the spirit of industry among them." Throughout the *American Universal Geography* "maturity," "progress," and "improvement" are by-words. They are tangible, one might almost say palpable qualities. It is as if Morse were pushing map tacks of moral-material social success from the Northeast in a widening fan that would eventually stop only at continental boundaries, themselves embroidered by island clusters off North and South America.[82]

Morse's wish that social dispersion be accompanied by terrestrial improvement leads him into a conundrum. On the one hand, he relishes the spread of settlers that reforms the American landscape but, on the other, frets when that reform falls short of his expectation. Of Vermont's settlers he can write, "Emigrants in general are active and industrious. The opposite characters have neither spirit nor inclination to quit their native spot." Yet elsewhere, reminiscent of Dwight, Warren, and Freneau, he laments that "emigrants, as a body, rarely compose the best part of a community." Fondly he returns to his New England paradigm and, in the face of discouragement at such slovenly settlement as he finds in Kentucky, pauses to remark on the occasional elegance of a brick or limestone house there and is cheered that "the state of society is ameliorated."[83]

Like his American literary confreres, Morse was much interested in possibilities of technology to hasten social and environmental change in America. He never misses an opportunity to describe canals, including those built, planned, funded, in the offing, or only dreamed of. The number of miles and of dollars, the maximum boat draft—all such figures appear in his accounts of canals in New England, the Middle Atlantic states, the South, and often with qualitative mention of the "immense importance" of the enterprise for trade growth. The canal does not take on for Morse the mystical meaning which, as we shall see, Joel Barlow attaches to it, but obviously Morse favors it as a means of transportation superior to the muddy and rut-prone roads.

He boasts, too, that "in the mechanick arts . . . there is as much native genius as in any part of the world" and for proof cites such clever American designs as a pre-Revolutionary Maine bridge copied throughout New England and imitated in Europe. He heralds an automated New England textile industry and particularly praises the ingenuity of a "gentleman [to whom] the world are indebted for the invention of a machine for cleansing upland cotton from its seeds." Eli Whitney's other enterprise, a firearms factory, draws Morse's praise for its "ingenious and peculiar" machinery, just as does David Bushnell's experiments with a submarine based upon sound "philosophical principles." Once again, Morse lauds New England for these "mechanick arts" while scorning the New York Dutch for following the old track of their forefathers, "seldom invent[ing] any new improvements in agriculture, manufactures, or mechanicks." Morse even inserts a section entitled "New Inventions," which he praises for their number and usefulness. Among them are "many manufacturing machines for carding, spinning, winnowing, &c. which

perform an immense deal of work with very little manual assistance."
Subtly Morse promotes automation, for there is no virtue in cottage
industry textiles, no moral values inherent in manual labor.[84]

In the details of Morse's statistics, demographics, and geophysical
survey, a reader is never for long let to lose sight of the moral
meanings inherent in reform of the environment. "The *Agriculture* of
a country," he writes, "is usually more the result of moral than of
natural causes." (He had decided to put agriculture under a heading
of "Natural" rather than of "Historical" geography only because he
felt obliged to discuss inherent qualities of soil, very few of which are
infertile, stony, or hopelessly awash.) Everywhere American "society
is improving" in such slothful outbacks as North Carolina and
Georgia and the barbarous Territories. Morse makes his act of faith in
the American future with a favorite adverb of continuity, "yet." The
character of Tennesseans is "not yet completely developed"; no
more have the salt marshes of Georgia "as yet been improved." But
progress in both is underway.[85]

If Morse stops short of geographical predestination, his *Geography*
nevertheless invites Americans westward with the lure of commercial
possibility and edenic plenty. Ohio's rivers "connect prodigious extensions of territory, and . . . we may anticipate an immense intercourse between them." Indeed, Ohio merchants will soon be trading
very profitably with the Floridas and West Indies. But commerce is
forecast in the territories too. In Michigan "the country is
improving," and "when the lands are put on sale, it is thought the
population will rapidly increase." Illinois is "commodiously situated
for inland navigation." And as for farming, there is ease and plenty.
Ohio's hills are "of a deep rich soil" covered, not with mere trees,
but with the more usefully attractive "timber." Morse's New England
readers, their farms fenced with stone reminders of slow and tedious
clearance, must have felt that truly an agrarian Canaan lay in the
Ohio, where "it is said that . . . a man may clear an acre a day."
Should acreage solely of Ohio Indian corn sound monotonous, a
reader need only turn to Morse's account of the Mississippi Territory
abounding with such variety of crops that it seems more like paradise
than a farmland. Staples of corn, rice, hemp, flax, and indigo mix
with plentiful oranges and lemons, herbs, wild hops, and "all kinds of
European fruits" brought "to great perfection" in a country that is

"delightful and well watered," its prospects "beautiful and extensive" with fine meadows and copses and trees. As for the Floridas,
Morse accurately predicts their value as rangeland for cattle, as well
as for coastline, rivers, and harbors. And he is struck by the "spontaneous" production there of produce common to the Carolinas and
Georgia.[86]

Throughout, Morse's geographies are "puritan" in the worst,
moralistic sense of the word. The idea of cultural plurality is
intolerable to this New Englander preaching normative social ideals
to a nation in "need" of guidance for spiritual and environmental
change. Such, however, is the response of a twentieth-century reader,
and presumably not of Morse's own audience, which evidently
warmed to his teachings. In a country where literary ventures were a
high-risk enterprise, where actuarial predictions for periodicals were
dire, and where authors realistically despaired of income from their
efforts, Jedidiah Morse supported his family for nearly forty years
largely on his earnings from geography books.[87] He offered an eager
public a "scientific" topographical survey as well as a cultural
miscellany. But, moreoever, he offered the nation a ministerial and
schoolmasterly lesson in what it might become. His ideal was both
spiritual and environmental, and Morse unsparingly prods his readers
toward it. His sales figures indicate that the public accepted the
didacticism, at the very least suffered it.

Without question Morse is geographically nearsighted. He does not
offer panoramic vistas but moves over the terrain like an inchworm
on a relief map. The American Far West exists only in the vague but
sententious phrase, "prodigious extensions of territory." It strains his
imagination even to conceive of the U.S. Territories, which appear in
his books as remote outcroppings largely because he had so little
information about these frontier antipodes (and so very much about
Connecticut hamlets whose citizens sent reams of local information
his way). Too, his themes are not presented systematically but
emerge as intermittent asides or reproofs or brief acts of faith in the
nation and continent. His are broken lines of argument which his
readers may or may not have synthesized. Indeed, it is not at all clear
that Morse himself understood how his suggestions converged—
whether, for instance, he knew how complementary were the

dredging machine and the steamboat, or was fully conscious that he saw material progress as a concomitant of moral progress.

Nor can we be certain to what extent Morse's categories of geographical features were meant to suggest a United States ultimately bounded by the two entire American continents. For Morse it is enough to cluster the rivers and bays of South and North America together, to list all the important cities of two continents under one heading, to discuss the navigability of the Oronoco River as thoroughly as he does that of the Mississippi, and to describe the agricultural Eden of Mexico as thoroughly as that of the U.S. South. It is enough for the Congregationalist Morse to frown unilaterally upon all of Roman Catholic America, be it New Orleans or Lima, and to remark suggestively that in Spanish America "two valuable provinces have lately declared themselves independent" and that "systems of revolt have been manifested in all the others," leaving readers with the tantalizing remark that "a part of one (West Florida) has been actually taken possession of by the United States."[88]

This, however, is Jedidiah Morse's message to popular America: the New England way will gradually inform the continent to its immense benefit, engendering social happiness in a uniformly industrious, independent, moral, and inventive society working for its own amelioration. At the same time, this social enlightenment involves a necessary and destined change to be wrought upon the New World environment. Forests will be cleared, their trees metamorphosed into ships' hulls and phaetons and banisters and countless other useful and lovely forms as everlastingly plentiful as America's trees. These will exist for endless "ages to come," yet simultaneously (and contradictorily) succumb to the axe destined to fell them all. For the time being, a primitive but progressing technology will enable Americans to rearrange the topography or overcome the "limitations" of the landscape. So taught the Father of American Geography.

4: *Joel Barlow and the*
Engineered Millennium

> *The earth to be spann'd, connected by network,*
> *The races, neighbors, to marry and be given in marriage,*
> *The oceans to be cross'd, the distant brought near,*
> *The lands to be welded together.*
>
> *Walt Whitman,* Passage to India

Amid raveled and desultory urgings of environmental reform in the American Enlightenment, one writer—Joel Barlow—brought forward a vision of the American New Jerusalem as comprehensive and programmatic as was that of Edward Johnson's *Wonder-Working Providence.* As a Yankee counterpart to his Puritan predecessor, Barlow chose heroic couplets instead of baroque prose and shed the vocabulary of orthodox Puritanism for the secular terms of the Enlightenment. Yet the American New Jerusalem of Barlow's *Columbiad* (1806) emerges in militant tones as fervent and zealous as were those of Johnson. And while James Woodress has spoken the valid obituary for Barlow's epic by calling *The Columbiad* a "dinosaur in the clay pits of literary history," the poem invites attention here for its own peculiar eighteenth-century rendering of the American New Earth, and for the power Barlow thought he could exert on its behalf.[1] The ideology of American environmental reform remains intact and enhanced in Barlow, who, like Johnson, combined the activism of an engineer with the utopian imagination that foresaw a millennial New Earth. He, too, thought of literature as a powerful instrument of social reform, though his convictions took quite different forms of expression from those of his predecessor.

Barlow has interested students of eighteenth-century America principally for his political attitudes, those of a one-time Christian and Federalist who converted to Jeffersonian republicanism and whose writings reflect the change.[2] Engaging, too, is Barlow's youthful fraternity with the Augustan Connecticut Wits, whose lives and writings are examined so splendidly in Leon Howard's unsurpassed work about that Revolutionary War group.[3] Barlow's biography well deserves its title, *A Yankee's Odyssey*, in which James Woodress gave his fine account of this very active envoy, businessman, litterateur, expatriate. But while Barlow's writings have been examined chiefly as the graph of his political career and his decline as a would-be poet sunk by epic pretensions, these writings compel attention here for their systematic and visionary concern about the relation between Americans and their two continents.

As an Enlightenment figure, Barlow had other devils than Satan and his witching crew. No less to be hated and feared were political tyranny, truth-obstructing superstition (including—in Barlow's maturity—revealed religion and its institutions), and the human torpor that could enslave mankind by leaving political vacuums filled by despots. But an earthly correlate of these Enlightenment demons was the palpable enemy of unreformed nature. As long as it existed there could be but limited American geographic expansion, a too-modest commerce of goods and spirit, and a constriction of liberty. The harmoniously apposite goals of moral and material progress were blocked. In sum, as long as there existed nature unsubdued—that is, a natural environment unreformed by human design—then there could be no Millennium, either of Patmos or of secular progress. Over the years Barlow's writings reveal his ideological conversion from belief in Revelation to faith in Jeffersonian republicanism, but the stanchion of his vision for this human apotheosis remained a reformed American earth.

The printer's copy for *The Columbiad* reveals Barlow's nearly life-long commitment to express this American imperative. The basic script is Barlow's earlier *Vision of Columbus* (1787), but interlined, emended, excised, amended. It is a book fattened by sewn-in leaves. Above all, it is worried over. The tip sheets of varying size, the papers of different stock, the alternately crabbed and free handwriting in inks from different wells—all suggest Barlow's compulsion to return to a poem that had been with him since his undergraduate days.[4] In one form or another it bracketed his adult life, and he never let it go, quite. (Even after *The Columbiad* had long been in print, he fussed to keep available a full complement of editions and mentioned it regularly, if "modestly," in personal letters.)

The book itself bespeaks vanity, for *The Columbiad* had the dubious distinction of being the most expensively manufactured book in American literature. Aggressive in format, it was so sumptuous in its paper, its leather, its gold stamping, that an embarrassed Barlow ducked responsibility for the extravagance by having his factotum and alter ego, the engineer Robert Fulton, appear to have made the choices. But beyond Barlow's pulsing vanity is the nationalistic need he evidently felt to have his book endure materially. The leather might rust a bit and foxing encroach upon the creamy pages, but Barlow needed to know that *The Columbiad* would last, since he believed it would initiate and sustain major social and environmental change ultimately on a global scale.

Significantly, Barlow's beliefs about America are cast not in prose narrative history but in the heroic couplets of this determinedly epic poem. Personal preference is less at issue than is a specific attitude about the power of literary forms. In the mid-seventeenth century the Puritan Edward Johnson could feel confident of exerting the greatest social influence through a history which, by its definition, revealed God's planned pattern of events in the cosmos from past to future. For Johnson history was intrinsically a Christian epic no matter how limited might be God's individual scribe. But late in the eighteenth century Joel Barlow felt otherwise. A lukewarm Christian even in his Yale days, Barlow could not share Johnson's center of conviction. He was reluctantly ordained for his chaplaincy in the Revolution and, before that, was a class poet in whose commencement verse a Christian retinue appear but ornamentally. (When his part-time ministry let him eke out a living, Barlow applauded one of his own sermons only on the ground that he could "do any thing from necessity."[5] Accordingly, in the *Vision of Columbus* his Christ became more of a reassuring sign of progress than a Messiah, and Columbus's guardian angel appeared as a better tour guide than celestial spirit.)

This lackluster Christian, however, was a fervent nationalist impelled to find a literary genre both congenial to his own faith and, in
his view, polemically powerful. In an age in which much of America's
literary imagination warmed to political prose, Joel Barlow held fast
to epic poetry as the only effective form in which to represent his
American New Earth. Barlow wrote his epic, not from ignorance of
other literary forms or from naiveté about the audience for poetry in
America, but from a sort of scholarly and zealous notion that the
epic poet could be a social force of incalculable power. *That*, finally,
was his stance as a fifty-year-old Great-Uncle of the Republic—
though getting to Parnassus had been a struggle.

The progenitor of *The Columbiad*, Barlow's *Vision of Columbus*,
had been conceived in an insular world of youthful misapprehensions
about prospects for American poets. Paradoxically, Barlow's talents
seem to have been advanced yet sequestered in the Yale atmosphere
Leon Howard calls a hothouse, and from which Barlow aspired to be
the professional poet America did not support until Longfellow's
day. At Yale he found encouragement from his poetasting peers,
Jonathan Trumbull, Timothy Dwight, and David Humphreys, among
whom, as Leon Howard reveals, he began to experiment with
different verse forms and with metaphysical and pre-Romantic
figures, in addition to his practice from Augustan models. Named
class poet and encouraged by his former tutor, Joseph Buckminster,
and by his friend Elizabeth Whitman, Barlow's private world was by
no means hostile to poetry. True, President Stiles regarded it as one
of the lower branches of literature to which he acknowledged
indifference. And Barlow's republican cohort Tom Paine conceded
his own suppression of poetic talent because he feared its dangerous
seduction of the imagination.[6] Moreover, when Barlow later translated Brissot de Warville's *New Travels in the United States*, he found
the French republican relieved to find a wholly utilitarian America,
blessedly free of the corruptive fine arts, themselves "a symptom of
national calamity." Much better, in the Frenchman's view, that the
"multiplicity of literary and Political Magazines" indicated a "culture of the sciences."[7]

But as a student and recent graduate of Yale, Barlow seemed not to
know how rarefied was the Poet's air in America. His very ignorance

nursed his ambition and enabled his experimentation. As his biography shows, Barlow was a man of very carefully calculated risks. His assumption that he could avoid the literary life of a minister and instead find a patron willing to support a fully professional litterateur was no doubt based upon his insular experience at New Haven and in the Continental Army.

James Woodress has traced out Barlow's disenchantment, begun once the young poet left the army and the parietal walls only to be rebuffed as he sought financial backing for his continued writing of poetry. His miscalculation led Barlow to reconsider the poet's place in American culture and ultimately to view it as socially reformist. In fact, it was his self-conception of the poet as social reformer that impelled Barlow to rewrite the *Vision* as the epic *Columbiad*. The first step toward his poetic social activism came from the admonitions of his former tutor, Joseph Buckminster, to whom Barlow had submitted his plan for *The Vision of Columbus*. Buckminster replied that success in poetry "requires an amazing universal knowledge to treat the great variety of articles that you propose." He added, "A man must be not only a poet and man of Letters, but a Lawyer, Politician, Physician, Divine, Chymist, natural historian and an adept in the fine arts."[8] To write comprehensively of America, it was insufficient to be *engagé* intellectually and spiritually. One must as well be an active participant and a credentialed authority. No critic of Barlow has ever said that a budding genius was irreparably hurt by this advice to become a savant-activist, but it is apparent that in the long run Barlow's greatest poetic failure was his inability to challenge Buckminster's position, indeed to refute it in his own literary life.

Unwilling to abandon his poetic aspirations, Barlow compromised by wedding personal ambition to fervent nationalism. No doubt he thought to

> Expand the selfish to the social flame,
> And rear the soul to deeds of nobler fame.[9]

His poetry could advance his own career together with that of the United States. As poet he became a polemicist, no man speaking to men but a director of the populace. The notion of singing the nation's praises through the recollected world of his Connecticut farm life presumably did not occur to him, though had he done so, the result would probably have resembled more closely Dwight's didactic *Greenfield Hill* than Whittier's evocative *Snowbound.* Barlow was eager, not to deny his origins, but to outdistance them. He asserted personal ambition in his bold, secret marriage to Ruth Baldwin, the daughter of a prominent Connecticut judge, thereafter proving with all energies that his personal progress was as feasible as that of his nation. In time Barlow became a Jeffersonian envoy, shipper, educational reformer, and propertied gentleman.

Through it all Barlow's attitude toward poets changed as he came to regard other writers as hobbyists but himself as a social planner with a mission. He even disavowed his poetic past, for in retrospect his youthful design of the *Vision* seemed to him but a boyhood building of [corn] cob houses, patently frivolous. In these midlife years Barlow cited the fine arts, poetry included, as a leisure-time occupation for those who, with "considerable vacancies of time and superfluities of wealth . . . otherwise will, in all probability, be worse employed."[10] By then, at fifty-two, Barlow had swung round completely to the utilitarianism that confronts art in bafflement. Never one to tolerate mystery (or quite to accept art solely as recreation), Barlow offered a one-hundred-dollar prize for the best essay on the *practical application* of the fine arts, thus revealing his belief that art was not socially fundamental but woefully ornamental.

Yet Barlow had developed messianic notions of his own role as poet, forging over the years a belief that epic poetry could be the greatest instrument of social power. To write an epic poem was to be not the scribe of God but a god oneself. Thus the eighteenth-century agnostic repudiated Christian history to embrace the more powerful epic poem in order, quite literally, to move men and mountains in America.

Barlow's views emerge clearly in remarks on Homer, who

> with his monumental songs,
> Builds far more durable his splendid throne
> Than all the Pharaohs with their hills of stone.[11]

Barlow's self-identification with Homer goes deeper than his wish to transcend the vicissitudes of time by annexing *The Columbiad* to the most enduring classical poetry. *His* Homer was no idyllic blind bard cum lyre but a figure of incalculable social power, and one whose ideas exerted the strongest influence on Western civilization after him. To gain Homer's enviable power, Barlow first felt obliged to adopt his genre. He intended his *Columbiad* to initiate a feat of social engineering on a cosmic scale, in fact to realize the New Earth. His preface to *The Columbiad* indicates that it was Barlow's belief in the power of the epic poem that led him to put his American history there. From Barlow's viewpoint Calliope was eminently stronger than Clio.

II

Barlow's views on the attainment of spiritual progress altered, but the need for a materially reformed American landscape remained his constant theme from undergraduate years. His changing ideas about the moral and philosophic basis for America's spiritual advance occasioned the revisions of his verse, but throughout his writings Barlow's stanchion of material progress was human reform of the two continents completed by nature, yet much in want of human correction or refinement. This attitude appears first in his Yale commencement poem, *The Prospect of Peace* (1778). A declamation of exactly twelve minutes by President Stiles's timepiece, the poem welcomes Peace, Virtue's "fair Nurse," and invites its domain continuously until the Millennium. The scene Barlow paints is of nature "methodiz'd." The plain is "furrow'd," and "Industrous crouds . . . improve the soil." The plains smile as harvests gild them, Nature is "kind," and luxuriant vines bow heads to drop "the clustering fruit." Here "Art vies with Art, ard Nature smiles anew."[12]

In effect there is established in America a millennial advent, one in which a civilized society has civilized the earth, even if the Second Coming finds the furthest corners of it populate by "prowling natives" in the "drear wastes." In these lines the young Barlow shar⸍ Edward Johnson's earlier convictions about site preparation for tne messianic New Earth. Some 130 years after Johnson wrote *The Wonder-Working Providence,* this Puritan theme of imperative reform of the environment remains a legacy intact in Joel Barlow's commencement poem. When he traveled in Europe for the first time (1788), Barlow confided to a notebook his disgust that the medieval habit of nighttime retirement to the walled city prevented

Europeans from making the best use of money and land. "They might have intersected every league with canals," wrote an indignant Barlow. "They might have levelled mountains & prepared the way of the Lord."[13]

But the preparation was itself too arduous to be glossed in poems. Barlow's *Prospect* embraced both the anticipated post-Revolutionary peace and the breadth of its landscape, but his ideal pan-American Connecticut village was, if true within the verse, very false geographically. And Barlow knew it. His portrayal had blithely over-arched environmental reality in America. He had been a verse drafts-man of the New Earth but could never afterward rest with poetic portrayal of an imagined America so at odds with the palpable one. For though he exploited visions in poetry, he lacked poetic vision. (Even the American future of his imagination was ever postulated upon measurable achievements from the past.) Barlow could all too easily see that his landscaped Canaan was, if proper within the couplets of a commencement poem, belied by the actual context of American geography. In subsequent poetry he would confront environmental problems and offer feasible solutions.

He had inspiration from a two-volume work whose importance he acknowledged in the preface to the *Vision of Columbus.* There Barlow commended the Scotsman William Robertson's *History of America* (1777), which he felt was undervalued and regrettably inaccessible and which, as Leon Howard points out, initially guided Barlow in his planning for the poem. Robertson was much more than a structural guide, for it was evidently he who brought Yale under-graduate to a keen sense of the awesome potential and the formidable obstacles of the two linked underdeveloped continents. "When we contemplate the New World," wrote Robertson, himself a vicarious explorer in the bibliophilic practice of the time, "the first circumstance that strikes us is its immense extent.... Nature seems here to have carried on her operations with a bolder hand, and to have distinguished the features of this country by a peculiar magnificence." Robertson lists instead magnificent peculiarities: perpetually snowcapped mountains, rivers like "arms of the sea," and inland lakes of sea size. But he is quick to point out the developmental possibilities of the two Americas. "A country of such extent," he writes, "passes through all the climates capable of becoming the habitation of man and fit for yielding the various productions peculiar either to the temperate or to the torrid regions of the earth." He states, "The New World is of a form extremely favourable to commercial intercourse," then likens its inland waterways, inlets, bays, and harbors to the best of the civilized world. Moreover, though various, the soil of America is naturally as "rich and fertile as in any part of the earth," a fact proven by the "vast number" and "enormous size" of American trees.

But Robertson does not stint the problems. "Countries where the grape and fig should ripen," he warns, "are buried under snow one half of the year." And lands in the same latitude with "the most fertile and best cultivated provinces in Europe are chilled with perpetual frosts, which almost destroy the power of vegetation." Up from the southern tropics "we meet with frozen seas, and countries horried, barren, and scarcely habitable for cold." The Laurentian Mountains so chill the wind in their "dreary region" that it becomes mild only when blown across America's "immense plains covered with impenetrable forests, or occupied by large rivers, marshes, and stagnating waters." Further, the vital life principle wastes its force in the propagation of "every offensive and poisonous creature, which the power of a sultry sun can quicken into life" unopposed by human society.

But the Scotsman offers a donnish object lesson from these observations about two virgin continents. "When we survey the face of the habitable globe," he writes, "no small part of that fertility and beauty which we ascribe to the hand of Nature, is the work of man," whose efforts "change the appearance and improve the qualities of the earth." The American problem, quite simply but hugely, is that human society has been too scattered, too small, and too rude to take dominion of the topography. "When any region lies neglected and destitute of cultivation," he says, "the air stagnates in the woods, putrid exhalations arise from the waters." Without purifying shafts of sunlight, "the malignity of the distempers natural to the climate increases, and new maladies no less noxious are engendered." The little native American tribes were "not capable to correct the defects . . . of the earth." And America's most fertile plains thus remained marshes or floodplains because "the hand of industry had not taught the rivers to run in a proper channel." Little wonder, from Robertson's viewpoint, that Europeans on the American threshold were astonished at what met their eye as "waste, solitary and uninviting," a *Wilderness* bereft of "the forming hand of industry and art." "The labour and operations of man not only improve and embellish the earth," he writes, "but render it more wholesome and friendly to life."[14]

For Barlow, Robertson's remarks imply the solution to America's problem. All that is wanting for the conversion of two virgin continents into a congenial, productive habitat is the infusion of a technologically advanced populace industrious enough to correct the topographical "defects" of North and South America. His is a solution as stunning for its simplicity as for its immensity. Essentially Barlow took it for his own, though he always made it part of the nation's spiritual biography.

His literary promotion of the American New Earth moved Barlow to some reading in geography, which in *The Columbiad* he called a "solid" (in contrast to "fine") art, legitimate among sciences in a modern world dispelling invidious ancient ignorance. Though he lived seventeen years abroad, Barlow's interest in American geography is evident at many points. From camp during his army chaplaincy he suggested that Noah Webster fill some back pages of his dictionary with geography, while later in Europe Barlow filled his own notebook leaves with titles he meant to acquire, among them

> Thomson, Voyages to N. America
> Kaimes Travels in America (2 vol)
> Danville's Atlas
> Smith's Large Chart of Chessapeak
> Fry & Jefferson's Map of Virginia
> Davis Travels 4 years in No. America
> Hutchinson—Hist Mass. 2 vol
> Hist & Acc't of Caroline & Geo.
> Hist & Pres. State of Virginia.[15]

In his translation of Brissot's *New Travels*, Barlow admired Jedidiah Morse's "American Geography," recommending it to those "who wish to be informed on this subject" and boasting that it "contain[ed] more information relative to that country, than all the books ever written in Europe." Too, while in Hamburg Barlow made the acquaintance of C.D. Ebeling, the European geographer of

America on whose behalf Barlow wrote a letter of introduction to President Stiles, evidently in the hope of encouraging European immigration to America, just as some thirteen years later the same possibility of increasing European immigration prompted Barlow to ask the London publisher Richard Phillips to bring out an English (and perhaps a German and French) edition of Capt. Meriwether "Lewis's Travels by the Missouri to the Pacific Ocean."[16] It seems to be not only the author but American settlement which Barlow was promoting. For to know of his continuous, if dillettantish, pursuit of geography is not only to see Barlow's homework for his poems but to gain a sense of his wider promotion of the American settlement and environmental reform which he believed to be an urgent rite of passage toward the American New Earth.

III

Barlow's promotional efforts warrant attention because, from his business venture to his literary translation, they reveal just how compelling were his needs to activate environmental reform of the American continents. Inspired by Robertson, he incorporated into his *Vision of Columbus* several themes of necessary environmental reform but, upon publication of the poem, seized a career opportunity (as it then seemed) to prosecute these very themes by expediting settlement of the West. Moreover, just as Brockden Brown made literary translation an occasion of nationalism, so in the guise of translation Barlow subverted Brissot's *New Travels in the United States* for similar ends by publishing in English only those parts of the Frenchman's vision congruent with his own.

It was from Paris that Barlow would be able—or so he must have thought—both to make his fortune and to spur the American land development that could lead to the realization of Columbus's vision. At twenty-four an ambitious Barlow was ill content to eke out a literary subsistence with a printshop, school, or editorial post, and happily he went abroad as the agent for Scioto Associates, a company whose avowed purpose was to sell Ohio land to French emigrants, thereby reducing the United States debt and settling the West. The moment was propitious, for one month after the fall of the

Bastille, Barlow, together with the Englishman William Playfair, formed the Compagnie du Scioto and sold frightened Frenchmen a dream of pastoral respite in Ohio.

The problem was that Scioto had no clear title to the lands being sold. Further, the French expatriates, many of them conservative aristocrats, were not made aware that their Ohio sanctuary lay hundreds of miles inland through stretches of hostile Indian territory. And despite Barlow's unanswered entreaties to his American partners to see that travel arrangements and accommodations were arranged for the emigrants (in order to insure a swelling, uninterrupted flow of emigrants, once glowing reports from Ohio reached France), still no preparations of the sort were made. In his naiveté (and perhaps his distracted eagerness to absorb French culture and French Revolutionary principles), Barlow did not seem to know until the end that Scioto was a fraud and he its dupe. (He was later exonerated of all blame when his fellow wit and Revolutionary War colonel David Humpreys examined the ledgers.)

For a man consistently impelled belletristically to clothe his worldly endeavors in principles, it seems odd that Barlow's extant letters and notebooks during this period (1788-90) are so sparing of the American millennialism rife in the *Vision*. Aside from the espoused virtues of respectability and solvency, Barlow's letters nowhere contain the territorial imperative of the *Vision*.[17] That imperative exists elsewhere, in his bowdlerized translation of Brissot de Warville's *New Travels in the United States* (1792), in which we find Barlow's philosophic justification for his territorial activities. This translation and "editing" of Brissot manifests Barlow's own self-conscious, active involvement in the eschatology evident in the *Vision*.

Personal travel narratives were of course a well-established literary subgenre long before Brissot's 1788 American sojourn, for the values and the domestic manners of the Americans had fascinated diverse Europeans eager to see what stirred in the new world crucible of European thought. Brissot, a Girondist later guillotined in the aftermath of the French Revolution, was a sympathetic onlooker to American life and an exponent of the republicanism Barlow espoused. But as Brissot's most recent editors point out, his was a distinctly European book, for intentionally the *Nouveau Voyage* was to be politically instructive to a post-Revolutionary France, to furnish it "more aliments to industry, more *data*, than can be found in Europe."[18]

Barlow's bowdlerization of Brissot made the *New Travels* a far more American book. Principally through excision, Barlow shifted the emphasis from the European illumination of America to an invitation to depart the Old World and be repatriated in the New. From his editorial pen emerges a clear pattern of changes designed to minimize the dangers of American settlement (and thereby to invite it) and to assert the salubrity of American life (again, an invitational emphasis). Gone are Brissot's descriptions of perilous ferryboats likely to capsize at midstream on windblown American rivers. Cut is the passage detailing the navigational hazards of the New York harbor—the first, the Pot, a gyre of two meeting tides that engulfs ships whose pilots lack experience or prudence; the equally treacherous Frying Pan on the opposite shore is a reef on which ships have shattered while avoiding the Pot. And midway between these two lies an enormous rock waiting to smash hulls sailing a careful middle course. It is Scylla and Charybdis rendered so literally that Barlow avoids them simply by omission.[19]

Indian danger, too, is unfit for the English-language edition of an otherwise favorable report on America. Barlow telescopes into a few sentences a Frenchman's account of Indian capture, murder, and torture on the Ohio River. In Brissot it is an account excitingly (though hardly enticingly) climaxed by a daredevil escape with an upstream swim amid whizzing bullets. Its result was to draw the escapee back to the sanctuary of Europe, hardly a denouement Barlow could relish. Brissot's remark that "Indians are still to be seen around Fort Pitt and infest the Ohio" is a statement no reader of Barlow's translation was to encounter.[20]

Nor would he have a chance to consider Brissot's remarks about dangerous variation in American temperatures, one day subzero and the next unbearably hot—indeed, a morning some twenty degrees different from the afternoon, and in Philadelphia itself. Worse was Brissot's contention that "consumption" is an unalterable "fact" of American life, and whether from outright disagreement or promotional bias, Barlow cut these passages.[21]

He also omitted Brissot's recurrent implication that westward-bent

Americans were sleazy nomads. Brissot said they were "afflicted" by the "ill" of "the wave of emigration to the West," which he imputed to sloth. The promise of easy success and status and a yearning to avoid hard work are what he felt lured Americans westward. Their "pleasure party" spirit surprises him, but their quest for "idleness" furrows his moralistic brow. Barlow, working to sell these very western lands (and somewhat on the same edenic basis Brissot deplores) rejected the notion of westward migration as an index of American moral laxity. After all, he held title to several thousand acres in the Ohio and urged his impecunious nephews to remove there and make their fortunes in the newest of the New World. The compass of the *Vision* reached far beyond the narrow strip of eastern seaboard which Brissot visited, and Barlow's excision of the Frenchman's remarks indicates a contrary point of view he could silence by lifting his pen for whole paragraphs.[22]

Barlow kept intact Brissot's bucolic landscapes, those described as radical conversions from bestial wood to prosperous rural civilization, sustained by the patience, industry, and labor that generated independence, plenty, and happiness. In large part this timeless portrait is one Brissot paints over and over as he travels and one Barlow leaves editorially unretouched. Although a great portion of the *New Travels* is made up of antislavery letters and of praise for the Quakers, there are also recurrent prospects—both geographic and futuristic—that Barlow translates with precision, since they so well accord with the environmental reform continuous throughout the *Vision*. "My principal object," Brissot had written, "is to examine the effects of liberty on the character of man, of society, and of government," and he suggests that liberty is the stimulus for territorial expansion, wilderness reclamation, and the technological progress that will lead to global harmony and happiness.[23]

But paradise is not only pastoral, "a charming cultivated country" with "neat elegant houses" and "vast meadows covered with herds of enormous cattle." It is additionally technological, a thrust Barlow warms to with his inclusion of Brissot's appreciation for bridges, canals, and the potential for steam power in a country where the labor force is small. The lesson of a New York-Newark road built across marshes is, the Frenchman says, one of extraordinary patience "of man who is determined to conquer nature." His description of "a floating dyke" that alters a river's course gives every reason to think that the Shenandoah Valley will be opened by river transportation once the "inconvenience" of navigational impediments is removed from the Potomac. Further, canals will "vanquish" the obstacle of waterfalls on the North River (the Hudson) since they are "so easy to construct in a country abounding with men and money." Indeed, America "in a little time may be intersected by canals in all directions."[24]

Brissot foresees a bicontinental American empire. In a rhapsodic conclusion to his *New Travels* he transports himself imaginatively one century hence to "see this whole extent of continent, from Canada to Quito, covered with cultivated fields, little villages, and country houses." This is his vision of "free Americans seek[ing] the advantages of the great family of the human race." (The native American, incidentally, poses no threat, for he will either be assimilated or annihilated.) "O Liberty!" Brissot cries, "how great is thy empire; how august and venerable does the aspect of liberty appear!" With power equal to will, "she commands, and forests are overturned, mountains sink to cultivated plains, and nature prepares an asylum for numerous generations."[25] No vision could have been more endearing to Joel Barlow, working to realize it both by translation and negotiation of the land sales that would move America westward and transform it into a secular New Earth.

IV

The Columbiad, Joel Barlow's great act of literary engineering, assumes from its beginning what the Puritan writers had worked to prove, namely, that American space could—if appropriately reformed—embody the idea of the New Jerusalem. But as a figure of the Enlightenment, Barlow necessarily confronted human problems he believed to be inherent in vast and various New World space unknown to the Puritan Edward Johnson who was uneasy about the antipodes of Connecticut. Johnson's New Earth, trumpeted in food and fiber acreage of thousands, is yet a kind of enclave for those "fit though few." But Barlow's expansionist imperative wholly opposes containment or social exclusiveness. On the contrary, Barlow so intimately connects the American experience with the two reformable continents that *The Columbiad* projects the building of a libertarian cosmopolis on two perfected continents.

The poem remained a personal obsession for Barlow because a very public America obsessed him. Roy Harvey Pearce points out that Columbus really represents the ideal reader, since the catechismic format of the poem permits Columbus to ask questions a reader is about to ask. But the format also permits Barlow to provide a program of answers. (In fact, he is far more a poet of programs for than of responses to America.) Pearce remarks that *The Columbiad*, subsuming the *Vision*, is real and earnest history and that Columbus and Barlow's readers are made Americans by it.[26] But it is a poem as much emeshed with American geography as with its history. As a Christian hierarchy recedes with each of Barlow's revisions, and the French monarchy is by degrees excised, concurrently humanity's shadow lengthens across the entire New World, and the imperative to reform that world becomes more fully stated and urgent.

The poem begins atop a second Pisgah where Barlow's Columbus looks upon the New World as a future Canaan that appears like a papier-mâché relief map of the two continents. "Nature's remotest scenes" roll before him, "and years and empires open" on his soul.[27] Barlow's is the problem of the propagandist because Columbus's geography lesson is political, its purpose to affirm the ultimate, bicontinental shape of the United States and to invite settlement. Barlow must render the topography on an epic scale while maintaining a topographical invitation to settlers, an assurance that the continents will not overwhelm them. Thus, his task is to evoke a sense of grandeur but not of foreboding, of majesty without imperiousness. Nor has he the option of avoiding description of inhospitable areas (polar, arid, volcanic), since he is committed to full settlement of both continents. He means both to consecrate them with republican form of government and physically to transform them by an intelligent (often technological) solution to their topographical problems.

There remains too the challenge to offer a geophysical survey that moves a reader to awed respect (but not to fear), that engages interest in natural wonders (without the titillation of a New World raree show), and that invites him into virgin terrain as a hard-working settler (but does not seduce him with a promise of paradisal indolence).

Barlow tries to keep balance by alternating emphases, really by having his own spokesman, the guardian spirit Hesper, move about focally so as to cheer, inspire, and fascinate the Columbus whom

Roy Harvey Pearce so aptly sees as the model reader. He is shown
Peruvian mountain peaks high as the nighttime apogee of stars, and
he·sees live volcanoes threatening Lima (although in the final book of
the poem Hesper predicts that men will learn to defuse the volcano
"ere his voice be tried.") Paraphrasing the Scotsman Robertson,
Hesper tells Columbus that nature formed the New World with a
"bolder hand," that indeed its sculpturing was the very consummation of all creation.[28]

Not merely for the thrilling sense of the sublime. Lest the reader
slip into subjective transport at description of cataracts, waterfalls,
and limitless expanses, Barlow endows the most dramatic
topographical features with a reserved patriarchal grandeur. That is,
he personifies them in order to suggest a human realm, if not a
human scale. Thus, for instance, "bold Erie's wave" stands sublimely,
and "Dread Niagara bluffs high his brow," frowning defiantly while
rainbows bend over the "dashing tide."[29] Networks of waterways on
both continents are described as cooperative teams of aqueous titans
who ultimately combat "Sire" or "Father" Ocean when they meet at
the sea. And Barlow works in the anthropomorphic terms standard in
geography: arms, mouths, heads, and so on, all embellished to enhance and dignify the personification.

Still, patriarchal splendor and wondrous topography do little to
entice man to attempt dominion of these continents. In the Southern
Hemisphere Columbus sees floods, whirlwinds, and lightning that
bends "forky terrors o'er the world." And in North America he views
"Maine's bleak breakers" along "the dangerous coast" whose isles
and shoals "boast" latent horrors. At a few points Columbus complains that even the grandeur seems useless, since it lies so far from
civilization and so difficult of access. "Far dim deserts," he calls this
northern virgin land, one ridden with "frost, crags, and cataracts"
and barely warmed by a "tired sun." At once Hesper agrees, but also
rebukes Columbus's lack of vision (of course an implicit jibe at any
reader predisposed to Columbus's views).[30]

Barlow's bicontinental New Earth is not all futuristic projection
but in certain locales is immediately accessible. Though Barlow has
dutifully cataloged geomorphic horrors, his guardian spirit
encourages Columbus with bucolic views at once charming and safe.
Indeed, for the most part, "a happy hemisphere invites [Columbus's]

view." Green hills lengthen, and bright rivers swell westward. The hemisphere may be "wild," its distant places "dim," but Columbus is jubilant that the new race will find "wide vales with every bounty spread." It is a topography suppliant to man's wishes and anticipatory of his wants. Mountain waters rush to the sea "lav[ing]" banks on which future South American towns will rise. (Throughout both the *Vision* and *The Columbiad* rivers wash banks in rites of preparatory ablution as nature readies for the new men.) In fact, "wild Rappohanoc seems to lure the sail," and the banks of the Patapsco, Susquehanna, and Potomac all invite settlers. In truth, says Hesper in reply to Columbus's complaints about remote and hostile terrain, this is the "happiest land," which, at the moment of human habitation, will reform itself to meet the needs and desires of the new race. "Streams obedient yield the heroes room" and spread broad passage for him, having sluiced lakes and formed soil just for him. In the ideal Mississippi Valley are regions "pregnant with a hundred states." It is a patient gestation, and the imminent parturition so easy.[31]

Barlow's America, if not intrinsically edenic, does offer paradisal potential. On untilled lands crops spring up and come to harvest spontaneously. (The produce report on spontaneous crops is impressive: rice, corn, bananas, dates, oranges, olives, apples, peppers, lemons, figs, cocoa, and, fibrously, cotton.) More important, there is no geophysical impediment to man's wish to prosper here. "Grassy lawns allure the steps of toil" in the Chesapeake Bay region. The colonists have an "instant harvest" with fields smiling at their tillage. Forests obligingly "yield" the colonists room, and "nature's care" will "repeople the tidal shoals." "Genial" is the word Barlow invokes repeatedly as the landscape's own adjective. Hills, plains, fields, tiles—all are "genial" and none combative, a relationship in accord with the post-Revolutionary environmental attitudes in which Americans and the continent were complementary, one with the other.[32]

One revealing word change from the *Vision* to *Columbiad* suggests Barlow's participation in these attitudes (as well as his promotional bias). In the early version Columbus gazes rapturously at American realms that "await" mankind; but in the later version those realms "invite" him.[33] There is much work to be done in reforming the topography of two continents, but eking subsistence from a meager soil forms no part of it.

Philosophically, Barlow's commitment to Americans' geographic destiny in the inaugural Millennium obliged him to account for "the various powers of soul and tints of face" that diversify mankind over the earth. Specifically, to present the American continents as inherently ennobling and morally regenerative, he had to suggest why the natives on such consecrated soil were as distastefully backward as he understood them to be. He offers a theory that deforming mutations ("crude atoms disproportioned") somehow fill the air with "sickening vapors" and genetically deform the "harmony of the human frame" over time until those confined to insular localities mistake themselves for the proper human norm. This is the unfortunate error of the North American native (the "bloody myriads" and "savage foes" convulsing the air with "discordant yells," "the war whoop's hideous blare"), and it was the flaw of the "feeble or fierce or groveling" South American natives before Manco Capac united them and brought them to an enlightened political state. Barlow's solution for this deforming insularity of human society is a vast communications network of river traffic and, later on, a webwork of man-made canals. The point is crucial with him, for the one-time Connecticut farmboy so hated parochialism that the word "local" is his epithet of greatest repugnance. All his most cherished metaphors point instead toward a cosmopolitan New Earth in easy access of itself.[34]

In fact, Barlow's values are so social as to be urban. Not that he values cityscapes; despite description of spires and domes, and vows of bustle and movement, his American cities feel like Connecticut villages. (It may be that this longtime resident of Paris and London was intellectually unable to separate urban architecture from the poverty, vice, and brutishness he felt went with it and so avoided tainting America with vivid urban detail.) But without question his are urban values. His Adam is "unhappy, unassociate, unrefined," a man who "wander'd wild, to every beast a prey,/ More prest with wants and feebler far than they." So much for Rousseau—but equally dismissive of two American continents geophysically primitive and harboring tribal travesties of man.[35]

Thus, pervasive settlement and the environmental reform of America are Barlow's highest priority, since the New Earth is possible only in a complex and interdependent human society: "the only state of nature is a state of society; and the more numerous the members, the more various their pursuits, the more populous the territory, the higher the improvements in every kind of regular industry and art." His is a circular argument, or perhaps a spiraling one, since all these components reinforce and magnify each other, blurring the distinction between cause and effect. In America "social man a second birth shall find, / And a new range of reason lift his mind." His intellect will be suffused with "purer light, / A nobler sense of duty and of right." Millennial nobility of course exceeds that of the past. Barlow is not so fatuous as to suggest that dense population over vast, genial terrain will in itself insure liberty and freedom, but it is prerequisite to them.[36]

Barlow's inclusion of South America in his reformist imperatives has gone virtually unnoticed, probably because retaining two books of its legends from the *Vision* through *The Columbiad* has seemed more like an act of poetic self-sabotage than of environmental activism. The interwoven legends of Manco Capac and Prince Rocha (the latter a composite of two figures bearing the name) were derived from Robertson and, as Leon Howard points out, from the Yale copy of Sir Paul Rycault's translation of *The Royal Commentaries of Peru* by Garcilasso de la Vega. Barlow's "Dissertation on the Genius of Manco Capac" appears in the text of the *Vision* and is, with some reworking, displaced into the notes of *The Columbiad*. It praises the civilized enlightenment of a sun-worshiping Inca who united scattered tribes in Peru, waged war "not to extirpate, but to civilize," and reached the highest level of monarchical rule. "The establishments of Manco Capac carry the marks of a most benevolent and pacific system; they tended to humanize the world, and render his people happy."[37]

Even when the *Vision* had been in print five years and Barlow was ready to revise it for the Paris edition of 1793 (thus indicating his readiness to "violate" the original text), he kept the two South American books intact, as he would fifteen years later in *The Columbiad*. He did so despite contrary persuasions of his London

publishers, Hayley and Clark, who urged Barlow to cut the *Vision* to
six books and especially to put the South American ones among the
notes in the back. Cheerfully they told him his poem was too long
and that "whenever we saw a passage that could be left out tho' the
Verses did not deserve such a Fate we instantly drew our Pen across
it." Whatever Barlow's reaction, it seems certain that, for all his
stylistic and structural revision, he kept the two South American
books intact as geographical balance to the others set in North
America. The North had its Revolutionary War heroes and its
proponents of political enlightenment. South America, too, must be
made to appear worthy of a millennial future in tandem with that of
the northern continent. Just as the colonial period in the North is a
historical preparation for the Revolution (itself the millennial beginning), so does the saga of Manco Capac and Prince Rocha impart to
South America a historical tradition of "benelovent and pacific"
politics. Capac's capital, Cusco, was designed "To reach o'er earth
and civilize mankind" just like its northern counterpart.[38] Barlow
means to assert parity between the two continents and in so doing
affirm the new nation's ultimate boundary lines as their joint
perimeter.

V

Because attitudes toward the environment changed in the
American Enlightenment, the quality of environmental reform in
The Columbiad marks a significant change from that of its Puritan
precursor, *The Wonder-Working Providence*. The imperative to transform the New World is just as urgent in Barlow as it had been in
Edward Johnson one and one-half centuries earlier. And certainly the
agnostic of the Enlightenment upheld the secular version of his
Puritan forbear's conviction about a prophesied reign of peace.
Barlow's eighteenth-century ideas, however, about man's relation to
the natural world so differ from Edward Johnson's that the very
experience of environmental reform is radically changed. Barlow
demonstrates how the Puritan's hard contention with the environment becomes instead cooperation with it in a context of nature's
bounty. No longer is the New Earth to be wrested from an inhospitable forest rotten with demonic savages. Rather, as Barlow's

Columbus dictates, "What nature fashions, let her sons refine . . . and work with nature on the line she drew."[39] The *effects* of environmental change might appear to be similar to those in Johnson (albeit on a larger scale), but the sensibility—and thus the experience itself— is redefined in Barlow. For among those post-Revolutionary writers redefining Americans' relation to their environment within the purview of the Millennium, Barlow shows in *The Columbiad* how this new race of Americans cooperates with the natural world by correcting and finishing the huge but primitive work of genesis and does so within assumed bounty of the earth.

The changed use of the word "waste" evinces the newer sensibility. In Puritan writings, as we have seen, "waste" land or ground reproaches colonists' insouciance or indicates God's reprimand. But in Barlow, the word is virtually a synonym for potential but unrealized use of the environment—for instance, use implicit in a navigable river through an unsettled forest. Indeed, waterways flowing without barge traffic, arable lands without farmers, fruit-bearing trees without gatherers—these are a categorical "waste," since they lack the one component that would complete and fulfill their existence: man. Barlow is no more the proponent of environmental rapine than is Johnson, but his is the view that only a human exploitation of the environment can properly finish it and bring about the New Earth.

According to Barlow's version of genesis, Americans inherit a kind of geophysical rough carpentry and commit themselves to the finishing work. To teach, tame, correct, refine, improve upon the topography—this in large part is the destiny of "Europe's better sons" who emigrate and sire the new race. The "millennial morn" that survived Barlow's loss of Christian faith (appearing as it does toward the end of Potomac's speech in *The Columbiad*) is unequivocally that of the secular New Earth.

In Barlow's post-Revolutionary genesis myth we find the reconciliation of a titanic American topography with the exigencies of settlement. In fact, Barlow's account of America's genesis anticipates the tall tales of the nineteenth century, for Hesper tells Columbus how, with an arm as long as the heavens, he healed an earth wounded by a rupturing birth of the moon. Then he calmed the elements and instructed them "where to mold their mass and rib the crusted sphere," before assisting in the elemental upheaval that wrought mountains and plains. He "led the long streams and roll'd the billowy main," and from low tide stole muck to fashion banks and inlets. Then he "strow'd the wild fruitage, gave the beast his place, / And form'd the region for thy filial race." Hesper then located the seats of government and scheduled them in time. Finally he retired to let the ocean waters work upon the continental boundaries to "create the shore, consolidate the soil." And he waited, his clock set and wound.[40]

The Potomac River describes its geologic genesis similarly ("from rock-ribb'd lakes I forced my birth"). And the Potomac, "garlanded with vines / and wreathed with corn," offers a composite statement of invitation, imperative, and future certainty. "Haste then, my heroes," he says, "tempt the fearless toil." He urges settlers to farm the river valleys, drain the fens, and break up rocks that impede navigation. And he predicts keels on every river branch and "contiguous towns on all my shores." Alluding to nearby Mount Vernon, he vows to nurture the military hero necessary to "drive the demon cringing from the coast," should "delirious war" occur.[41]

From this rough draft of creation and these predictions of human polishing (as the Potomac terms it, a coronation), Barlow tries to show events moving forward in the destined pattern of environmental reform toward the New Earth. When among darkening Revolutionary clouds Columbus asks anxiously, "Where then the promised grace?" Hesper offers a litany of achievements of the new men. As the Potomac had foretold, Americans have planted the intricate branches of the Chesapeake and straddled the Roanoke River. Felling Appalachian pine and building levees along the Pimlico, they send barks "groaning" with commercial materials down the waterways toward the sea (there to "seek distant worlds and feed and clothe mankind"). Rice, indigo, and corn float downstream to the holds of those ships, as does ore dragged from "Toconnok hills."[42]

This is no portrait of American colonists as titans duplicating Hesper's feats or those of the anthropocentric Potomac. Nor, on the other hand, is continuous reform of the American landscape arduous or debilitating. The domestication of a majestic country is heroic, but its tenor is of patient steadiness. It is a "patient plow" that divides the earth; it is a groaning bark "labor[ing]" to the sea. As Hesper reminds Columbus, "slow proceeds the work. Long toils, my son, / Must base the fabric of so vast a throne." One's first impression of the reform of the American landscape in *The Columbiad* is of instantaneity, since Barlow returns to the subject intermittently and with the suddenness of a photographic slide, or perhaps of a hasty landscape limner. But within the sudden panorama from the "pencil [that] moves and calls the whole to life," there are statements of persistence and slow steadiness.[43]

To move pictorially from landscape to landscape in the order of Barlow's presentation is to see the realization of the geographical predestination he asserts intermittently. The new race are refining the work of genesis toward the utopian perfection characteristic of the New Earth, and in so doing they are clocked by verifiable milestones in American history. Barlow enjoys linking his American prophecy with past events which Columbus himself sees prophetically but which Barlow's reader knows have already happened. In this way Barlow assures readers that the futuristic projections of the tenth book of *The Columbiad* will also come true. The matter of American history is in this sense a basis for Barlow's divination of the American future, and he is careful to show it as a consummation of processes long underway.

These processes—of titanic genesis coupled with settlement and environmental reform—make up one myth of the New Earth in *The Columbiad*. But, unknowingly, Barlow undermines this happy connection (and thereby his myth) with contradictory themes of ominous social and environmental relapse. For unconsciously Barlow partakes of a version of that American cultural paradox whose origin Sacvan Bercovitch locates in New England Puritanism and which we have examined in some writings of Cotton Mather. This paradox, one of Congregationalists on a historic mission, had for Puritans embraced a City of God together with that of earth.[44] In Barlow the paradox disintegrates into outright contradiction. For the agnostic Barlow's secular City of God is strictly earthbound; yet within this one literary work it vies for material space with that other nation, the one which is vigilant against new antichrists of monarchy and tyranny, yet vulnerable to backsliding in its own laxity or complacency. The cohabitation of these two "Nations" in American space reveals Barlow's confusion. For he acknowledges that the republican experiment might fail and bring on environmental cataclysm—yet asserts simultaneously the idea of a *destined* spiritual apotheosis necessarily inclusive of environmental paradise that is both discovered and in part man-made.

The destined, paradisal nation is one of a mutually enhancing New World landscape and the new men come to inhabit it. "Freedom's unconquered race" shall "plant with men the man-ennobling shore."[45] This is a race broken free of benighted time past, one violent, superstitious, and ignorant, one in which man's grasp of the physical universe far exceeded that of his own moral nature.

The central question about the destined apotheosis, in both the *Vision* and *Columbiad*, is not whether environmental reform will occur but only *when* it will. As we have seen, its inevitability is assumed, though processes can be quickened by human industriousness. ("Tame the soil," Barlow says repeatedly, a phrase seldom more than a few lines removed from some tribute to "honest," "enlighten'd," "healthy," or "fearless" toil.) Still, in his ebb of Christian faith a key millennial conviction remained, one asserted at several points in *The Columbiad* as Hesper declares the certainty of a full reign of peace to Americans "predestined." Viewing scenes where "frowning forests stretch the dusky wing, / And deadly damps forbid the flowers to spring," an impatient Columbus demands, "*When* shall my children cross the lonely tide?" Smitten with sense of place, the explorer thrice repeats that it is "here" his progeny will implant culture. The colonial presence will teach lawns to smile and groves to sing. The navigable rivers will not long flow in vain but will flow with purpose, laden with harvests and logs that proclaim peace and plenty through waterborne products. The Americans are "predestined" to tame flood waters and thus to transcend nature's vagaries. In this manner will paradise be won. The New Earth is by nature decreed, reassuringly fixed and beyond vicissitudes of time.[46]

But not so for that other nation, the provisional one proving itself through conjoint moral and material progress in the United States, yet ever subject to relapse. In colonial American history, Barlow found solid basis for his fears that the nation could go either way and that moral apostasy would include environmental havoc. In *The Columbiad* he proves the point with contrasting portrayals of the English and French colonial experience, the first as exemplary for its ascendant strength as the second, France, was for its dissipation and ultimate ruin.

For the French colonies, "Gaul's migrant sons," provide a grim object lesson. They build a post on the "sylvan Wabash" and spread a "mantling host" over the Mississippi. They bid Louisiana's "lovely clime" to prepare to rear "infant states" and to prove out new arts. Exploration of the Great Lakes reveals "paths of trade," and waves of the Ohio River smile as if conscious of the approaching fame and honor of that water route. But (critically) the French have only scouted the landscape and not civilized it. Any why?—because "Gallic planters still their trammels wear, / Their feudal genius still attends them here." Theirs is the cramped soul fearful of independent thought, looking anxiously to France for prefabricated laws and generals. The institutions (schools, judiciary, and church) and their slaves "spread thick the shades of vassalage and sloth," sponge up the energy, stunt the colonies, and damp libertarian thought.[47]

Because of this, the French "keep the vast domain a desert and a grave"; that is, they fail to make a mark of environmental reform.[48] The lesson is clear: the American New Earth is possible only when inhabited by an enlightened society progressing in justice and liberty. Barlow's presentation of this socioenvironmental contrast between colonial Britain and France just on the eve of the French-Indian War of course allows him the tactical advantage of implying British victory as one predestined step in America's progressive enlightenment.

In a footnote in *The Columbiad* Barlow sings a dirge about the environmental price paid by the French for benighted feudal practices. They "had greatly the advantage in point of soil, interior navigation and capability of extension," he writes. "They commanded and possessed the two great rivers which almost met together on the English frontier." Further, New Orleans predated Philadelphia and was better situated to become a great commercial center, and Quebec and Montreal were older cities than those of the eastern seaboard and of comparable advantage (conveniently, nothing here about the northern Canadian climate). Too, France had twice the population of England and could better spare a colonial population.[49]

But, because the French lacked libertarian traditions, they squandered their advantage and atrophied, their geographic resources becoming little more than a trading commodity in "the capricious vicissitudes of European despotism." Conceding that his remarks are written at the moment of the Louisiana Purchase, Barlow plays the republican chanticleer: "The world will see how far the above theory will now be confirmed by the rapid increase of population and improvement in that interesting portion of our continent." The improvement of "our continent" is inextricably connected with its political traditions, and, typical of millennial thinking in the American Enlightenment, Barlow so structures *The Columbiad* that one cannot go forward without the advance of the other.[50]

Nor was the example of France Barlow's only source of disquiet about the direction in which his nation was moving. William Hedges has pointed out how very worried were the Early National writers about failure of their enterprise—and Barlow was no exception.[51] As a document intended to incite the nation to social progress, *The Columbiad* offers specific solutions to American problems. But its prevalent optimism ought not to obscure the tangle of Barlow's own fears and reservations, which he confided to footnotes, to notebooks, and to his correspondents.

In the final note to *The Columbiad* he implicitly acknowledged his verse propaganda and the motive behind it. Deploring pointless longing for a Golden Age or a foolish idealization of the primitive, Barlow suggests that "one of the most operative means of bringing forward our improvements and of making mankind wiser and better than they are, is to convince them that they are capable of becoming so."[52] He concedes that societies lacking this conviction may desultorily progress anyway but that those suffused with it (inspired by its presence in educators and public leaders) "would greatly expedite our advancement in public happiness and virtue." Yet he worried about whether elected officials would be the pragmatic muses of the new nation. To his brother-in-law, Abraham Baldwin, Barlow wrote from Europe in 1801: "Will [Jefferson] give more of his attention to the native and internal sources of improvement, to the encouragement of agriculture, to roads, canals, useful arts & domestic manufactures?" Barlow fretted that Jefferson might not pay serious attention to improving the nation's educational system and added, "Very few men think of these things, but thousands would think of them and labor at them if they were set agoing and the [impetus] were given them by a great man in power." He concluded, "I dwell on these subjects with great anxiety, because America, though young, is growing old in wrong habits & prejudices, which have not yet become inveterate but will soon if not corrected." Then, portentously, "It depends on this generation, perhaps on that one man, to say whether America shall rise to real greatness and true glory, or retrograde & dwindle into the ape of every error that has hitherto degraded & tormented the human race."[53]

The greatness and glory of America is bonded to its environmental improvements, but Barlow worries about Jefferson's possible failure to galvanize the nation to them. Its political tenuousness haunts him. He had confided to his first travel diary that the British Westminster election was of great moment for America, since, strenuously contested and drawn out, it served as "a *momento mori* to the freedom of election in his own country." The author, who was to conclude his *Columbiad* in an allegorical sculpture garden of human fulfillment, projected his final chapter of the aborted U.S. history as one wholly cautionary. "A most useful chapter by way of conclusion," he wrote: "Draw a detailed & impressive picture of the dangers that threaten the destruction of our brightest hopes as to the duration of the Constitution & the preservation of liberty." These dangers include too few "objects of laudable ambition," lack of encouragement to "Science, literature & other elevated pursuits," and the defeat of the meritocracy, with distinction conferred only for wealth and genealogical prominence. *The Columbiad* would end nonetheless with a vision of serene and majestic topography as a setting for the four-gated city populated by a delegation of "guardian guides," all in a "monumental clime" and "rear'd by all realms to brave the wrecks of time."[54]

Barlow's interlocking moral and material values made it perhaps inevitable that his anxieties about the nation's backsliding should surface in his poem as environmental threats. Should the nation slip into despotism, it has the alternative of quietly sinking in thrall or

> of throwing off like a vast volcano the accumulated mountains by a dreadful explosion; when a great part of what was good & a small part of what was bad are buried in the ruins, & the remaining mixture of materials are left to jumble for their places, with a miserable prospect of ever being able to reduce themselves to order.[55]

This notion of volcanoes disturbed Barlow, among others. As

Frederick Somkin observes, "The idea of a violent breakdown of the social order during an age of prosperity . . . easily utilized the metaphor of volcanic eruption."[56] The cost to an America whose sociopolitical system fails through civic laxity is massive geophysical upheaval. Because spiritual and environmental progress are inseparable, the republican New Earth—including a lacework of canals, endless farm vistas, tamed rivers, staunched floods, and drained fens—will not survive if liberty atrophies.

In this sense Barlow is an environmental Manichean, offering his reader a landscape dyptich of luminous pastoral goodness hinged to opposing cataclysm. The first presupposes the success of the political experiment in a montage of the tumescence of spring, the ripeness of summer, and the fulfillment of waterborne harvest, but without hint of approaching winter (nary an empty husk or pod, nor stubble field). The floods are "of day" and not of overflowing banks, and the seas are calm and stormless. Barlow, once a farmboy in the short growing season of Connecticut, where he endured some quarter-century of New England winters before departing for Europe, might well envision nature perfected as a montage of three mild seasons in a perpetually genial climate and topography.

But because the New Earth depends upon moral-political progress which is by no means certain, Barlow presents a vision of environmental holocaust. For instance, the continuance of slavery, the subject of a speech by Africa's guardian spirit, Atlas, will surely lead to a geophysical cataclysm as retributive Nature

> Waits but the fissure that my wave shall find,
> To force the foldings of the rocky rind,
> Crash your curst continent, and whirl on high
> The vast avulsion vaulting thro the sky,
> Fling far the bursting fragments, scattering wide
> Rocks, mountains, nations o'er the swallowing tide.

Finally, after the holocaust, America shall exist only as "a dim lone island in the watery waste," one that "stands the sad relic of a ruin'd world."[57]

As much as Barlow's own lines plunge and surge, it is clear that he meant to evoke a sense of geophysical horror equal in power to that of earthly repose in his vision of America's bountiful future.

Tactically—both as propagandist and rhetorician—he weighs the prospects in favor of the luminous vision, no doubt to inspire readers to its realization. But that smoking, tumultous scene of destruction is no mere attempt at a tour de force. To Barlow the nation (and by extension the world) was "growing old in wrong habits & prejudices" and could regress to just such an end. America's spiritual biography (again, ultimately the global Millennium) was in doubt as long as there existed such salient indices of its failure as legal slavery.

Barlow conveys his sense of personal urgency by his sudden reversion to the "I" pronoun at this point in the poem. It is as if he felt such surrogates as Atlas and Hesper had insufficient authority in an eighteenth-century culture that viewed physical science as the real repository of truth. His decision to address his audience directly in a didactic narrative voice is really some indication of his own crisis of confidence in fictive modes of truth telling and moral suasion. To take the poem in hand polemically after his two-book account of the nation's birth, the American Revolution, is to issue imperatives enabling America to avoid the brink of geophysical collapse. Moreover, it reveals Barlow's Olympian effort to will provisional America into conformity with the predestined, elect nation, though the two are never poetically reconciled in *The Columbiad*.

VI

As personally liberating as it was for Joel Barlow to pare away the language of Scripture in each revision of his poem, he left himself no ready symbolic means by which to convey faith in the reform of the American environment. Replacing the Christian Trinity with a "holy Triad" of "EQUALITY, FREE ELECTION, and FEDERAL BAND" enabled him to express ideals of social and spiritual well-being but went nowhere toward embodiment of the earthly imperatives congruent with spiritual ones. The Puritan Edward Johnson's soldiers of Christ and the plowshares and pruning hooks—these were archaic figures for Barlow, a social reformer burdened with the future, a self-appointed agnostic maker of myth. Responsible to what he knew about the geography of two continents, Barlow did not shrink from explanation of tasks to be faced in its reform. But we must look further for the vessels of Barlow's faith that human effort "would make a garden of the United States . . . a garden extending over a continent." What we find in *The Columbiad* is that, as environmental tasks loom largest, Barlow enacts faith through imitation of scenes from Homer and through a symbolic use of the new technology.

Curiously, the cold climate provoked Barlow's Homeric imitation. Since precious little of the continents was climatically as mild as the Mississippi Valley, he was head-on with the vexing problem of severe cold and its hammerlock on vast areas of the New World. Others had proposed forest clearance as the means of changing cold climates, and Barlow agreed. But the magnitude of the required effort drove him to Homeric imitation as an act of faith in future possibilities for climate control that might liberate vast continental acreage. Specifically, Barlow elevates frost to the godly status of Frost and vanquishes him in epic battle. The lower-case frost is irksome throughout Columbus's lesson in geography. In South America it invades and perennially hides mountain peaks. Ice fields continuously deflect the sun's rays in a blinding glare, while in the Northern Hemisphere (upper-case, Frost now) holds its victims in "ice-bound jaws." Icebergs flow sluggishly downstream to threaten "insidious death," a contemporary instance of which Barlow recounts.

Even though Hesper at that point distracts the anxious Columbus with more heartening topographical features, Barlow returns to the mythified enemy that seasonally or climatically impedes water transport, itself his personal sine qua non of America's Millennium. While Hesper can boast that "vain proud Frost has no domain in the Mississippi Valley" or over any of its waters, the Hudson's Bay region, however, provides somber contrast. Snow chokes the vegetation, and human life is reduced to a primitive level. Here "joyless seasons hold unequal sway." And here Barlow resorts to Homeric imitation, for he writes into his account of the Revolutionary War an epic battle scene in which Frost is put to rout.

The scene is that terrible Trenton winter. The Delaware is frozen, though Washington and troops cross it undaunted by the enemy Flood, whom they virtually vanquish with their oars but who in demise calls to "Almighty Frost" for aid. True to form, "the monarch mounts the storm" and in a swirl of snow and hail freezes the waters. The very waves "conglaciate," by which Barlow intends that they look fixed, like those of an inept seascape. It is Hesper, the continent's guardian genius, who rises to oppose Frost. "I come," the spirit announces, "not to insult the brave, [but to] teach the proud stream more peaceful tides to roll." He adds that "this land, these waters and those troops are mine" and vows to dispatch Frost to its proper polar domain. The chill foe lets loose one pine-tree javelin, which falls harmless. And though Barlow tries for epic effect with Hesper pulverizing ice chunks, it is really unexciting heat that vanquishes the mighty foe—the very solution that land clearance and cultivation offer on a mundane level.[58]

The battle is a typical confrontation between contending epic gods, but important in that it occurs in the American Revolution and involves Washington. The battle for liberty is thus connected with the battle to reform the environment. Poetically the episode is unsuccessful, but Barlow asserts in it a relationship between the Revolution and the freeing of vast continental acreage to man's reforming hand. It is a concurrent liberation of the spirit and of the land itself. For Barlow it is a symbolic act in attempted emulation of the Homer whose social power he felt to be unequaled.

Barlow's other symbolic—even mystical—act of faith is his use of technology. Mechanical processes had fascinated him at least from college days and from his first European sojourn in the late eighties when he jotted observations about whale-oil processing, gun-shot harpoons, a mangle, and above all the steam engine then used in smelting and in powering boats.

This intrigue with gadgetry appears in his notebooks alongside statistical entries about United States population, acreage, agricultural production, electoral votes, and so on (most of which he got from Morse's *Geography* and from correspondents). And though his notebooks are a topical stew, Barlow's technological and demographic entries reveal an important pattern of his concern. The nation was growing, and his data confirmed it. But the progressive growth over the continent contained the built-in threat of giantism in which distant parts of the body politic and its correlative body geographic would lack a sense of cohesive identity, perhaps at last to destroy the nation by dismembering it.

This was Barlow's great fear, but one he allayed with faith in technology. The mangle might be a useful gadget to bring to

Kalorama, his Georgetown estate, but the steam engine could be literally instrumental in binding the nation together commercially and spiritually. Barlow put faith in that engine.

More than that, he became a close friend of its leading exponent, Robert Fulton. In the autumn of 1788 the young Barlow on his first European sojourn had made note of "the great canal that extends in different directions all over the low countries & unites all the ancient trading towns that gave birth to the commerce of Europe under the name Hans Towns." Just a few years later Robert Fulton, a working engineer with an aborted art career behind him, was in England devising plans to interconnect English towns and cities with the very canals whose possibilities had so long intrigued Barlow. When the two men met, the *Clermont,* whose trial run against the Hudson current would prove the feasibility of steam power on American waters, was still a decade into the future.[59]

Were it not for the projected Barlow-Fulton poem, "The Canal," the friendship between the two men would but verify Barlow's engagement with technology. More than a "younger brother," the ten-years-junior Fulton appears to have been Barlow's engineer alter ego. Barlow's faith in Fulton's well-engineered submarine and side-wheel steamboat was proven by his financial support of both inventions.

Together the two planned their literary project, "The Canal: A Poem on the Application of Physical Science to Political Economy." Mercifully, from an aesthetic standpoint, the rupture of the Barlow-Fulton friendship terminated the poem midway in its first book. But 290 lines were completed, a fragment Barlow thought substantial enough to warrant publication. In the original plan, Barlow was to supply the philosophy and Fulton the technical information. Plans for the poem in Barlow's own notebooks reveal, as they often do, the engineer and litterateur seeking some synthesis. "In the poem of the Canal," he wrote in a notebook dated 1802,

> describe the Canal of Athose cut by Xerxes, and its destructive object. . . . The ships might have been drawn over; and at less expense, supposing the Canal was not meant for future use, but only for passing the fleet once. . . . Carry roads and canals under rivers, instead of going over them with bridges or aquaducts.

... Canal of Languedoc—makes two oceans salute each other. . . . Compare the turning of rivers into calals [*sic*] to the Labor of Hercules—cleansing the Augean Stables by turning the river Alpheus thro' them.

From these jottings it is clear that Barlow's conception for the poem was at once historic, technically pragmatic, and epic.[60]

The extant fragment suggests that this conception held. Recently it has been argued that philosophically Barlow owes much to Constantin de Volney's *The Ruins; or, A Survey of the Revolution of Empires* (1793), which attacked religions and appealed for a return to understanding and reverence for the animating force that moves the material world.[61]

Barlow's fragment, arcane in its zodiacal patterning after Volney's argument, continues to express faith in the technological expedience of the American New Earth. In the midst of heroic couplets on ancient Egypt he fairly bursts forth with his expectation that some "future Franklin" will not only comprehend the nature of electricity but master it for a reform of the environment. Desert sandstorms will no longer rage, since man will compel rains to convert the desert to a greening nursery. Blasting drought (to which Barlow attributes the Philadelphia plague of 1793) will also be vanquished. "Ah, speed thy labors! Sage of unknown name," cries Barlow. Impatient with his slow, methodical trek through history, he usurps time to assert technological mastery of the natural world.

In the union of natural waterways with canals and steam-powered craft, Barlow found his cherished metaphor for coherence of the New Earth. In fact, canals, so feasible for economic growth and social dispersion, become for Barlow an obsessive and mystical symbol, a worldwide river of life connecting all nations in spiritual and commercial harmony:

> Canals careering climb your sunburnt hills,
> Vein the green slopes and strow their nurturing rills,
> Through tunnel'd heights and sundering ridges glide.
> . . . .
>
> And plant new ports in every midland mound.

Barlow goes on to say that the "lawless Mississippi, who now slimes

/ And drowns and desolates his waste of climes," will be contained as civilization ("glad nations") prospers on both sides.[62] Further lines indicate that he saw the Mississippi as America's Nile which, when anciently "tamed," spawned science and art of global influence.

At several other points in the poem Barlow hearkens to the Mississippi, which obviously is of great symbolic value to him. Its civilization is tantamount to human control over all the North American waterways (and implicitly looks forward to similar subjugation of those in South America). This picture of a rehabilitated river points toward a body politic unified, literally, with a circulatory system of naturally and artificially created waterways. "System of Canals," he jotted in a notebook (1802), "& the activity it would give to Commerce, compared to the veins & arteries & the circulation of the blood. The power over this object ought to be in the federal gov't."[63]

The symbolic, the very mystical, power of these waterways proves Barlow's faith, especially when against his lines we see Jedidiah Morse's list of navigational horrors of the Mississippi. First, "sawyers, the bodies of trees . . . inevitably destroy the boats against which they strike." Then, planters, "trees firmly bedded in the soft muddy bottom . . . are peculiarly dangerous at night," not to mention "falling banks" undermined by the current, so that pieces of them (frequently more than an acre in extent) fall into the stream, often wrecking boats, which are "sometimes crashed in pieces." More treacherous still are the bayous of the Delta, since boats there can "be carried away by the current, and lost in the swamps."[64] Undeterred, Barlow kept faith in a "tamed" Mississippi and enjoyed thoughts of the Potomac, Ohio, Missouri, and Columbia rivers as

> . . . four brother floods, like a garland of flowers, [who]
> Shall entwine all our states in a band,
> Conform and confederate their wide spreading powers,
> And their wealth and their wisdom expand.[65]

Moreover (and typical of the eighteenth century), the rudimentary technology that Puritans hoped would ease hard lives becomes in Barlow the greater power to compel the natural world to conform to human wishes. Armed with "new engines," man will command the elements, "lay the proud storm submissive at his feet," and "change, temper, tame all subterranean heat." He will "brew" soft showers to repair the "labor's land," spread "fruitful soil" over the sandy desert, and "clothe with culture every mountain's head." In a Fourth of July oration Barlow reminded hearers that "Several of the great arts that are now grown familiar in common life were once thought visionary" and that America must not become skeptical about "the higher order of mechanical combinations." Elsewhere he wrote that "while it continues to be necessary to make use of animal force to move heavy bodies in any direction by land or water, we have a right to anticipate new discoveries." And the American Homer yearned for a homebred Francis Bacon to inspire engineers to become midwives of the Machine Age, itself one of a transcontinental garden. Barlow longed to see the machine help to bring about the American New Earth.[66]

The Columbiad reveals Barlow's prejudice and confusion as well as his foresight. He vanquishes Indians without qualms and contradictorily allows both a destined and a provisional nation at once the assured luxury of environmental paradise and yet the possibility of cataclysm as well. Poetically, as is well known, Barlow's opus smelled more of the lamp with each revision. As with the figure of Jason on the Chesapeake, he spread decals of classical myth on a new and naked landscape and seems to have used the *Iliad* like a cookbook. James Russell Lowell could have spoken of *The Columbiad* when he said that "the mistake of our imaginative writers generally is that, though they may take an American subject, they *costume* it in a foreign or antique fashion. The consequence is a painful vagueness and unreality."[67]

It is pointless to beat the carcass of a literary dinosaur but noteworthy that Barlow felt the need to find a new language for the new land. In his notebooks are to be found attempts at literary mimesis of the American topography. "To say of a river," he jotted, "his vast earth-draining bed.—Mountain miming wave.—pine-crested hills—Snow crested mountains—isle-encumber'd bed—isle-encircling bed—earth-disparting bed—heaven-reflecting flood."[68] Such adjectival lumpen spelled disaster for the poem catching it, though Barlow's scribblings indicate his awareness of the challenge to find a special vocabulary for the literary vivification of America. (Walt Whitman was not born until twelve years after *The Columbiad* splayed into the better libraries of America, there to stand with uncut pages.)

Yet Barlow was our first American writer to think systematically about the complete relationship between American society and the two continents. On the cusp of the nineteenth century, he went the logical step beyond the spatial confinement of Edward Johnson's American New Earth. His view on Americans and their environment is best revealed in Barlow's one lasting contribution to the English language. While he meant *The Columbiad* to enrich American English with such stillborn terms as *coloniarch*, *heliosebia,* and *burin,* Barlow's real contribution was the word he never boasted of in letters or footnotes. Yet, adopted from the French, *utilize* began with him, defined when he coupled it with *improve*. To render useful, to turn to account—this was his semantic innovation.[69] More than that, it was the essence of his programmatic American vision. In order to construct a New Earth ultimately "fill'd with happiness and peace," it was imperative both to improve man's moral sense and, conjointly, to utilize two entire continents.

5: Questioning and Chronicling: Thoreau, Cooper, Bancroft

> *Below, the mainfold grass and waters, animals, mountains, trees,*
> *With inscrutable purpose, some hidden prophetic intention,*
> *Now first it seems my thought begins to span thee.*
>
> . . . .
>
> *Ah who shall soothe these feverish children?*
> *Who justify these restless explorations?*
> *Who speak the secret of impassive earth?*
> *Who bind it to us?*
>
> *Walt Whitman,* Passage to India

Writing of American "Nationality in Literature," James Russell Lowell offered this literary lesson in 1849: "We have . . . a continent to subdue with the plough and the railroad, before we are at leisure for aesthetics. . . . Our spirit of adventure will first take a material and practical direction." Lowell was attacking the Young America movement, whose members renewed in the Romantic era the idea that a great national literature would come largely from the "rolling rivers, dark & green woods, boundless meadows, and majestic peaks" of the American landscape. The New Englander Lowell had an object lesson in American literary history for the New York-based Young America of Evert Duyckink, William Alfred Jones, and Cornelius Mathews, with whom he had had a contentious relationship for nearly a decade. Already (in 1843) he had attacked the democratic Young America for promoting an elitist literature far from the democratic ideals of brotherhood. Now, to prove how false was their manifesto on nationalism in literature, he presented his case against Joel Barlow.

As Lowell presents him, Barlow is an ersatz poet who "made the lowest bid for the construction of our epos, got the contract, and delivered in due time *The Columbiad*," an experiment that "should have been enough." Lowell held all America blameworthy for *The Columbiad*, which exemplified for him the fallacy of basing literature nationalistically upon an intimate relation of the poet to the national landscape. Lowell wrote, "Nothing has hitherto been demanded of rivers and lakes in other parts of the world, except fish and mill privileges, or, at most, a fine waterfall or a pretty island." In the geographical context, he added wryly, "so monstrous a conception as that of a poet is nowhere on record."[1]

In a few strokes Lowell dismissed Barlow (and implicitly cast doubt on Young America's expectations of an American literary Master Genius). But he did not so easily dispose of the difficult relation of American literature to the land and to the energetic—increasingly technological—change to the American environment in the first one-half of the nineteenth century. Lowell, however, did broach the mimetic problems central for those writers who, in the years following the Revolutionary and Early National era, tried to represent the American New Earth with factual accuracy and aesthetic power. These were writers who faced the romantic dilemma of mediation between the material and the imaginative worlds. But their problem of literary representation was compounded by a new cultural onus which their predecessors had not faced, that of interpretation of the success or failure of the American New Earth.

Exuberant rhetoric in American periodicals in the 1820s and 1830s shows us once again the endurance in American thought of conjoint values of spiritual and environmental reform. In the Era of Good Feelings that followed the War of 1812 and included two economic panics, of 1819 and 1837, we find much quasi-literary rhetoric espousing ideals of democracy and Christianity as they were thought to fit the stunning new technology that promised to consolidate the nation and ameliorate the lives of its people. This age becomes, as everyone knows, one of the steamboat and canal, preeminently of the railroad. President John Quincy Adams remarked in his First Annual Message to the Congress (1825) that civil government was obliged to promote internal improvements by "roads and canals" as it was duty-bound to encourage improvement in the "moral, political, intellectual" life of the nation. Joel Barlow and his confreres of the Enlightenment would have been heartened to read that America of 1827 was building according to the cosmopolitan blueprint of *The Columbiad.* Now "enterprising mechanics spread the products of their industry up and down our almost interminable streams . . . [and] a steam boat, coming from New Orleans, brings to the remotest villages . . . a little Paris, a section of Broadway, or a slice of Philadelphia." What's more, "the country is charming, with the pleasant alterations of fertile valleys, and cultivated hills, dotted with a number of considerable towns and pleasant villages."[2] "Abundance" and "comfort" are now bywords.

Not surprisingly, the vocabulary of this new phase of millennial America differs somewhat from that to be found in the rational discourse of the Enlightenment. Within the shibboleth of progress in the 1820s and 1830s, writings in praise of environmental and spiritual reform ring kinetically with the words "prosperity," "vigor," and "energy," of "astonishing rapidity of ———" (here, constructive changes of many sorts), and too of the "industry" and "industriousness" beloved of writers of the Enlightenment, cherished especially by Crèvecoeur. Yet American writers' understanding of the environment necessarily undergoes important change in this so-called Era of Good Feelings. For by proclaiming the Revolutionary inauguration of the Millennial Age of Liberty, writers of the Early National period had left their new literary heirs in an extraordinary position. Now the generation of the Transcendentalists, of the historian George Bancroft, and of James Fenimore Cooper had the obligation to take the true measure of the New Earth, to say how the Millennium was faring.

We must recognize this new onus for writers confronting together the ideographic and geographic America in the earlier nineteenth century. These were the first group of American writers to inherit the idea that, as of the Revolution, the Millennium had begun, that the New Earth was actual. One-half century after the Revolution came the incumbent duty to assess the national spirit and, correlatively, to judge the progressing environmental changes in this American New Earth.

That these changes were rapid and "extraordinary" is made graphic in John J. Audubon's sketch of "The Ohio," written between 1810 and 1834. Audubon recalls the past "Grandeur and beauty of those almost uninhabited shores, . . . the dense and lofty summits of the forest, that everywhere spread among the hills, and overhung the margins of the stream, unmolested by the axe of the settler." Then Audubon observes the absence now of Indians and the disappearance of "vast herds of elks, deer and buffaloes which once pastured on these hills and in these valleys, making for themselves great roads to the several salt-springs." He reflects that the Ohio "is now more or less covered with villages, farms, and towns, where the din of hammers and machinery is constantly heard; that the woods are fast disappearing under the axe by day, and the fire by night; that hundreds of steam-boats are gliding to and fro, over the whole length of the majestic river, forcing commerce to take root and to prosper at every spot." Audubon sees "the surplus population of Europe coming to assist in the destruction of the forest, and transplanting civilization into its darkest recesses," all in a twenty-year span.[3] His concluding tones of wonder resonate criticism of the new civilization, though Audubon declines explicitly to judge "whether these changes are for the better or for the worse."

Native Americans, however, felt few constraints in interpreting the changes. From the irrepressible periodical literature came both doubts and hosannas on the New Earth. Repeatedly in this Era of Good Feeling we hear celebrations of the American Revolution as

> a baptism of a great nation, the political regeneration of a great people . . . [of] the great panorama of our country's progress from her birthday to the present hour . . . [of] the firm walls of a mighty and enduring empire, destined to exert a most momentous influence . . . [of] cities lifting spires and turrets amidst the gloom of the scarcely trodden forest . . . [of] a nation enter[ing] on the race of glory, and unfolding all the moral and physical capacities demanded by the new position.

We read that in America "a fertile soil, and a mild climate, and their native enterprise, fostered by the stimulant effect of freedom and mild laws, will overcome every impediment," that "great enterprises" indicate "a new era in the world, and that this Union starts into being under the auspices of this new era . . . in which mankind have wisely resolved to devote the fruits of their industry, as a means of their further prosperity, [and] in which the energy of the whole human family will be employed in improving their condition as a mass."[4] These orotund phrases, formally loosed from the severe discipline of the heroic couplet, nonetheless survive semantically intact from the Enlightenment. The ideas that America (in particular the Union of States) is the redeemer nation, that the driving transformation of wilderness into civilization must proceed in the interest of social progress—these are a commonplace, really a cliché.

One figure in particular expounded these ideas in grandiloquent oratory. Especially between 1820 and 1840 New England's Daniel Webster found in public occasions the opportunity to state from his protectionist, Whiggish perspective the idea of a New Earth emerging within the American political system. Characteristic of the time, Webster's is the language of accelerated progress. True, his sonorous sentences build slowly in ways we must imagine to have been powerful in open-air speeches (to say nothing of the U.S. Senate chamber in which he declaimed by the hour). Yet his metaphors for American progress are strikingly kinetic. Echoing Federalist sentiments, Webster nonetheless believed that human progress had accelerated enormously from the time of English settlement of America. Declaring his to be an extraordinary age, he wrote that "events so various and so important that they might crowd and distinguish centuries are, in our times, compressed within the compass of a single life." At the laying of the cornerstone of the Bunker Hill Monument, Webster proved American social progress by citing the Revolution, the establishment of twenty-four states, and the growth of population from two or three to twelve millions of Americans. Over the years, in speeches responsive to the Hartford Convention's proposals for secession and to John C. Calhoun's argument in favor of the states' nullification of federal statutes, Webster emerged as the exponent of Union and of its safeguard, the federal government. He praised a safe, wise, free, and practical federal government and verified national progress in vignettes of rapid environmental reform. He sees, for instance, "the great forests of the West prostrated beneath the arm of successful industry; and the dwellers on the banks of the Ohio and the Mississippi became the fellow citizens and neighbors who cultivate the hills of New England."[5]

Rather like Joel Barlow, Webster is an apologist for technology, a point which Leo Marx has examined closely. But unlike his literary predecessor of the Enlightenment, Webster assumes that in important ways technology already has bound the United States into a geographic whole. He does not foresee cultural conflict as machines take over the labor previously performed by men, since "Providence" has wisely "adjusted men's wants and desires to their condition and their capacity."[6] In this way Webster offered his hearers welcome anodynes in which, evidently, he himself believed.

Typically, Webster portrays the progress of American civilization by emphasizing the inexorable, fateful march of American settlers westward. The population has "rolled backward and filled up empty spaces, after which it has overflowed those boundaries" and moved west unchecked. In phrases echoing Jedidiah Morse, Webster imagines the model New England farms covering the terrain from the Ohio to Lake Erie and beyond, and he intones, "Two thousand miles westward from the rock where their fathers landed, may now be found the sons of the Pilgrims, cultivating smiling fields, rearing towns and villages, and cherishing, we trust, the patrimonial blessings of wise institutions, of liberty, and religion." He concludes, "The world has seen nothing like this," and adds prophetically that "ere long, the sons of the Pilgrims will be on the shores of the Pacific."[7]

As is apparent, Webster views American environmental change as a correlate of the nation's political virtue. As a Unionist he insists that American progress is assured by "wise institutions and a free government."[8] Significantly, Webster invokes conjoint environmental and spiritual reform in his most politically strategic speeches, for instance, in his replies to Hayne, which turned specific matters of the tarriff and of federal policy on public lands into a defense of national power against states' rights. On those occasions Webster said that, in passing the Alleghenies, colonists "did not pass beyond the care and protection of their own government," that "wherever they went, the public arm was still stretched over them" More than public, that federal arm is "parental," and Webster added that since 1794 it has had "an entire ability to protect those who should undertake the conquest of the wilderness." That "fresh, untouched, unbounded, magnificent wilderness" was but "bare creation" when General Wayne "conquered the Savages" and freed "hundreds and thousands of square miles [of a] surface of smiling green" to an astonishing transformation of settlement.[9] As much as Webster appreciates the pristine landscape "crossed [by] mighty rivers flowing in solitary grandeur," his great pleasure is in the western census of one million people in the Ohio, people bringing the internal improvements of farms, industry, canals, and the railroad.

Webster, then, is exultant on the issue of national geographic expansion and progress. He wrote that "the *Principle* of Free Governments adheres to American soil" and "is bedded in it." This literally fused soil and spirit admit no doubts on American geography as political destiny. Yet, as is so well known, Webster keenly understood the danger of sectional rivalry on ideological grounds. He wrote that "Mind is the great lever of all things," that "human thought is the process by which human ends are ultimately answered."[10] Webster did not, in short, fear for a nation scattered westward (as much as his opponents accused him of New England protectionism). He did fear the fraternal divisiveness based in regional chauvinism, and of course the Civil War validated those fears.

Significantly, the conservative New England legislator seems to have regarded his own rhetoric as transcendent of politics as he drew analogies of his work with that of poets. Commemorating the landing of the Pilgrims in his Plymouth Rock discourse (one address that established Webster's public reputation as an orator), he spoke of poetry as vivifying the past for the present. More, poetry "shows us the long continued result of all the good we do, in the prosperity of those who follow us, till it bears us from ourselves, and absorbs us in an intense interest in what shall happen to the generations after us." The poet, then, is the historian who enlivens human consciousness through time. He telescopes segmented periods or epochs, brings them into simultaneity, and incites both reverence for the past and a vibrant pleasure in progressive goodness. Webster sees himself in that office. Declaiming on the virtues of the American system, he said, "We are not propagandists," perhaps suspecting that he was (or could be thought to be) just that.[11] From 1835 onward (as we shall see), the Democratic historian George Bancroft took up themes of the American New Earth in rhetoric much like Webster's, and with similar covert declarations of poetic purpose and stature. It seems significant that on these themes the ardent Whig and the professed

Jacksonian Democrat sound so much alike. In promoting internal improvements in the name of national destiny, Webster takes his place as a celebrant in political rhetoric of the American New Earth.

Yet there is a contradictory and countervailing tone elsewhere. Resonant of the jeremiads of the Puritan seventeenth century and of those eighteenth-century writings lamenting America's moral degeneracy (intermittently, for instance, in John Adams or Benjamin Rush), writers of the so-called Era of Good Feelings speak their fears and doubts about a nation whose materialism and avarice have out-distanced humane sociality. The western editor-essayist-geographer, Timothy Flint, and the New York minister, Elihu Baldwin, as well as Lyman Beecher, William Ellery Channing, and Orestes Brownson variously deplored the commercial spirit and idolatry of wealth that seemed to characterize the American public. Much periodical literature took up the same theme. One essayist feared that "national wealth . . . may be the destroying poison of that civiliza-tion which is of the spirit." He added, "To have canals, and rail-roads, and mines, and to be devoid, as a people, of the spiritual purity and spiritual strength, is to sell, not our birth-right, but our souls themselves, for a mess of pottage."[12]

Because such lamentations cross-cut regions and span a wide spec-trum of political, philosophic, and religious views, we are hearing deeply national sentiments when we read that

> the study of the powers of man—more especially of his moral powers . . . is neglected, as of no practical importance, [that] "the spirit of the age and country is . . . pre-eminently an age of gross and absorbing avarice, . . . [that] the physical im-provements of the country have infinitely outbalanced the ad-vances in morals . . . [and that] to produce a rail road, a canal, a joint stock company, is felt to confer more national renown, as well as advantage, than to rear a Milton.

One writer of distinct utilitarian bias even suggests, with canals in mind, that "we are too much prone to spend money for objects, and engage in enterprises which are not required by the exigencies of the country."[13] Writing to his daughter of American government, Albert Gallatin spoke of the private self-interest and factionalism masquerading as "a species of political millennium," while Orestes

Brownson held up for Americans the caveat of wanton England "gorged with spoils, and drunken with the blood of the poor, the weak, the defenseless," all victims of "astonishing industrial truimphs."[14]

Thoreau and Emerson joined this chorus decrying a commercial, materialistic America. In "The Transcendentalist" Emerson pleaded, "When every voice is raised for a new road or another statute or a subscription of stock; for an improvement in dress, or in dentistry; for a new house or a larger business; for a political party or the division of an estate; will you not tolerate one or two solitary voices in the land, speaking for thoughts and principles not marketable or perishable?" That second voice, of Thoreau, had warned at a Harvard Class Day conference in 1837 that "a blind and unmanly love of wealth" is a "ruling spirit" from which originates the "commercial spirit." He advised, "Let men, true to their natures, cultivate the moral affections . . . and we shall hear no more of the commercial spirit."[15]

We may recognize once again in these countervailing tones of lamentation and celebration that paradox which Sacvan Bercovitch finds to be central in American culture. On the one hand, America is thought destined to be the redemptive nation of biblical prophecy but, on the other, is felt to be a nation continuously on trial, as capable of regression as of progression, and yet in that dynamic way susceptible to endless possibilities for the renewal of its spirit.[16] Cotton Mather implied a certain resolution of the paradox in his sermons, while in *The Columbiad,* as we saw, these two visions of America are not held in paradox but jostle in contradiction, since Barlow seems not to have been aware of the disjunction of his two viewpoints and so vacillates between them even as he tries to remain convinced of the destined success of a redemptive America. But to see the nineteenth-century version of this cultural paradox is to recognize as well the aesthetic and ideological problems for American writers confronting a supposedly actual New Earth. For that millennial legacy literally left no middle ground to those confronting together the ideographic and geographic nation. The new writers had the alternatives only of concurrence with the millennial assertions of their predecessors (and therefore of assenting in amplified celebration) or of dissent that could only sound nihilistic (and therefore find expression in lamentation or repudiation). Either view would tend toward the polarities ever destructive to literature, propaganda or polemic. Tonally the danger was of literary monochrome without the rich tension of ambiguity or ambivalence.

And without originality of vision. For the imaginative conception—the myth of the actual New Earth—came into the nineteenth century intact. Vis-à-vis the writer and the New Earth, the literary task ahead was reportorial rather than visionary, one of repudiation or verification but not of conception. (One difficulty of mimesis may be grasped at once if we but recall that when faced with the implied continuum of progress that characterizes the New Earth, the Puritan Edward Johnson had reverted doctrinally to the prophesied Battle of Gog and Magog that meant the end of the world, while Joel Barlow, apparently unable to think up additional marvels of technology or synonyms for peace, fixed the consummation of human progress in a garden of statuary.) The New Earth could be very heavy baggage.

Thus, in the 1820s and 1830s many writers confronting the American landscape might be said to be in a state of future shock, to borrow Alvin Toffler's phrase. The epoch of the New Earth had been asserted, and ineluctable material changes were everywhere. Monumental and palpable, they demanded the scrutiny which Audubon sidestepped. Steamboats, "fairy structures of oriental gorgeousness and splendor," too fabulous even for "the imaginative brain of a romancer," now "rush[ed] down the Mississippi, as on the wings of the wind, or plow[ed] up between the forests." Wondrous, certainly, but to what good end? On board were "pianos, and stocks of novels, and cards, and dice, and flirting, and love-making, and drinking and champaigne," all in some waterborne mission to "ferment in the minds of our [rural] young people the innate propensity for fashions and finery."[17] These frivolous uses of steam power Barlow never mentioned when he envisioned the high-minded, cosmopolitan efficacy of the steamboat.

In fact, this very disparity between projected intention and the evident outcome brings us to a crux in American thought on the environment in the Era of Good Feelings. The reform of the American earth had been intimately joined since 1650 with spiritual regeneration of the nation. Writers were obliged now to consider the quality of this nexus in the 1820s and 1830s. In so doing they had to face up to the obvious disparity between moral and material progress. By definition, within the aegis of the New Earth the reform of the environment was utopian, in that it was utilitarian for ameliorative social purposes. But when the land became a speculative commodity, its minerals inciting schemes for riches, its canals a profiteering opportunity, and, withal, the burgeoning prosperity closed to the populace at large, then the writers of democratic vision were in a bind. Celebration of the New Earth would be flatulent (as those foregoing samples of exuberant rhetoric demonstrate) or, worse, hypocritical or callous. Yet to denounce the failure of the New Earth (or deny its existence) would, at the other exteme, indicate the very failure of democracy. These extremes are, as we shall see, the very alternative positions which Bancroft and Cooper reached, respectively.

II

For their part, Emerson and Thoreau moved in another direction and avoided confrontation with ideas of an actual New Earth. True, their writings are flecked with figures from it, as in Emerson's remark that "the land is the appointed remedy for whatever is false and fantastic in our culture," a sentiment enabled by the millennial suffusions of the American Enlightenment. Too, Emerson intermittently partakes of the celebratory spirit of a utilitarian New Earth, as when he calls the steamboat and locomotive the shuttles that weave "threads of national descent and employment and bind them fast in one web."[18] Similarly, Thoreau writes that the American makes himself "stronger and in some respects more natural" because he "redeems the meadow." "The weapons with which we have gained our most important victories," he continues, "are not the sword and the lance, but the bushwack, the turf-cutter, the spade, and the bog hoe."[19]

But Emerson and Thoreau shunned confrontation with the New Earth as a phenomenon of sociological realism. Emerson's was the doctrine of "the infinitude of the private man," of "the individual [as] the world." F. O. Matthiessen wrote that what stirred Emerson most deeply was man's "capacity to share directly in the divine superabundance" and that accordingly Emerson felt capable of writing both "about Universal Man and about man as a democratic citizen."[20] Emerson's true democracy, to be comprised in maturity of the beloved "young men" of his address, is quite separate from the "magazine of chattels" he feared the nation could become. For his part, while Thoreau celebrates reclamation of American land unmarked by the Indian's clamshell, he scorns the docility of American society whose spirited members have their "natures broken" before joining the "dogs and sheep" who are "fit subjects for civilization."[21]

In his study of the literary qualities of Transcendentalism, Lawrence Buell explains the mobility of these writers' positions in this way: "Transcendentalist literature refuses to commit itself either to a straightforwardly literal or an out-and-out metaphorical approach to the subject at hand. It is constantly trying, failing, and trying again to balance and reconcile the external world with the world of the imagination." It is not surprising that Bronson Alcott should have felt that Emerson's Nature, while "caught from our own woods . . . [was] never American, nor New English, . . . but some fancied realm, some Atlantides of this Columbia."[22]

Alcott may or may not have considered these figures apt for Thoreau's own conception of nature, one principally turned toward the individual as Thoreau too worked to reconcile the life of the imagination with phenomena of the outside world. Notoriously skeptical of programs for societal change, Thoreau nonetheless on one occasion drew upon traditions of conjoint environmental and spiritual reform in American writings. For in an early review-essay Thoreau confronted one plan for a kind of legislative New Earth and repudiated it by affirming a necessary relation between moral and material progress in America. More, he restated for his own visionary purposes the double imperative of spiritual and environmental reform.

Thoreau's review, entitled "Paradise (To Be) Regained," was occasioned by the reprinting in 1842 of part 1 of a two-part work call *The Paradise within the Reach of All Men, without Labour, by the Powers of Nature and Machinery*. Originally published in 1833, the book was written by J. A. Etzler, a German immigrant living in Pittsburgh. It presented a materialistic utopian plan which Etzler hoped that President Jackson and the Congress would enact. At

Emerson's suggestion, Thoreau agreed to review the book for the *Democratic Reviw,* and after some revisions reluctantly undertaken at the behest of the editor, John O'Sullivan, the review appeared in November 1843.

"Paradise (To Be) Regained" addressed Etzler's promise that with concerted human will, men within a decade could create a paradise on earth. Etzler proposed that "the whole face of nature shall be changed into the most beautiful forms, and men may live in the most magnificent palaces, in all refinements of luxury, and in the most delightful gardens." This plan entailed the kinds of environmental change which had become commonplace in writings since the Enlightenment: leveled mountains, dipped valleys, drained lakes and swamps, engineered canals and roads. Etzler's premise was that men could legislate a program for "a life of continual happiness, of enjoyments yet unknown." Not surprisingly, Thoreau labeled Etzler's program "a transcendentalism in mechanics," an impulse to "reform nature and circumstances," after which "man will be right." Contrarily, he observes, transcendentalists of ethics, that is, *the* Transcendentalists, urge "reformation of the self," after which "nature and circumstance will be right."[23] In such remarks we hear unmistakable echoes of Cotton Mather's visionary *Theopolis Americana,* one following from the spiritual regeneration of its citizens.

Thoreau does use the occasion of the review to lament men's shirking of the hard work of improvement of the earthly "fair homestead." Having decided against westward migration for himself, he chides those off to the Canaan of the Ohio: "Would it not be more heroic and faithful to till and redeem this New England soil of the world?" Further, as Henry Seidel Canby noticed years ago, Thoreau's imagination really did expand with Etzler's. The review genuinely entertains possibilities for solar, wind, and waterpower—as Thoreau put it, "all that blows, all that shines, all that ebbs and flows, all that dashes."

But Thoreau comes to this crux of the *Paradise within the Reach of All Men,* a problem of motivation. To Etzler, labor, no matter how elaborately mechanized, devolves from the turn of some crank. And Thoreau seizes upon this figure for his own metaphysical purpose, to define the motivational "crank within," that "certain divine energy in every man . . . the prime mover in all machinery." In the economics of the physical and metaphysical, "no work can be shirked. . . . not one particle of labour . . . can be routed without being performed." Here Thoreau dismisses the power of technology by saying that no "really important work [can] be made easier by . . . machinery," a sentiment anticipating (in *Walden*) his indictment of inventions as distracting "pretty toys," an "improved means to an unimproved end."[24] His recourse instead is to personal "Industry," to the "small private, but both constant and accumulated force, which stands behind every spade in the field." Thoreau's faith lies in this inner divine energy manifest in the farm spade. He writes, "This it is that makes the valleys shine, and the deserts really bloom." Greater than the "physical power" of a mechanical system is the "moral power" that comes from reforms of the inner life. Thoreau criticizes Etzler for aiming solely at objectives of "gross comfort and pleasure." He asserts, "A moral reform must take place first . . . and we shall sail and plough by its force alone." It is "the power of rectitude and true behavior" that can "fill up marshes, . . . secure agreeable environs, diversify the land, and refresh it with 'rivulets of sweet water.' "

In his response to Etzler we see both Thoreau's debt to writers of the past, notably Johnson and Barlow, and his difference from them. For he appropriates the conjoint values of spiritual and environmental reform as a Romantic writer working to reconcile the imagination of the individual with the external world. It is true that from the retrospect of the twentieth century Thoreau's remarks on human alienation in a materialistic utopia sound prophetic. His skepticism of a culture abounding in physical power but lacking self-insight was obviously well founded. Of interest here, however, is not Thoreau's prescience but his recourse to the two prior centuries of the American literary nexus of spiritual and environmental reform. (He may in fact have recognized this nexus in *The Wonder-Working Providence,* which Thoreau quoted in *A Week on the Concord and Merrimack Rivers* and later in *Walden* as well.) Challenged to consider a purely materialistic New Earth and the likelihood of human satisfaction in it, Thoreau instead affirms the primacy of reform of the individual inner life. For him, that prophesied Isaiahan landscape can be achieved in a visionary way by the divine energy of moral reform from within the individual. Dubious of a societal Millennium,

Thoreau yet draws from the traditions of the New Earth in order to help define an individuated paradise of the personal vision. In this respect he stands midway between Mather and Whitman.

In his emphasis upon the individual and especially in his valuation of the pristine natural world, Thoreau remains in other important respects outside the literary tradition urging programs of environmental reform in America. In his mature writings he did not advance environmental ideas on the New Earth within his own ethos. Rhetorically, he enjoyed opposing the free and vital searchings of the individual soul to the procrustean, mechanized town life that enslaved its citizenry. This opposition disallowed Thoreau the social-individual confluence Whitman exploited and made contemporary social change—including environmental change—suspect at best. *His* Maine lumbermen were necessarily "demons" whose "mission" seemed to be to "drive the forest all out of the country . . . as soon as possible."[25]

While Thoreau stands outside the socially centered tradition of American environmental reform, one point needs to be borne in mind. It is his presupposition of a particular middle landscape—one of wildness within distinct domestication, and fundamental to *Walden.* Just as Cotton Mather presupposed a civil landscape for the New Earth whose spiritual essence absorbed him, so Thoreau presupposes a marked degree of environmental domestication within which he celebrates his cherished wildness. *Walden* is in fact filled with reminders of civil settings and of Thoreau's profound connection with them. His house, located in the woods between the towns of Concord and Lincoln, is of milled boards and quite near to that railroad of his gnawing ambivalence. Too, from the village on public occasions he hears in his bean fields the cannon and martial music, and intermittently he recounts episodes of his boyhood in Concord and brings to life those who in the past lived in the vicinity of Walden Pond. Every day or two, by his own account, Thoreau went into Concord for the village rounds integral to his woodland life.

It is true that Thoreau injects irony, and often bitter denunciation, into these accounts. He slips in and out of Concord as if in fear to run its gauntlet. And the martial music stirs him momentarily to spear a skunk or woodchuck, just as the American army skewered those "trifles," the Mexicans. And for the ruins of old houses, "Alas!

how little does the memory of these human inhabitants enhance the beauty of the landscape!" There is an ironic dimension to his query on whether these sites might not have supported cottage industries and farming to make "the wilderness blossom like the rose."[26]

Though his irony glances from American town life and its values, Thoreau still needs a measured, domesticated landscape of the sort the Concord environs typify. His philosophic vitality much depends upon such a setting. From the village to Thoreau's house in the woods a traveler might lose his bearings in the nighttime or in snow, but Thoreau can only proceed to his philosophic point—that "not till we have lost the world, do we begin to find ourselves"—from the premise of geophysical security for life and limb, and mind.[27] Thoreau calls it "very pleasant" to "launch" himself in the "dark and tempestuous" night and "set sail from some bright village parlour or lecture room" for his "snug harbour in the woods." He continues these nautical figures, but readers never are subject to the oceanic void that drives Melville's Pip mad or to the "cold malicious waves" that push the helmsman Bulkington toward the enslaving shore. Thoreau's reader does not experience the threat of annihilation in (or by) a hostile or overwhelming geography.[28]

On the contrary, it is the premise of a domesticated environment which frees Thoreau to explore and to celebrate wildness as a tonic for thought. Thrilled in "savage delight" when tempted to seize a woodchuck and "devour him raw," Thoreau is at once drawn toward a "highter . . . spiritual life" and "toward a primitive rank and savage one." He "reverence[s] them both," loving "the wild not less than the good." As the seasonal cycle of *Walden* moves into spring, Thoreau writes that to prevent the stagnation of village life, "We need the tonic of wildness." And he boasts of aspects of nature "mysterious and unexplorable," "infinitely wild, unsurveyed and unfathomed because unfathomable." He speaks of "inexhaustible vigor, vast and Titanic features," and of "Nature so rife with life that myriads can afford to be sacrificed and suffered to prey on one another." But Thoreau's settings are quiet marshlands, his exemplary wild animals the waterfowl and little mink. Too, his speculation on the recesses of wildness is explicitly pastoral, and his exemplars of predatory sacrifice are the tadpoles, toads, and one dead horse.[29] All this is to say that Thoreau's rhetoric of wildness is extravagant but held in check by the smallness or by the domesticity of his illustrations. On the subject of wildness he thus achieves counterbalance in his language. His wildness is held in a domestic embrace.

It is well recognized that for Thoreau unremitting wildness could block the imagination as much as did the material paradise he despised in Etzler. There were clear geophysical bondaries beyond which wildness was not tonic but paralytic. In "Paradise (To Be) Regained" Thoreau refuted Etzler by saying that "surely a good man need not be at the labour to level a hill for the sake of a prospect," since from within himself "he enjoys better prospects than lie behind any hill." He added this fillip, that "where an angel travels it will be paradise all the way."

But Thoreau found limits even to the paradise of personal vision. His journey to Mount Katahdin in the summer of 1846 included not only his anticipated pleasure in vivifying wildness but the dread, desolation, and sense of diminution before the enormity of the "howling wilderness." Thoreau had rejected Etzler's mechanized Millennium, but at the other extreme he shrank from the "savage and awful . . . Earth . . . made out of Chaos and Old Night." Extremes both of materialism and of "Matter, vast, terrific," repelled him. Thoreau complained that Maine's Mount Katahdin was "no man's garden, but the unhandseled globe."[30] And this point seems crucial for the kind of geography to which his imagination could respond freely. Through his seven sets of revisions of *Walden* Thoreau kept his record of the handseled world, that of good omen, of a pledge for the future.

Thoreau's quest for deeper dimensions of wildness in Maine during his second summer at Walden Pond led him, unexpectedly it seems, to desolation and derangement. On the peak of Katahdin, "Vast, Titanic, inhuman Nature got him at disadvantage, caught him alone, and pilfers him of some of his divine faculty." On Katahdin, Thoreau experienced such extreme wildness as throttled his imagination. Intermittently in the essay he had spoken of "savage and dreary scenery," of "the grim, untrodden wilderness . . . even more grim and wild than you had anticipated" in a country predominately "stern and savage." It is "the most treacherous and porous country" he ever traveled, and at one point Thoreau even likened himself to Satan in Chaos.[31]

Then, on the peak itself, he feels the measurable loss of his "divine faculty," of the "vital part." Here man can "freeze or starve, or shudder his life away," without succor or memorial or any communion with this geography so reminiscent of scenes of genesis in ancient epics. This "primeval, untamed, and forever untamable *Nature*" is fit only for men of closer kinship to rocks and to "wild animals." Sobered, Thoreau concludes that America *is* "exceedingly new," that the continent remains "unsettled and unexplored," and that its very shores at either end are "like a desolate island, and No-Man's Land." Just sixty miles from the railroad, the cosmopolitan traffic, and the city of Bangor "like a star on the edge of night" is "that very America which the Northmen, and Cabot, and Gosnold, and Smith, and Raleigh visited." "Unmapped and unexplored," it is "the virgin forest of the New World."[32]

Awed by it, Thoreau yet kept it out of *Walden* because the experience of it threatened both life and self. The idea of creative disorientation, of losing the world in order to find the self, emerged in *Walden* in a careful pattern as Thoreau developed the trope from the notion of losing one's bearings quite near to Concord. But the voice crying from Katahdin—"rocks, trees, wind on our cheeks! the *solid* earth! the *actual* world! the *common sense!* Contact! Contact! *Who* are we? *Where* are we?"—this voice represents the deracinated mind. It is not a state of mind able to seek the higher laws, those conceived to be immanent in the seasonal change in the domestic environs of Walden Pond or along the shores of the Concord and Merrimack rivers.

Thoreau had no affirmative use for the ideology of the reformed environment, it is true. But essential to the work of his imagination —the divinity that makes the "valleys shine" and the "deserts really bloom"—was a distinct degree of environmental domestication in America. Dubious of Etzler's program for paradise, he retreats at the other extreme from "the unfinished parts of the globe." No partisan of the societal New Earth, Thoreau yet needed for his own imagination the presupposition of domestication, which is to say, the environmental reform of the "unfinished . . . New World."

III

For other writers, however, the idea of nineteenth-century America as the *actual* New Earth was salient. And this idea only secondarily compelled balance and reconciliation of the external world with that of the visionary imagination. Primarily it required personal judgment that confirmed or denied the existence of a redeemer nation located geographically in North America and evincing in its landscape those material changes that were irrefutably progressive. In important ways the Transcendentalists made way for the individuated New Earth of Whitman's poetic vision. But meanwhile, in the 1820s and 1830s, Cooper and Bancroft addressed the subject of the actual New Earth. Cooper recorded its failure in his fiction, while Bancroft celebrated its authenticity in historical scholarship. Both appreciated the pristine American wilderness, but both were committed beyond it to environmental reform concomitant with the spiritual (specifically political) growth of the nation. Their stances—one as denunciatory as the other was celebratory—were irreconcilable.

Taken together, their representations of the American landscape really suggest to us the aesthetic impossibility in the nineteenth century of enmeshing the conceptual New Earth with the accomplished material changes of the American environment, one increasingly appreciated, in F. O. Matthiessen's term, by "rising forces of exploitation."[33] The New Earth in the writings of Cooper and Bancroft warrants attention because these writers show the disintegration of what for more than one and one-half centuries had been a continuing emphasis on the American chiliad in the national literature. In Cooper and in Bancroft we see the breaking apart of the ideographic from the geographic America that Edward Johnson had welded together in *The Wonder-Working Providence,* and which in *The Columbiad* Joel Barlow had represented anew within the changed sensibility of the Enlightenment. Ultimately this desintegration enabled Whitman to imagine America as his own "heart's geography's map," a symbolic New Earth of singular poetic vision—yet one built upon cultural imperatives furthered by Cooper and by Bancroft.

In Cooper's fiction, environmental reform is a national imperative authorized by the American gentleman who is Cooper's national paragon. While the Leatherstocking Tales collectively affirm the aesthetic and ethical values of the pristine wilderness, principally through the character of Natty Bumppo, the novelist's American gentlemen mandate environmental reform in the name of civilization. Through them Cooper locates opportunities for progress and stability in a democratic America. For Cooper's gentlemen—his Marmaduke Temple, his Effinghams and Littlepages—are the exemplary Americans. They are at once its representative men and the stellar achievement of its civilization. These are political paragons, not autonomous romantic American "nations" of the individual self alone. They head up the social hierarchy and are both models for emulation and dutiful respondents to the needs of yeomen less culturally gifted than they. Theirs is the duty to uphold abstract ideals —liberty, justice, equality, and so on—valuable because such terms at once inspire and yet reproach a society that ever falls short of them. Cooper is no subscriber to what John L. Thomas calls a nineteenth-century "romantic perfectionism," that is, "an educational crusade based on the assumption that when a sufficient number of individuals have seen the light, they would automatically solve the country's problems."[34] There are no such mass conversions possible in Cooper's America. This is an author who finds "the foundations of great events remotely laid," not in high-minded philosophy but "in very capricious and uncalculated passions, motives or impulses."[35] As one writer points out. "Cooper directly contradicted Bancroft's basic premise that all men possess an equal ability to discern truth."[36]

His true gentlemen do possess such power of discernment, and the spiritual biography of the nation devolves upon them. In the "mysterious void . . . of an interminable forest" there are "high civilization, a state of infant existence, and positive barbarity . . . brought so near each other within the borders of the Republic."[37] It is a delicate ecological balance tipped in favor of civilization only by the authority of the gentlemen-democrats and the consent of those they govern. Cooper well understood how precarious was his scheme for the spiritual biography of the nation. Discursively and structurally, his writings abound in cautionings, doubts, caveats, provisos. It is thus not surprising that he should find most congenial to his thinking that part of the national myth that defines a nation ever provisional, ever on trial and susceptible to backsliding, to regression, to the ultimate failure of its mission. In fact, Cooper worked with zeal to help sustain an imperiled historic mission. Needless to say, he is no less the historicist and reformer for being a writer principally of fiction.

Not that Cooper abandoned all ideas on the destined redemptive success of America. Defending the nation against character assassination by European travelers, he closed his celebratory *Notions of the Americans* (1828) with this millennial anticipation:

A new era is now about to dawn on this nation. It has ceased to creep; it begins to walk erect among the powers of the earth. ... Europeans may be reluctant to admit the claims of a competitor, ... but Nature will have her laws obeyed, and the fulfillment of things must come.[38]

Even in 1849, eleven years after publication of his severe social criticism, *The American Democrat* (1838), Cooper wrote that "a great change has come over the country since [1821]," that "the nation is passing from the gristle into the bone, and the common mind beginning to keep pace with the growth of the body politic." He concluded that there was "reason to hope that the same Providence which has so well aided us in our infancy, may continue to smile on our manhood."[39]

In Cooper's thought this imminent spiritual fulfillment of a mature America is based substantively upon the conversion of wilderness to civilization. In *The Wept of Wish-ton-Wish* (1829) he imagined the seventeenth-century colonial experience to be one in which "necessity, prompted by an understanding of its wants, incited by a commendable spirit of emulation, and encouraged by liberty, gave early birth to those improvements which have converted a wilderness into the abodes of abundance and security, with a rapidity that wears the appearance of magic."[40] Important are the drives of necessity and additionally of liberty. Once again we see the necessary connection between spiritual life and environmental change. As for "improvements," Cooper defines the term in his desultory American lexicon which readers discover throughout his works. "*Improvements* is used by the Americans," he writes, "to express every degree of change in converting land from its state of wilderness to that of cultivation. In this meaning of the word," he concludes, "it is an improvement to fell the trees."[41]

By whose authority those trees are felled is, however, of paramount importance because nothing less than the survival of American democracy is at issue. In a little book by Cooper's father,

A Guide in the Wilderness, itself a landlord's handbook to wilderness settlement based principally upon the senior Cooper's own experience at Cooperstown, one William Sampson wrote in his preface to William Cooper, "Leave to Caesar the boast of having destroyed two million men; let yours be that of having cut down two million of trees. [Caesar] made men disappear from the fruitful soil where they were born; your labours made a new and happier race appear where none before had been."[42] Probably with Sampson's remark in mind, Cooper reiterated the point when in *The Chainbearer* (1845) he burst into this song which, as E. Arthur Robinson observes, anticipates Whitman:

> The American Axe! It has made more real and lasting conquests than the sword of any warlike people that ever lived; but they have been conquests that have left civilization in their train instead of havoc and desolation.[43]

Even in *Wyandotte,* that brooding dark novel, Cooper wrote, "There is a pleasure in diving into a virgin forest and commencing the labors of civilization, that has no exact parallel in any other human occupation. . . . [It] approaches nearer to the feeling of creating."[44]

Yet the question of who authorizes that creative axing is central to Cooper's conception of democracy. The issue is not one of conservation (though in part it is focused there) or of aesthetics (though that too plays a part). The crucial matters are moral, political, and social. The question of who authorizes "improvements" in the wilderness is one of liberty and human rights under law. The success or failure of Cooper's American democracy—of the spiritual biography of the nation—depends largely upon legitimate authorization of the use of the American axe.

That legitimacy rests with Cooper's morally exemplary gentleman, whom he identified as "one elevated above the mass of society by his birth, manners, attainments, character, and social condition." He added, "As no civilized society can exist without these social differences, nothing is gained by denying the use of the term." No provincial or rustic imitating European antecedents, Cooper's American gentleman is bred to superiority by social progress. Maintaining "his own independence of vulgar domination," he is rightfully a man apart from others in "education, manners, accomplishments, tastes, associations."[45]

All this is familiar ground to readers of Cooper. It is significant here because, as Edwin Cady remarked years ago, "the most important fact which Cooper wanted to show about [his gentleman democrats] was that by their talents, wealth, good-will, social and political power they had created in the American wilderness the possibilities for civilization."[46] In fact, Cooper obligates his gentry to that transformation of wilderness to civilization. His gentlemen are not permitted to remain in their comfortable family houses in Westchester County or in Manhattan. Fathers send sons into the wilderness to superintend settlement and assert property rights or, moved from private ambition for wealth and self-respect, go by themselves to civilize the wilds.

Preeminent is Cooper's obsessive connection of his gentry with the American landscape, a point numerous critics have argued.[47] These gentry have all a sensitive appreciation of the wilderness they are obliged to transform. While it is true that Natty Bumppo is Cooper's most eloquent spokesman for the ethos and the aesthetic of the American wilderness, his gentlemen see and describe wilderness as beautiful, wondrous, and grand. Their acceptance of the wilds forms one part of a nationally broad-based, growing appreciation of wilderness which Roderick Nash describes as a phenomenon of the first decades of the nineteenth century, in which a developing acceptance of wilderness prepared the way for the Romantics' fullest exploitation of its thematic and epistemic possibilities. Nash notes especially that by the 1840s the capacity to appreciate wilderness was one attribute of the gentleman.[48] And Cooper had helped to establish that norm. In Marmaduke Temple's reverie on the pristine Lake Otsego, in the young Corny Littlepage's description of the wild Mohawk country, in Cooper's own narrative in *The Wept* on "the bosom of a deep and dark wood" for readers confined in settled eastern states, we come to understand how sensitive are Cooper's gentry to the beauty and grandeur of the American forests. They speak of it, not in Natty's voice of "the primitive poet" but certainly with deepest respect.[49] It is a point that transcends the Leather-stocking Tales to be additionally verified in Cooper's decidedly political novels and essays. He thus makes certain that those Americans qualified to authorize the "improvements" of the broadaxe in the widerness well understand and value the scenes they will supplant with civilization.

With fullest credentials to transform the wilds, Cooper's gentry nonetheless find their efforts thwarted by the factional strife, greed, self-interest, and demagoguery that become the stuff of conflict in all of Cooper's plots, and that accordingly have compelled much critical attention. In all, *Home as Found* and the Littlepage Trilogy (*Satanstoe, The Chainbearer, The Redskins*) have most often been the focus of such studies,[50] with Cooper's early *The Pioneers* (1823) until recently exempted as a tonally nostalgic novel whose importance lies in its introduction of a conflict obsessively recurrent in Cooper's mature work, namely, the opposition between wilderness freedom and civil order, represented by Natty Bumppo and Marmaduke Temple.

Yet *The Pioneers* is the work in which Cooper most clearly presents another crucial conflict, one central to the survival of America's historic mission, in fact to the progression of its New Earth. It is the struggle of the gentleman to realize his civilizing vision (and his moral imperative) of wilderness transformation. In Cooper's scheme of American history it is nothing less than the struggle for the survival of democracy. Wilderness transformation is the enormous and problematic task whose potential failure spells failure for the democratic nation itself. The structure of *The Pioneers* indicates Cooper's deep doubts that American society would respond adequately to the civilizing imperatives urged by the sapient gentry, though the young novelist seems not to have been prepared to confront that enormity directly in *The Pioneers* and so glossed his dreadful conviction evident in the story itself by enclosing the world of the novel in a pastoral contemporary setting, circa 1823.

Inadvertently, perhaps, Cooper abets readers inclined to accept his glossed world of *The Pioneers,* since in a short essay included subsequently in *Home as Found* he offered a nostrum from the past by calling the initial period of wilderness settlement in America a happy time of communal and cooperative social struggle to which social distinction is irrelevant. Cooper calls this first period one of "fun, toil, neighborly feeling, and adventure."[51] Not surprisingly, since *The Pioneers* concerns initial settlement in the upstate New York wilderness, and since (as Robinson notices) it begins and ends with echoes of Crèvecoeur in phrases on "man's conquest of nature . . . of man's mastering the environment,"[52] interspersed with images of placid and bountiful agriculture, commerce, and social cohesion, readers have been quick to call *The Pioneers* a pastoral and nostalgic novel exemplifying this first period of settlement and based verifiably upon Cooper's own family experience in Cooperstown.

Structurally, however, the novel works in a different direction. And it suggests how precarious is Cooper's scheme for a national spiritual biography dependent—as he believes it to be—upon the authority of the gentry. For there are two visions within *The Pioneers,* one of Natty Bumppo and one of Judge Marmaduke Temple. These two represent the difference between the vision creatively appreciative of the virgin land as it is (a vision typically romantic in its active passivity) and the vision that requires social implementation in order to bring it about. Unequivocally can Natty say that what meets his eye from a Catskill mountaintop is "Creation!"[53] But to Temple falls the onus of the civilized vision of his *mind's* eye. His is the rightful authority of the broad-axe, and his the imagination and judgment and energy to realize that vision. Problematically, however, the success of his vision depends upon the holistic assent and cooperation of society. And that is the haunting uncertainty for Cooper because it lies at the very heart of his doubts on American democracy. In *The American Democrat* he wrote of the self-evident "impossibility of raising all men to the highest standard of tastes and refinement" and added that "the whole embarrassment on this point exists in the difficulty of making men comprehend qualities they do not themselves possess." Cooper concluded that "when it comes to a question of the difference between ourselves and our superiors, we fail to appreciate merit of which we have no proper conception."[54] This, for Cooper, is the crucial weakness in American democracy, and one of course central to the Enlightenment idea of the social contract. Though Cooper believed that legitimate government exists by the consent of the governed, he doubted in the populace the sufficient wisdom requisite to consent. In the dramatic structure of *The Pioneers* he enacts his doubts.

Cooper opens his novel in the bucolic upstate New York of 1823. We see arable mountains with "romantic" outcroppings, narrow, rich, and cultivated vales plentifully watered, "beautiful and thriving villages," "neat and comfortable farms," a splay of roads in all directions, and the customary public buildings that are the signs of social cohesion. The scene set, readers are moved back to 1793, to the post-Revolutionary years of America's first national energy. As he elsewhere called environmental changes "magical," Cooper refers to "that magical change in the power and condition of the state" and tells us that Judge Temple's founding of the Otsego settlement is antedated by another seven years.

These markings of time are important, for as the creation of the judge's mind and energies, Templeton is a vision which predates actual settlement. Only much later in the novel are we privy to that progenitive vision—that is, long after we have accompanied Miss Elizabeth Temple home from boarding school with her father in the sleigh; met the old hunter, Natty Bumppo, and his mysterious, culturally divided companion Oliver Edwards (really Effingham) who is equally comfortable with piano and powder horn; met all the cosmopolitan mixture of villagers; learned the pecking order; visited the manor house and public house; and become involved in the mystery of young Edward's anger and in the thematic complications of Natty's freedom in a community cohering in law—only then, in a chapter of reminiscence between Judge Temple and his daughter (with Edwards listening in and Temple's cousin, the sheriff Richard Jones, participating) do we learn of the visionary Templeton, the creation of the mind of the judge.

He describes the district as "it lay in the sleep of nature" and afterward "awoke to supply the wants of man." Then (acknowledging his motive to accumulate wealth), Maramaduke Temple describes how he took leave of wife and infant to "survey these uninhabited mountains." "God has been pleased to smile on my efforts," he says. He recounts how on his first morning in the area he left his surveying party and by himself rode a deer trail to the summit of a mountain from which he looked upon the primordial scene that filled him with "a mingled feeling of pleasure and desolation." This of course is the famous "Mount Vision" passage in which Marmaduke Temple is thought to superimpose upon this wilderness scene his vision of settlement, though, interestingly, we must infer the actual vision from his active surveying and exploration of the shores of Lake Otsego. For when he looks upon the lake and forests from his treetop perch, he recalls only the wildlife and vegetation and remembers the vista as one made memorable by the lack of human presence ("not the vestige of a man could I trace"). Soon thereafter he sees the curl of smoke that leads him to Natty Bumppo's hut. By Temple's admission, it is only later (sometime "since") that he named the site Mount Vision.[55]

In a major sense the "vision" is one earned through its realization. For there is not a sense of destiny in it, no sequence of events by which the "boundless forest" will inevitably become Templeton. Settlement requires the creative energies of Marmaduke Temple. It is not attainable by passivity, by awaiting the inevitable fanning out of population from the eastern seaboard. It must be sponsored, undertaken, brought about by design and driving energy. And we learn from Marmaduke Temple's reminiscence what was the cost of that effort. In an account nearly verbatim from that of Cooper's father in his *Guide,* Cooper speaks of the deprivations and, importantly, of the responsibility of Judge Temple for those yeomen whose settlement he had encouraged with generous leases to good land. An incredulous Elizabeth asks how in "the beautiful and fertile vales of the Mohawk" there could be "actual suffering," a rhetorical device by which Cooper can establish legitimacy and real respect for Temple's position (and by implication for all the landed gentry he defends in his novels). "Remember, my child," the judge says, "it was in our very infancy, we had neither mills nor grain, nor roads, nor often clearings;—we had nothing of increase, but the mouths that were to be fed." He recounts that he had "hundreds at that dreadful time, daily looking up to me for bread," and that the very suffering of the foraging and enervated populace had "paralysed" the efforts of the settlement. Says Temple, "It was not a moment for inaction." And he recounts buying Pennsylvania grain and arranging its transport to his tenants. He tells, too, of a near-miraculous migration of lake herring seined in abundance for immediate use and, doled out with salt, dried for home larders and for sale elsewhere. That epoch of settlement is remembered as "the starving-time," one in which wild garlic became the dietary staple. As its benefactor, Marmaduke Temple was also its hero.[56]

Cooper emphasizes that Temple's authority rests precisely in this sense of responsibility and, through wealth and connections, in the sponsorship of social growth. It rests, moreover, in his foresight, for

the comprehensive "mind of judge Temple . . . had a bias to look
into futurity, in speculations on the improvements that posterity
were to make in his lands. To his eye, where others saw nothing but a
wilderness, towns, manufactories, bridges, canals, mines, and all
other resources of an old country were constantly presenting themselves, though his good sense suppressed, in some degree, the exhibi-
tion of these expectations."[57] Here Cooper shows the continuous
development of Mount Vision as it exists in the mind of Marmaduke
Temple.

I emphasize the existence of the vision in the *mind* of Temple,
because there is tremendous disparity in *The Pioneers* between the
pure conception of Marmaduke Temple's mind and the development
of Templeton, Cooper's emblematic America, as we observe it in the
novel. It is true, as McWilliams has written, that Natty Bumppo and
Marmaduke Temple are equally admirable characters whose ideals are
unalterably opposed. The crucial difference between the values of
the two is that Natty's wilderness ethos requires only the receptivity
of his own mind and a virgin land from which human society is
excluded. But Judge Temple's vision, one of civilization (meaning
building, land-use planning, conservation, etc.), cannot—absolutely
cannot—be realized without the participation and cooperation (at the
very least the assent) of others. And the others with whom Cooper
populates his novel suggest thematically that the vagaries of human
nature are at work to subvert and despoil that pure vision. Cooper's
Americans are finally in the aggregate too self-willed, greedy, obtuse,
dangerously whimsical, contentious, arrogant, and jealous of individual prerogatives to bring about the vision of Marmaduke Temple.
In large part *The Pioneers* is a story of a vision of environmental
reform that is subverted in the process of its attempted enactment.

There are three principal areas in which Cooper focuses his theme
of subverted vision, namely, in the society of Templeton, its use of
land and natural resources, and its architecture and town planning.
For this last, one must first recall that Cooper shows a continual
interest in architecture, that his writings abound in detailed description of buildings, especially dwellings. To linger in all his works with
shingling, siding, chimney design, roof overhang, heights, floor plans,
and so on, is to grasp the author's life long interest in the aesthetics
of architecture and to appreciate what thematic uses he might make

of it in his fiction. In *The Pioneers* the one asset of Templeton's architecture is its comfort and abundance. The interior of the manor house is warm, its banquet table filled with dishes various enough to win approval of any Victorian cook, its furniture a comfortable mix of urban and rural American woods, design, and craftsmanship.

But architecturally Templeton is an aesthetic botch for which direct responsibility belongs to Hiram Doolittle, a sleazy lawyer and self-proclaimed architect, and his collusive mark, the ambitious Richard Jones who is Temple's cousin and factotum (officially the sheriff). Their design for the mansion house, pretentious and impractical, has left "four little columns of wood," intended pillars, hanging from the roof when the porch foundation and stairs buckled. Too, by error in design "the roof was left the most conspicuous part of the edifice," oddly high and every shingle an optical attraction. Remedially, Doolittle and Jones attempt a *trompe de l'oeil*, painting the roof sky-blue, then cloud-blue, and when it blends with neither sky nor cloud, trying a green which they hope will make it disappear in a background of pines. All these failing, they leave it an equally unsatisfactory sun-yellow, with gaudy railings, "divers urns and mouldings," and four "extremely conspicuous chimneys" to complete the embellishment of Temple's manor house.

Cooper makes it clear that Temple's own taste is superior to that of his house, that he "bore this deformity in his dwelling with great good nature, and soon contrived, by his own improvements, to give an air both of respectability and comfort to his place of residence." And Cooper's own remarks on the house might be thought no more than the digression of an architectural dilettante did he not pursue the twosome of Doolittle and Jones through construction of several other buildings and draw conclusions on vanity, vulgarity, and the evil of bad taste. For, once past the mansion house, we watch through Cooper's own sarcasm the building of a public edifice, the Academy, "a comfortless open place" burdened with a "multitude of ornaments" and "lighted with a vast quantity of blurred and green-looking glass." Cooper puts *steeple* in quotation marks, calls the cupola a bottomless "inverted tea-cup," and notes that from lack of public funds the blinds are left the somber color of lead. Thereafter, the Academy done, we move with Doolittle and Jones to the site of the church, one "*New* St. Paul's," a "somewhat lame" imitation of its London antecedent, its "proportions but indifferently observed." Cooper says it bears "a prodigious resemblance to a vinegar cruet."[58]

Through the heavy irony, Cooper has serious points to make. He hates this proliferation of bad taste, for the mansion house inspires imitation from prosperous citizens of no aesthetic judgment. Jones's "mortification" turns to pride in the house once his eye becomes accustomed to it, and he finds that his boasts on its behalf draw commissions to reproduce it elsewhere in the village. Those not affluent enough to build imitation mansions share still the responsibility for the spread of bad buildings, since "the people" endorse the Jones-Doolittle Academy and, based on its success, unanimously commission the two to design and build the "*New* St. Paul's." Despite the superiority of Marmaduke Temple's taste, it does not prevail; bad taste proliferates, and its sponsors gain in stature.

Moreover, though they form no part of Temple's vision, these wretched buildings endure. The "vinegar cruet" of a church is brick, as the mansion house is of stone—durable materials even in what Elizabeth calls "this changeful country." She notices that in her five-year absence "the very houses seemed changed," altered by additions or painted or newly erected on the site of a predecessor "which had been banished from the earth as soon as it made its appearance on it."[59] Yet we have no evidence that each metamorphosis brings architectural improvement or even that the present buildings, those on which Cooper exerts satiric energies, are razed or replaced. In fact, when at the end of the novel Cooper disarms Richard Jones in penitential humility and literally moves Doolittle westward and away from a Templeton whose wealth and intelligence are now said to be no match for him, Cooper concedes that "vestiges" of his legal learning and his professional science (architecture) are scattered through the land. Thus Cooper concedes the power of a vulgar populace to impose its will on the land. These offenses to aesthetic judgment linger on, "corrected" only in words, in the only trenchant voice left to one powerless to change events, that of the ironist.

In town planning, too, we get the keen sense of disparity between Temple's vision of the future and the citizens' compulsions to act for present and shortsighted convenience. The village, some fifty buildings, architecturally "bore not only strong marks of the absence of taste, but also, by the slovenly and unfinished appearance of most of the dwellings, indicated the hasty manner of their construction." Houses are parti-colored, overly ambitious in windows that are cut but unglazed, and grouped together "in a manner that aped the streets of a city." Pitifully landscaped with a few spindly door-front saplings, the Templeton dwellings (including the "pretending dwellings" of "the better sort of building") are most charitably called "incongruous."[60]

Cooper tells us that the houses of Templeton were "arranged by the directions of one who looked far ahead to the wants of posterity, rather than to the convenience of the present incumbents." But once again the will of the populace prevails over the gentlemanly authority of the visionary mind. "In the original plan" for Templeton, "it was ordained that the village should stretch along the little stream." But "convenience frequently frustrates the best regulated plans." A house (one of the imitation mansion houses) blocks the planned throughfare, and the much-used short-cut becomes the permanent highway lined with dwellings that "effectually prevent any subsequent correction of the evil." Cooper calls this an "insidious change in the regular plans of Marmaduke." "Evil," "insidious"—Cooper's is opprobrious diction for those who subvert Temple's plan, even as his novel records the very process of that subversion. At one point a resentful Richard Jones says sarcastically to Elizabeth, "We must run our streets by the compass, coz, and disregard trees, hills, ponds, stubs, or, in fact, anything but posterity. Such is the will of your father."[61]

But as willful as he is thought to be, Temple is powerless to persuade his subordinates to imagine the future, even though Cooper emphasizes how necessary is such imagination. When Elizabeth exclaims, "The enterprise of Judge Temple is taming the very forests!"[62] we know it is enterprise coupled with visionary foresight, itself tempered by prudence. Yet apart from the admiration of Elizabeth and occasional hints that the angry Edwards shares Temple's utilitarian vision, the judge is alone and his influence clearly waning since that "starving-time."

In the husbandry of natural resources, therefore, Temple finds among his villagers an audience that will suffer him but cannot really hear him imaginatively. Though Cooper so carefully distinguished the gentleman from the man of wealth alone, we find in this early novel that the character who typifies the mentality of Templeton, Richard Jones, respects his cousin, not for his wisdom, but because he is a rich man. Not surprisingly, Temple is often at loggerheads with the villagers over questions of resource management, that is, of conservation with utilitarian motives. When Jones urges immediate sugar production, Temple replies that his first concern "is to protect the sources of this great mine of comfort and wealth from the extravagances of the people themselves." Interested as he is in the business of sugar production (and we remember that Temple made his fortune in commerce before underwriting the costs of settlement of the patent), it is not he but Jones who would produce sugar loaves big as haycocks. Temple is the proponent of natural resources carefully cultivated, though Jones hoots at the notion of tree farming. It "grieves" Temple "to witness the extravagance that pervades the country, where the settlers trifle with the blessings they might enjoy, with the prodigality of successful adventurers." Even as burning maple logs ooze sap in his fireplace, he reminds Jones (too late now, of course) that he forbids the use of sugar maple as firewood. "It behooves the owner of woods so extensive as mine, to be cautious what example he sets to his people, who are already felling the forests, as if no end could be found to their treasures, nor any limits to their extent." He concludes, "If we go on this way, twenty years hence we shall want fuel." Predictably, Jones scoffs and in so doing represents the response of the populace.[63]

At other points, too, Temple offers lessons his hearers do not understand, for instance, when he censures the woodsman, Billy Kirby, for slashing the sugar maples when a neat tap would do as well and seems to regret the wartime conditions abroad that make timber and especially potash so valuable that acreage is stripped for them. When Kirby wonders at tales he has heard of wealthy Europeans ornamenting their lands with trees, Temple hastens to say that his concern is not with arboreal ornamentation (for which, interestingly, he has imported poplars from Europe) but with utilization. "It is for their usefulness. . . . They are the growth of centuries, and when once gone, none living will see their loss remedied. . . . We are stripping the forests, as if a single year would replace what we destroy." Then he speaks of his personal consolation: "The hour approaches, when the laws will take notice of not only the woods but the game also." That may be his consolation, but Cooper ends that scene (and chapter as well) ominously with the picture of Kirby against a "background of stately trees" bawling a song about "the proud forest falling." Whether buyers of these lands choose highland oak or "silvery" pine lands, "it matters little" to this man who has "chopped over the best half of a thousand acres" and has on his side the momentum of settlement over and against Temple's belief in the abstraction of law.[64]

Through social dissension, too, Cooper dramatizes the subversion of Temple's vision. So pervasive is the squabbling, bickering, and quarreling in the novel that we see those moments of sociable pleasure as aberrations from the querulous norm. In an important essay which traces this pattern of "resentment, rivalry, and hostility" in *The Pioneers,* Thomas Philbrick warns that if the novel "must be associated with the pastoral, it is best viewed as an ironic treatment of the genre," since "the episodes of the novel reveal anything but harmony and living cooperation in the affairs of men." Philbrick demonstrates carefully how contentious are human relationships in the work, from the major dispute between Natty and Judge Temple over primitive freedom and the institutions of civilization, down to the resentment of the housekeeper, Remarkable Pettibone, toward her newly arrived mistress Elizabeth. As Philbrick says, "Everywhere in the novel one encounters bickering and baiting, grudges and grumbling." He shows how communal unity is but "pretence," and that the conflagration at the end of the novel, the eruption of anger seething in the townspeople all along, "is an emblem of the fierce passions that have engulfed the human world."[65]

To better understand the social impasse between Temple and the villagers we must also acknowledge the disparity in *The Pioneers* between what is stated and what is rendered. To move to the very end of the novel, to the Lake Otsego of 1823, we find that symbolically the ancestral rift between Effingham and Temple is healed in the marriage of "Edwards" to Elizabeth and that a wise landed gentry live on to guide public affairs. In his final chapter Cooper ties up all loose ends. Natty serves his prison sentence for killing the deer out of season and is pardoned by the governor. The couple are married, and Major Effingham dies, making way for Oliver Edwards. Of course Richard Jones is silenced for a decade, Doolittle moved west, Natty voluntarily gone west, the old Mohican memorialized with a proper grave. Elizabeth's influence has got her maiden friend, Louisa, a probable relief from spinsterhood as she and her minister-father prepare to move to a town on the Hudson. And Natty goes west as Cooper heralds him (in the often quoted line) as "the foremost in that band of Pioneers, who are opening the way for the march of our nation across the continent."

Yet the problems that lie at the very center of this novel are not resolved. Cooper can move people to the banks of the Hudson, exile them westward, bury them, marry them to one another, silence them in humility. There remain, however, at the very heart of this novel the two opposing and equally respected sets of values, one of which —that of Judge Marmaduke Temple—consistently is subverted because it lacks the popular assent and cooperation necessary to its survival. This is a matter not only of social compromise but of the consistent challenge to, bafflement at, scorn for, skepticism of Temple's greater wisdom—in fact, of his vision. This is a story of persistent thwarting of Cooper's own sociopolitical ideals. Emblematically it is really the story of the failure of America in its errand, though Cooper refuses to carry out these implications structurally, retreating as he does into a happier future engineered in mechanical plot devices.

Thematically important in this regard is the great fire toward the end of the novel, a fire that claims two lives, that of the greedy, rootless, self-seeking Jotham and of the Indian sage, Chingachgook, whose pyre marks the end of the Indian epoch. But the fire also consumes the mountain from which Marmaduke Temple envisions the future. As McWilliams writes, "Mount Vision, the hilltop from which Judge Temple had foreseen the glorious setting and future of his new community, is consumed in flames," and "Cooper indicates that the destruction of Mount Vision is neither a providential judgment nor mere chance, but arises out of the actions of the townspeople."[66] It is poignantly fitting that the citizens in pursuit of Natty Bumppo ignite the fire that consumes the mountain, essentially Marmaduke Temple's own vision of social consent to his mild laws, to utilitarian conservation, to provident change. The fire climaxes processes of subverted vision in the novel, for Templeton has grown desultorily, its architecture foolish and ugly, its citizens argumentative and heedless, all the while Marmaduke Temple's powers of civilizing leadership are waning. To the townspeople, represented by Richard Jones, Temple is the impediment to progress, preachy, a blocking character. Worse, to Billy Kirby he is simply irrelevant, which makes Temple powerless to stop the axe he himself first set in motion in the American forest. As Kay House observes, "Whereas the settlers had once been completely dependent on him for food, Temple is now little more than the community's first citizen, and his only power is derived from the law."[67]

Law, however, is no safeguard when the citizens of Templeton join in emotional holocaust and become what Cooper feared at base they were, a mob. Fifteen years after publication of *The Pioneers,* he said it explicitly:

> A body of Americans, . . . collected under what is popularly called an "excitement," losing sight of that reason and respect for their own deliberately framed ordinances, which alone distinguish them from the masses of society, is neither more nor less than a rabble.[68]

He had already demonstrated that point in *The Pioneers.*

Nor, as all critics of Cooper have understood, could he ever rid himself of that dread conviction on human nature as unalterably base. His notorious lawsuits, his bitterness at demagoguery and the press, his advocacy of long-term tenantry in a nation that embraced the freeholding of land, his very inability in his world of fiction to believe that legal entitlement to land conferred safeguards of control over it (even as his polemical voice in *The Redskins* turned churlish on American folkways and vernacular speech)—all point to the conclusion which McWilliams states succinctly, that Cooper was deeply angry "at the impossibility of solving the dilemmas underlying his twenty years of political speculation," that his fiction finally acknowledged formally that "a republican polity could neither perpetuate an agrarian hierarchy nor control the demagogue," and that "a republic cannot sustain both minority rights and majority rule."[69]

We find Cooper thus disengaging from the linear movement of American history—and with important environmental ramifications. No longer did he work on behalf of the American society which he understood to be, as one writer puts it, "a purely human creation, secular in conception and essence and moving toward a city of men rather than of God."[70]   Instead, as of the end of *The Redskins,* Cooper prepares his withdrawal from that temporal city of men into what Bercovitch identifies from Melville as chronometrical time, atemporal, fixed, above all safe from the terrible vicissitudes of human events that had so deeply wounded him. Thus, at the end of *The Redskins* the gentleman, Hugh Littlepage, is bound for Washington to test the purity of Constitutional law and, that failing him, to become an expatriate in Florence—each move a retreat from the contention of active social engagement and at the same time a search, as McWilliams identifies it, "for an unchanging code of political justice that would correspond to timeless divine laws."[71] It was in chronometrics, in the "timeless divine laws" of the Constitution, that he sought his respite. In *The American Democrat* Cooper had explicated that document as if it were a realm unto itself.

And with important environmental results. Since the reformed environment of the New World is inextricably bonded to the progression of human society (manifest in the political life of the nation), the failure of one requires the failure of the other. Specifically, as one writer remarks, "to destroy the American gentleman or to drive him abroad . . . is to rob American society of its supporting substance and leave it vacant at the core."[72] Spiritually exiled, Cooper was impelled to show literally, that is environmentally, just how vacant was America. Thus, in *The Crater* (1847) he destroys the very world to pronounce the fate of the nation that has failed in its mission. With an earthquake he simply sinks it beneath the sea. This earthquake is not simply an artistic device with which to dramatize the social failure of America; it is in the material world the correlate of the nation's spiritual failure. The lush gardens and farms wrested from mud swamps of the emblematic (and edenic) New World are consigned to the very destruction that Joel Barlow had feared and warned against in *The Columbiad.* The nation whose spiritual biography fails is swallowed by the sea. As one critic says of *The Crater,* "Here, finally, the apocalyptic strain that has been present beneath the surface in Cooper's work since *The Pioneers* becomes the controlling theme." Cooper's Apocalypse occurs offstage, to be sure, but it is outright cataclysm. It is at once Cooper's leave-taking and his vengeance upon the temporal America that has failed him. The mills, the flocks, hedgerows, buildings, the once "broad plains of mud" now "converted into meadows and arable lands"—all sink in a perceptible "terrible truth" as Cooper's persona, Mark Woolston, apprehends what has happened. There is a "new convulsion," a "dire catastrophe," as the errant America is effaced from the earth, its only monument a guano-covered rock peak. Thus in the world of fiction Cooper takes a vengeful, apocalyptic leave of the world that has failed him.[73]

As a polemicist Cooper leaves this bleakest marker of the failed New Earth. Tested politically, it was irredeemably flawed, and he repudiated it. He abandoned, too, the artful persuasion of the fictional chronicle and resorted to moral allegory and to diatribe unleavened by satiric skill. In his fecal commemoration of a rotten New Earth, Cooper himself seems finally to be made speechless on the subject. He enacts his nihilism in a nonverbal symbol. In his father's generation the Revolutionary writers had proclaimed the Millennium, but a skeptical and disappointed Cooper felt hoaxed and so exposed the myth. To him this cosmic American lie deserved only holocaust.

IV

Unlike Cooper, George Bancroft embraced from the first the idea of a destined, "chronometric" America whose spiritual apotheosis transcended calendric time even as it was verifiable within human history. While Cooper grew certain that America was failing every opportunity for democratic redemption, Bancroft was unwavering in the inverse conviction. He believed that events of history proved the inevitable progression of democracy, culminating in the formation of the United States of America. In several ways Bancroft wrote the very history of America for which Joel Barlow had begun to take notes and make outlines. Or, to be precise, Bancroft wrote the history Barlow would have wished, since the nineteenth-century historian recorded as verified truth the epic vision which Joel Barlow projected hopefully but with doubt into the American future. The spiritual biography of America was not for Bancroft problematic or doubtful of outcome. His redeemer nation had been proven, its origins traceable to antiquity. The history of the United States was thus no inductive experiment whose results were yet unclear but a demonstration of irrefutable truths.

Bancroft saw "general laws" which influence the moral world. Amid incongruous incidents and "checkered groups" he found a "guiding principle of civilization," a "clear and harmonious order" apparent to the discerning historian. Bancroft complains that in the past "history has ever celebrated the commanders of [victorious] armies," heroes of "scenes of carnage and rapine." From the misdirection on the part of earlier historians came his own clear purpose: to offer a corrective focus on "the founders of states; the wise legislators who struck the rock in the wilderness, so that the waters of liberty gushed forth in copious and perennial fountains." [74] He knew that tireless and disinterested research was mandatory and that the historian who swerves from exact observation becomes "absurd." Yet Bancroft was confident of a "sure criterion" for success. Since every false statement contains contradiction, "truth alone possesses harmony. Truth, also, and truth alone, is permanent." He relies on factional, partisan, that is, spurious history to be ephemeral. "But the facts faithfully ascertained, and placed in proper congruity, become of themselves the firm links of a brightly burnished chain, connecting events with their causes, and marking the line along which electric power of truth is conveyed from generation to generation." [75] Enviably, his work was neither discredited nor seriously challenged in theory or method until Bancroft was in his grave.

His premise from the outset of his multivolume *History* (1834–74) is that the American environment has been progressively reformed even as America's spiritual progress (manifest in its political life) has been brought toward perfection. All Bancroft's research into the American past brought forth facts that he reconstituted as legend and symbol, a process which Bercovitch has examined in detail. [76] Moreover, a close study of Bancroft's *History* suggests a strong Whig bias, in that he blames the British crown for constricting traditional liberties, thus compelling the American colonists necessarily to revolution. Like the Federalists and like his contemporary Whigs in America, Bancroft could thus view the Revolution as a corrective or reparative measure, one reinstating libertarian progress and order and not itself subject to repetition. Yet over all is his premise that the millennial epoch is actual, that America is the apotheosis of civilization and utopian refuge. Europe may be in flux, but America has established: popular sovereignty, equal rights, prosperity, just laws, inventiveness, free competition, domestic peace, commercial expansion, a diplomacy of friendship abroad, intellectual freedom, satisfying work, responsive government, safe dissent, and a dynamic Constitution that retains its "energy" and is thereby safe from "decay."

The American landscape is the perfect correlate to this ideal—or redemptive—life of the spirit. Material changes on the American continent only verify spiritual progress. "New states are forming in the wilderness," Bancroft writes in the introduction to his first volume. "Canals, intersecting our plains and crossing our highlands, open numerous channels to internal commerce; manufactures prosper along our watercourses." Bancroft reiterates the view which President Jackson had expounded in 1830 in this purely rhetorical question: "What good man would prefer a country covered with forests and ranged by a few thousand savages to our extensive Republic, studded with cities, towns, and prosperous farms, embellished with all the improvements which art can devise or industry execute, occupied by more than 12,000,000 happy people, and filled with all the blessings of liberty, civilization, and religion?"[77] As a professed Jacksonian Democrat (and apostate among the Boston Whigs), Bancroft made his *History* a kind of exegesis of Jackson's view.

Thus a utilitarian Bancroft outlines in his introduction the primeval and the reformed landscape of America. In "little more than two centuries" America has metamorphosed from an "unproductive waste." Back then, "throughout its wide extent the arts had not erected a monument." The only inhabitants "were a few scattered tribes of feeble barbarians, destitute of commerce and political connection. The axe and the ploughshare were unknown." Too, "the soil, which had been gathering fertility from the repose of centuries, was lavishing its strength in magnificent but useless vegetation. In the view of civiliation," he concludes, "the immense domain was a solitude."[78]

This historian finds no human repose in such "solitude," only unrealized potential. As he says, the purpose of his multivolume work is "to explain how the change in the condition of our land has been accomplished," that is, to explain a regenerative spiritual life that occasions material progress. It hardly needs stating that his will be no history of demographic patterns, technological development, or agricultural change. On the contrary, given that "the fortunes of a nation are not under the control of blind destiny," Bancroft will "follow the steps by which a favoring Providence, calling our institutions into being, has conducted the country to its present happiness and glory." Central to Bancroft's purpose, and echoing Whig principles, is the discovery of the libertarian spirit of America in its political institutions.

He keeps the reader mindful of the reformed topography because those environmental changes prove out the power of liberty in the political structure of the state. George Bancroft is really using material change to verify destined spiritual progress. The conversion of primordial "unproductive waste" to the bustling scene on view to all Americans is proof positive of the spiritual vivification of America.

Because he believed in the *destined* success of American democracy, Bancroft embraced both the reformed environment of civilized life *and* the American virgin land. Two kinds of America's primeval landscape, the garden and the forest, proved Bancroft's Redeemer Nation, and for different reasons. In his forests, or wilderness (two virtually interchangeable terms in the *History*), inhere the natural laws which America's representative men both learn and affirm during their youthful sojourns in the recesses of the forest. Their identity is predicated upon selfhood informed by the "book" of nature there. As for the garden, though its customary geographic locus is the South, its conceptual definition as hospice and refuge enables Bancroft to cite it literally as the predestined nursery of liberty.

Central to his belief in the national garden is Bancroft's idea that liberty flourished alike in the colonial South and in New England. The historian's beloved New England may be preeminent ("The bloom of immortality belongs . . . let us hope, to the institutions of New England"), but despite the quasi-feudal design for the Carolinas which he blames on the perniciousness of Locke and Shaftesbury, Bancroft documents the advance of civilization in Virginia and in the Carolinian "twin stars" beyond it. Sectarian Puritanism made no headway in the Old Dominion, he says, but Puritan ideas, "which the instinct of freedom had already whispered to every planter, and which naturally sprung up in the equalities of a wilderness," took firm hold in the South. Since freedom is indigenous to all of North America, Bancroft can use the actual garden as a national nursery of American liberty. Conceptually it transcends the regional South of its location and its literary origins.[79]

Thus an appreciative Bancroft eulogizes the pastoral full-sufficiency of the American garden in mid-seventeenth-century Virginia. It is a land of "genial climate and transparent atmosphere," and full of natural wonders from forests to streams to fecund earth. "There was no need of a scramble," Bancroft writes, since "abundance gushed from the earth for all." Just in passing he offers a phrase on plenty encouraging indolence, but his emphasis is abundance. The flora and fauna are diverting curiosities but never alienating in their exoticism. Too, Bancroft emphasizes the garden as a refuge. Against the backdrop of the percussive revolutions in Europe of the 1830s and 1840s, Bancroft could cherish the Carolinas of the late seventeenth and mid-eighteenth centuries as scenes of respite from the European tumult. "What though Europe was rocked to its centre by commotions?" he asks. The "planters of North Carolina recovered tranquility so soon as they escaped the misrule from abroad." Set among "noble prospect[s] of spacious rivers, of pleasant meadows enamelled with flowers," and of "primeval forests," Bancroft's planters (and accordingly his readers) breathe jasmine and honeysuckle and magnolia. The peaches measure in "heaps," the cattle "multiply." "Freedom, entire freedom, was enjoyed without anxiety," and "the charities of life were scattered at their feet, like the flowers on their meadows."[80]

Accepting as he is—indeed, as he must be inclusively—of the American topography as a suitable site for the culmination of human civilization, Bancroft could not represent the forest wilderness as treacherous or hostile. He offers instead a wilderness conceived as an extension of the garden refuge. If at one point a reader sees Father Marquette and his companions face "captivity, death from the tomahawk, tortures, [and] fire," he is barely given pause to appreciate the dangers before Bancroft moves to countermand them with the idea of American wilderness as refuge, in fact as temple. There is "simplicity and freedom of life in the wilderness," which has its "charms."

Marquette's heart swells with delight at the limpid waters, serene sky, and mild temperature, and the wilderness becomes a deer park as hunting for food becomes the "pleasure of the chase." Then suddenly the missionary in his tent turns biblical patriarch whose stone pillow hearkens to that of Jacob. Then he is an Abraham under an oak tree of Mamre breaking bread with angels. He is a pilgrim whose daily journey ends at "a new site for his dwelling, which the industry of a few moments would erect, and for which nature provided a floor of green inlaid with flowers." Bancroft adds the finishing touches: "On every side clustered beauties, which art had not spoiled, and could not imitate."[81] In a very few lines the historian moves us from the tomahawk to the green cathedral of floral respite. His is a benign and hospitable American forest, a refuge at its wildest and a garden at its most remote.

For excellent reason does Bancroft make the wilderness a kind of temple, not only for Marquette but, additionally, for the Founding Fathers Washington, Jefferson, and Madison, and for the folk hero Daniel Boone. As Bercovitch has pointed out, "from the Revolutionary period onwards, the Lives of public leaders constitute a progressing spiritual biography of America." Their lives not only exemplify but embody the American ideal and idea. Moreover, in a crucial epistemic emphasis which Bercovitch locates in American romanticism, the American Romantic "interpreted the self through the medium of nature." And it was nature transcendent of past and present, one intrinsically regenerative. In a direct line from Jonathan Edwards to America's consummate Romantic, Emerson, Bercovitch finds that the image of the new World "invests the regenerate perceiver with an aura of ascendant millennial splendor" and that the perceiver "must prove his regeneration by transforming himself in the image of the New World."[82] He goes into American nature in a pilgrimage for his identity, which is then validated as representatively American.

Bancroft takes care to emphasize this education in nature on the part of the founders and of Boone. In mid-eighteenth-century Virginia the "child," Madison, "round whose gentle nature clustered the hopes of American union," sports on the lawn among "half-opened forests." Still "deeper in the wilderness" young Thomas Jefferson, diligent student of classical languages, "dwelt on the skirt of forest life . . . treading the mountain side with elastic step in pursuit of game." But beyond the bourn of wilderness is Washington, the Virginia "stripling" whose "robust constitution had been tried and invigorated by his early life in the wilderness, [by] his habit of occupation out of doors, and his rigid temperance." In the wilderness at sixteen as a surveyor, "the forest trained him, in meditative solitude, to freedom and largeness of mind; and nature revealed to him her obedience to serene and silent laws."[83]

To grasp the full meaning of that young American's education in the wilds (one only sketched for Madison, Jefferson, and even Washington), Bancroft's reader must go to his account of Daniel Boone, the young man cheerful, meditative, careless of wealth, and "ignorant of books, but versed in the forest and forest life." His foray into Indian-infested Kentucky heralds settlement and is warranted by Kentuckian beauty and luxuriant fertility, by the very "wonders." Emphatically, Boone "was no more alone than a bee among flowers, but communed familiarly with the whole universe of life." Similarly, Bancroft's Washington was "a man of action, not of theory or words . . . [and] his whole being was one continued act of faith in the eternal, intelligent, moral order of the universe." Of Boone, Bancroft goes on, "Nature was his intimate, and, as the roving woodsman leaned confidingly on her bosom, she responded to his intelligence."[84]

Significantly, neither Boone nor the Founders enter the American forests to learn survival skills. Theirs is not a study in forestry or woodlore or even in Indian fighting (or aboriginal diplomacy). That part of their identity formed by the American wilds is different from the self-testing of the rite of passage into manhood. For American nature and the representative American are complementary, reciprocal, and mutually defining of the nation. In Bancroft's imagery (Boone "held unconscious intercourse with beauty/Old as creation") is the attempt to conjoin this American folk hero with a landscape inclusively fecund, informative of the self, and thereby intrinsically educational toward self- and national self-realization. The multivolumed book of nature is Boone's Kentucky. And his life is validated by this wilderness education, as are those of Madison, Jefferson, and Washington.

It is, however, vital to Bancroft's scheme of history that Founders

and folk hero alike so qualify themselves only by reemerging from
the forests into public life (in the mode of Washington) or (like
Boone) by taking society into the wilderness in civilizing progress.
That is, the figural America embodied in the lives of representative
Americans is valid for Bancroft only when those lives contribute
explicitly to sociopolitical America, including the reform of the environment. Bancroft has no sympathy with American lives of
isolated retreat. Like Daniel Webster's, his is a progressive story
of gardens socially cultivated, of wilderness enjoyed initially
for itself but in the longer view valued for its utilitarian potential. A "half-opened forest" is one midway to civilizing progress.
Those "glooms" of the American forest will yield to the radiance
of the reformed landscape. After all, New Englanders were a
"dauntless community," who turned "the sterility of New England into a cluster wealthy states."[85] Thus Bancroft's essential
America of democratic ideology is mirrored in public institutions of
government, commerce, agriculture, education, and so on. The two
realms—of idea and of social reality—are inseparable and mutually
obligated. He is markedly unsympathetic to the buckskinned woods-
men who retreat endlessly into the forests, submit to no governance,
and make no civil contribution.

For Bancroft is ever utilitarian in his judgments and in his vision of
America. The primeval garden and wilderness bespeak millennial
destiny when identified as refuge, cornucopia, and temple. But under
a rubric of progress they compel reform as the very spring compels
vegetation. "Nothing could restrain the Americans from peopling the
wilderness." As "masters of their own free wills," the colonists
"spread more and more widely over the mild, productive, and en-
chanting territory" and "through the boundless wilderness." The
Illinois of 1769 "invited emigrants more than ever," while in the
Alleghenies "the old home of the wolf, the deer, and the panther"
becomes the new domestic site of "packhorses and droves of cattle."
The process of settlement is to Bancroft as inherently progressive as
it is inexorable. We notice what glee the historian attributes to the
very Kentucky valleys that school Boone in natural laws even as they
are by his presence readied for settlement: "the valleys of Kentucky
laughed as they heard the distant tread of clustering troops of adventurers, who . . . prepared to take possession of the meadows and un-

dulating table land that nature has clothed with its richest grasses."
In the offing in these valleys are "companies of honest farmers,"
"iron works, a salt manufactory, grist-mills, and saw-mills." These
"men who are now to occupy 'that most desirable territory,' will
never turn back, but, as we shall see, will carry American independence to the Wabash, the Detroit, and the Mississippi."[86]
It is well to recall Bancroft's millennial convictions on America.

> To the forests of America . . . came a free people, . . . separating
> itself from all other elements of previous civilization. . . . Like
> Moses, they had escaped from Egyptian bondage to the wilder-
> ness, that God might there give them the pattern of the taber-
> nacle. Like the favored evangelist, the exiles, in their western
> Patmos, listened to the angel that dictated the new gospel of
> freedom.

Bancroft is not here talking about the parochial New Englanders'
self-identity. He is using a figure prominent in Puritan sources to
characterize *all* the American colonies. Bancroft mixes biblical history with that of Western Europe in the typological scheme for
human redemption. Thus is Marquette the patriarch Abraham. "The
people of Palestine," he writes, "from the destruction of their
temple, an outcast and a wandering race, were allured by the traffic
and the candor of the New World; and not the Saxon and Celtic races
only." Shunning to name those other races (probably from his
Teutonic bias), Bancroft alludes to those who "worshiped near Cal-
vary" and who have finally "found a home, liberty, and a burial-
place on the Island of Manhattan." Untroubled by the Augustinian
distinction between the cities of God and men, Bancroft resolves
them on the banks of the Delaware where settlers "build the city of
humanity by obeying the nobler instincts of human nature."
Bancroft's Quakers expect "Christ's kingdom on earth, his second
coming at hand." Under the excitement of libertarian hopes, "the
blissful centuries of the millennium promised to open upon a favored
world."[87]
Significantly, Bancroft does not pronounce these beliefs as myths
of the past now repudiated in the enlightened 1830s (or 1840s and
1850s). He admits that such phrases as "Christ's kingdom on earth"
typify "the language of that age," meaning the 1670s. But if the

phraseology is outdated, the idea remains valid, because to Bancroft it is truth. All America is his millennial "city of humanity." Thus his prelude to the three-volume account of the American Revolution rings with millennial fervor:

> The hour of the American Revolution was come. The people of the continent with irresistible energy obeyed one general impulse, as earth in spring listens to the command of nature, and without the appearance of effort bursts forth to life in perfect harmony. . . . For the first time [freedom] found a region and a race. . . . When all Europe slumbered over questions of liberty, a band of exiles, keeping watch by night, heard the glad tiding which promised the political regeneration of the world.[88]

Bancroft takes care to show that the "political regeneration" accompanies utilitarian development of the environment. His Canadian "noble forests invited the construction of log cabins." Near the Gulf of Mexico his La Salle "heard in the distance the footsteps of the advancing multitude that were coming to take possession of the valley." And in the North and East "armies fought in the wilderness for rule over the solitudes which were to be the future dwelling place of millions." In New Orleans, though three years of French settlement had resulted in no visible signs of progress, still, not only were the "unsubdued canebrakes" free of the historical sorrow of "ruins of a more prosperous age," but the "enlightened traveller" could see a happy America because he looked with a cheerful eye into the future and predicted "the opulence and vastness of the city which was destined to become the emporium of the noblest valley in the world." The utilitarian prophetic eye is vitally important to Bancroft. (After all, his was the historiographical tradition that sought from the past a grand theme, a controlling idea which made coherent the disparate events in diverse locales; thus, from the past he is the very diviner of truth, the mirror image of the prophet.)

So Bancroft's young George Washington, the Virginia "stripling" destined to change the world, is gifted with the utilitarian vision of the American New Earth. Traveling inland toward the confluence of the Allegheny and Monongahela rivers, moving "through forest solitudes, gloomy with the fallen leaves and solemn sadness of late autumn, across mountains, rocky ravines, and streams, through sleet and snows," Washington arrives at the fork of the Ohio, "How lonely was the spot so long unheeded of men," writes Bancroft. But his Washington is the prophetic genius: "At once Washington foresaw the destiny of the place," as his imagination filled with fortress and city. Throughout December, delayed by rain, snow, mire, and swamps, Washington's "quick eye discerned all the richness of the meadows." It is an important discernment. Joel Barlow's Columbus might cry out in near-despair at the uselessness of a rich and a sublime landscape hopelessly remote from men. But Bancroft's hero needs no Hesper to counsel patience and urge foresight. Bancroft's hero is innately gifted with prophetic powers to know the utilitarian future of the American landscape.[89]

Not only does he endow La Salle, Washington, and his "enlightened traveller" with such prophetic powers, but Bancroft himself steps forward unabashedly to contrast the Hudson Valley of his own day with the primeval scene he imagines Henry Hudson to have looked upon in 1609. The contrastive passages on environmental reform are extraordinary for two reasons. First, Bancroft bursts his disciplined chronology to hasten readers from Henry Hudson's view to that of George Bancroft himself. This is the only point in all the ten volumes of his *History* in which Bancroft so violates his time line to focus readers in a detailed scrutiny of the same site utterly transformed in two centuries. It is a passage well worth seeing in its entirety. First, we have the primeval view, supposedly from Hudson's lookout:

> Sombre forests shed a melancholy grandeur over the useless magnificence of nature, and hid in their deep shades the rich soil which the sun had never warmed. No axe had levelled the giant progeny of the crowded groves, in which the fantastic forms of withered limbs, that had been blasted and riven by lightening, contrasted strangely with the verdant freshness of a younger growth of branches. The wanton grape-vine, seeming by its own power to have sprung from the earth, and to have fastened its leafy coils on the top of the tallest forest-tree, swung in the air with every breeze, like the loosened shrouds of a ship. Trees might every where be seen breaking from their root in the marshy soil, and threatening to fall with the first rude gust; while the ground was strewn with the ruins of former forests, over

which a profusion of wild flowers wasted their freshness in mockery of the gloom. Reptiles sported in the stagnant pools, or crawled unharmed over piles of mouldering trees. The spotted deer couched among the thickets; but not to hide, for there was no pursuer; and there were none but wild animals to crop the uncut herbage of the productive prairies. Silence reigned, broken, it may have been, by the flight of land birds or the flapping of water-fowl, and rendered more dismal by the howl of beasts of prey. The streams, not yet limited to a channel, spread over sand-bars, tufted with copses of willow, or waded through wastes of reeds; or slowly but surely undermined in groups of sycamores that grew by their side. The smaller brooks spread out into sedgy swamps, that were overhung by clouds of mosquitoes; masses of decaying vegetation fed the exhalations with the seeds of pestilence, and made the balmy air of the summer's evening as deadly as it seemed grateful. Vegetable life and death were mingled hideously together. The horrors of corruption frowned on the fruitless fertility of uncultivated nature.[90]

We notice in the passage a tone of revulsion at the rankness and stench. Bancroft moves from the romantic cliché of "melancholy grandeur" into relentless figures of atrophy, decay, mortality, and death. Clearly, as he imagines the primeval scene, he loathes it.

Utilitarian values determine this judgment. Nature's magnificence is "useless," its former growth in "ruins," its flowers wasting their freshness. Mere animals harvest the herbage of the "productive prairies," and streams without proper channels flow "through wastes of reeds" and undermine stands of sycamores that grow at the waterline. The comingling of life and death is, in a word, "hideous." Unutilized fecundity distresses him; natural resources in want of use appall him. This is the landscape not of an angry man but of one in disgust. The more closely he imagines the primeval scene, the more loathesome it becomes in his mind's eye. This is one of very few places in the *History* where Bancroft does not represent landscape in conventional phrases—which makes this passage all the more extraordinary, since it reveals his personal feelings toward the primeval American scene. In the manner of the best known of the Hudson River school of painters, Thomas Cole (whose work Bancroft must have known), the historian accumulates detail upon detail. But

Bancroft's is no landscape of psychic projection or of the aesthetic sublime. His sole criterion for evaluating the Hudson Valley is utility. By that standard the landscape holds no aesthetic appeal, no appeal of any kind.

Bancroft has now to present his successful outcome of landscape reform. And in a sense it is the very success of civilization in the Hudson Valley (as he understands it) that enables him to release his utter loathing at the scene of its past. For he has an environmental success story to tell, one so compelling that he leaps ahead by 228 years to the present moment to present to his readers the utilitarian culmination of environmental reform:

And how changed is the scene from that on which Hudson gazed! The earth glows with the colors of civilization; the banks of the streams are enamelled with richest grasses; woodlands and cultivated fields are harmoniously blended; the birds of spring find their delight in orchards and trim gardens, variegated with choicest plants from every temperate zone; while the brilliant flowers of the tropics bloom from the windows of the greenhouse and the saloon. The yeoman, living like a good neighbor near the fields he cultivates, glories in the fruitfulness of the valleys, and counts with honest exultation the flocks and herds that browse in safety on the hills. The thorn has given way to the rosebush; the cultivated vine clambers over rocks where the brood of serpents used to nestle; while industry smiles at the changes she has wrought, and inhales the bland air which now has health on its wings.

And man is still in harmony with nature, which he has subdued, cultivated, and adorned. For him the rivers that flow to remotest climes, mingle their waters; for him the lakes gain new outlets to the ocean; for him the arch spans the flood, and science spreads iron pathways to the recent wilderness; for him the hills yield up the shining marble and the enduring granite; for him the forests of the interior come down in immense rafts; for him the marts of the city gather the produce of every clime, and libraries collect the works of genius of every language and every age. The passions of society are chastened into purity; manners are made benevolent by civilization; and the virtue of the country is the guardian of its peace.[91]

By contemporary, twentieth-century standards Bancroft's personal vision is environmentally arrogant, insensitive, supremely anthropocentric. In retrospect it may reveal (and may indict) the mentality that has heedlessly exploited the landscape in damaging ways, as George Perkins Marsh was to recognize just a few years after Bancroft published this second volume of his *History*. And indeed, if confined to considerations of material progress, Bancroft's reformed Hudson Valley does signify an obtuse mind. Only if we additionally consider his beliefs that America's spiritual regeneration is connected to its environmental reform does Bancroft's hymn to the railroad, to commerce, and to deforestation sound tenable within an intellectually coherent system of thought.

Clearly, in such tributes as this to the reformed environment (which appear, abbreviated, at regular intervals through the ten volumes), the historian was not trumpeting the virtues of materialistic America per se. Further, reform of the American landscape is not in Bancroft an imperative for the future but an already-achieved part of the nation's destined progress. American vigor and energy were but a necessary force behind the process. David Levin remarks that "torpor and languor seemed subversive . . . to a nineteenth-century American who knew that his continent has to be 'improved.' "[92] But landscape change was much more than a matter of improvement. It was an integral part of America's spiritual biography. This is why Bancroft concludes his picture of the transformed Hudson Valley with "the passions of society . . . chastened into purity," its "manners . . . made benevolent by civilization," and national virtue as "the guardian of its peace."

Aesthetically, however, Bancroft pays as dearly for his total celebration of the American New Earth as had Cooper in his misanthropic despair of it. In amplifying the ideological legacy of the Enlightenment, Bancroft did not work to find his own, individual voice. He represented the American landscape designatively but not evocatively. We have *noble* forests, *majestic* mountains, *inclement* weather, all the stock phrases of established romanticism, none of them inviting readers to engage imaginatively in the personal lexicon of a visionary mind. His rhetoric is what Lowell called "the mere torpid boon of education or inheritance." Further, in his art Bancroft lets his acceptance of geographic America as the millennial nursery restrict his range of human experience in the pristine continent. While he does cite the "savage forests" and their "appalling silence" and thinks of the Mississippi Delta one century after its settlement as a cacophony of mosquitoes, snakes, frogs, and alligators, Bancroft offers no reader the harshness of the American environment in his accounts of pioneering or settlement. ("Hardy emigrants" is his concession to the necessary rigors of colonial life.)

A keen example of this restrictive softening of experience is his representation of the exploration of three missionaries, including Marquette, in the upper Great Lakes. Bancroft concedes that they mingle happiness with misery and suffer certain "inclemancies" from nature and from the Indians. They defy "the severity of climate," lack "the comfort of a fire," have "no bread but pounded maize" and no "food but unwholesome moss from the trees." They live "without nourishment" and sleep "without a resting place." But in all such phrases Bancroft insulates his audience from the direct experience of privation in the American wilds. His are normative terms of full-sufficiency (comfort, nourishment, resting place, wholesomeness), from which he suggests mitigation. Yet apart from maize and moss there are no words upon which to focus (and therefore to measure) privation. There is no diction which verifies the experience or which shapes imaginative participation in it. The reader's mind is not taxed to leave the armchair.[93]

In some part Bancroft's softening of harsh experience pertains to his literary theory. As he wrote in tribute to the popular and prolific American versifier, Mrs. Felicia Hemans, "Happy the nation, of which the writers are filled with elevated thought and tastes!"[94] (Longfellow spoke similarly of "clothing the real with the ideal" and so provoked ethnologists who complained of his prettified Hiawatha, even as he pleased a vast reading public.) With elevation of taste as a literary desideratum, Bancroft may have avoided documentary immediacy in favor of what he understood to be "ennobling" or elevated phrases, many in latinate constructions.

Yet, we must consider that for the romantic historians the landscape was not ornamental but integral to the historic vision. Levin argues this point, emphasizing that Bancroft and his cohort (Jared Sparks, Francis Parkman, William H. Prescott, John L. Motley) were not only scholars but men of letters. If their literary landscaping often failed aesthetically, that was because the very topographical features once stylistically so fresh as to indicate awe (for instance in Scott or Cooper) had by now petrified into cliché. Levin suggests, too, that readers of Scott and Cooper need only find in the histories certain phrases resonant from their novels in order to grasp the emotional value which the historians intended their scenery to convey. Thus could participants in sublime scenes in the Scottish highlands or in Cooper's Adirondacks transfer their literary experiences into events of American history.[95]

For Bancroft there was another good reason not to evoke the awesome dread of the aesthetic sublime or the palpable harshness of wilderness life. Because the American landscape formed an integral part of his historic vision of America as redeemer nation, he must have felt that it would be thematically destructive to elicit strong feelings of dread or of mortal threat. Thus, when he involves readers in the American landscape, he does so in the rhetoric of a genteel romantic.

His all-inclusive celebration of the American New Earth also leads Bancroft into self-contradiction within the *History*. He seems not to recognize that the Kentuckian forest temple in which Boone communes with "the universe of life" is conceptually opposed to the primeval Hudson Valley with its hideous comingling of life and death. Too, in time the wilderness green cathedrals of Madison, Jefferson, Washington, and Boone will disappear, transformed to the America exemplified by the Hudson Valley of 1837. Untroubled, Bancroft neither acknowledges nor interprets a process structurally inevitable (and at thematic cross-purposes) within his work.

More, Bancroft's commitment to the spiral of human progress prevents human satisfaction in the results of environmental reform. This problem comes clear, curiously, in his treatment of English rural life of the later eighteenth century. Bancroft praises the temperate English climate, the fruitful and perpetually green, wooded, and arable land, the soft grassy walks, and the cottages "carefully neat, with roses and honeysuckles clambering to their roofs." Here Aristocrats live among Yeomen who are affectionately deferential to (but neither dissembling nor cowering before) their betters. "The very lanes," writes Bancroft, "were memorials of early days, and ran as they had been laid out before the conquest; and in mills for grinding corn, water-wheels revolved at their work just where they had been doing so for at least eight hundred years." Too, both flocks and herds graze "on freshly springing herbage." We have here a pastoral ideal of rural English life.[96]

Understandably, Bancroft cannot approve its aristocratic (and plutocratic) foundation. But beyond that, he frowns upon his own pictorial ideal. The pleasant country life has its cottage industries, husbandry, horticulture, and farming in a mild climate with congenial society. Its problem is that, once established, it is unchanging. It is not dynamic; it shows no spiral of progress. The democrat Bancroft is understandably critical of the political ideology of monarchy and nobility, and critical too of a mortgaged nation in which quit-rents prevent yeomanly freeholding of land. Yet he criticizes his ideal village for its lack of change per se. No matter that it is virtually perfect as he describes it—it wants change. The rich irony is that Bancroft is caught in that perpetual screw thread of progress. There is no surcease even when life is brought to agrarian and communal perfection. Material change has become in itself some necessary evidence of progress, not the handmaiden of progress but progress itself.

Thus, English rural life, the apotheosis of contentment and full-sufficiency between Englishmen and their land, is errant in its very endurance over time. Progress mandates change, and change in turn proves progress. Bancroft does not confront this philosophical bind in his idealized portrayals of American village life, though the ominous implications exist for America when the historian envisions industrial parks free of all hints of satanic mills.

A point remains, namely, Bancroft's own relation to the America of his *History*. As a successful politician and litterateur he had solved the problem that ever plagued Joel Barlow, that of one man combining the two careers in America. But Bancroft evidently sought to be the spokesman of his nation, an ambition that surfaces recurrently in his writing. The English poets interest him chiefly because he felt they had discovered not only the transcendent spirit of humanity but the quintessence of nationality. His Milton belongs in the constellation of ideal scholars, those "high priests of nature"; his Shakespeare "unfolded the panorama of English history." (Dryden is his caveat: "least read because least profoundly national."[97]) As historians of

England, these poets are for Bancroft embodiments of their nation, representative men in the Emersonian sense. It is true that Bancroft and his confreres were affirmatively, consciously literary. Both David Levin and Russel Nye have written extensively on this point. But in accepting fellowship with the greatest English poets Bancroft seems to intend transcendence of the nexus of scholar-litterateur conventional for his time. His definition of these poets as high priests and historians indicates his own place as America's high priest and diviner of the "inmost character" of the American national mind. His rite of divination is performed in ten volumes, virtually in one and one-third millions of words.

And Bancroft marvels that these are words in English, a language which "but a century and a half before, had for its entire world a part only of two narrow islands on the outer verge of Europe." Now it is *his* language, summoned to fit the new continent. Just as Edward Johnson struggled to define amorphous terrain in America by imposing upon it images of familiar shapes, and Joel Barlow after him worked into his heroic couplets those Gallicisms which he hoped would make America in the image of his own verbal icons—so Bancroft utters his own imperatives that language define the American continent and reform it in the very act of representation:

Go forth, then, language of Milton and Hampden, language of my country, take possession of the North American continent! Gladden the waste places with every tone that has been rightly struck on the English lyre, with every English word that has been spoken well for liberty and for man!

He insists that language animate American geography as he commands it to "give an echo to the now silent and solitary mountains," to "gush out with the fountains that as yet sing their anthems all day long without response," to "fill the vallies with the voices of love in its purity." Transcontinentally, the English language heralds and propagates democratic values of the American New Earth as Bancroft bids it "Utter boldly and spread widely through the world the thoughts of the coming apostles of the people's liberty, till the sound that cheers the desert shall thrill through the heart of humanity, and the lips of the messenger of the people's power, as he stands in beauty upon the mountains, shall proclaim the renovating tidings of equal freedom for the race."[98]

So it is the English language that vivifies the topography, that makes America in words. Bancroft here broaches the idea of the poet, the maker of a metaphoric America—but only that. Constrained in the vocabulary of genteel romanticism, he remains the propagandist for the New Earth. At the bourn of metaphor, Bancroft retreats from it and, finally, with Edward Johnson, Joel Barlow, Daniel Webster, and in certain respects Cooper, takes his place in literary history as yet another prologue to the American New Earth of Whitman.

6: Walt Whitman, the Literatus of the New Earth

After the seas are all cross'd, (as they seem already cross'd,)
After the great captains and engineers have accomplish'd
their work,
After the noble inventors, after the scientists, the chemist,
the geologist, ethnologist,
Finally shall come the poet worthy of that name,
The true son of God shall come singing his songs.

Walt Whitman, Passage to India

It seems inevitable that American imperatives of environmental reform should culminate aesthetically in the poems of Walt Whitman. This pivotal figure in American literature, the paterfamilias of the moderns as well as the apotheosis of American romanticism, Whitman assumed the heritage of the American New Earth by his very determination to be "the spokesman of American democracy" —more, the persona embodying or incarnating America itself.[1] In Whitman we have at last the writer in whom the ideology present in American literature since the mid-seventeenth century is realized as aesthetic achievement. *Passage to India, The Song of the Broad-Axe,* and *The Song of the Redwood-Tree* stand at the end of two centuries of American thinking (and American myth making) on the New Earth. These are the poems in which environmental reform is a successful and a fully stated theme, though of course Whitman's American New Earth is everywhere implicit in his poems and emerges too in unsuccessful verse, for instance, in the sentimental rhymed statement, *Pioneers! O Pioneers!* and in *By Blue Ontario's Shore.*

Whitman's earth is made new in words, in language resonant from, but not mimetically correlative with, the actual environment. This is an important point because by it Whitman departs radically from those of his American predecessors who espoused imperatives of environmental reform but made them one part of a doctrinal social program for the nation.

Of course, as a newspaper journalist Whitman too had tried to be a social programmer. But after those years of social advocacy in editorial journalism (all the while frustrated at his inability to effect social change), Whitman's own temper changed in the late 1850s to that of the poet we now recognize. As Floyd Stovall describes it, "The activist has become an observer, the reformer a philosopher, the journalist a poet."[2] This complex of observer-philosopher-poet is yet reformist but, unlike Cooper and Bancroft, is not sociologically or politically so. The journalist Whitman had castigated William Gilmore Simms in 1846 for the coarseness and indelicacy that he felt made *The Wigwam and the Cabin* unfit literature for the edification of the American family. But, by the late 1850s onward, Whitman the poet had not only repudiated such constraints of normative respectability but urged "individual regeneration" as the only valid means to social reform. His ideal America became that in which "outside authority enters always after the precedence of inside authority," and where "children are taught to be laws to themselves."[3]

Thus the poet-priest becomes the reformer, not by writing social programs but by first informing (and thereupon reforming) the individual from within. James Miller, Jr., calls attention to our underemphasis of this poetic concept on Whitman's part and reminds us of the poet's consciously strenuous demands upon his reader, his likening the experience of reading to a gymnastic struggle. The poet-Literatus is therefore a "priest of man, and every man shall be his own priest. . . . They shall arise in America, and be responded to from the remainder of the earth." Whitman reiterated the point in *Democratic Vistas* and emphasized that "the mind, which alone builds the permanent edifice, haughtily builds it to itself."[4]

Such a mind yet needs a sense of place, and we have ample evidence that Whitman, no less than Joel Barlow, was interested in the study of geography and history and that his poetic New Earth was informed by it. Edwin Fussell writes that "in the early years Whitman was wonderfully superficial, conventional, and chauvinistic about

geography, and especially about the geography of Western America."
And he lists those titles which, as editor of the *Brooklyn Daily Eagle*
(1846–47), Whitman placed in review, among them *Life and Adven-*
tures in California, and Scenes in the Pacific Ocean; Julia Ormond,
or, The New Settlement; Sam Houston and His Republic; and *Jour-*
nal of an Exploring Tour beyond the Rocky Mountains. Writing, in
Fussell's term, "endlessly and recklessly" of the political, military,
and demographic expansion westward, Whitman was an exponent of
America's geographic outreaching during his years as a journalist.
Thomas Brasher, who has made careful study of Whitman's tenure at
the *Eagle,* concludes that although Whitman never used John
O'Sullivan's exact phrase, Manifest Destiny, he adhered to the spirit
of that concept, for instance, in his support of the Mexican War and
his yearning to see the Union flag decked with additional stars.[5]
   Whitman's interest in geography is to be found, moreover, in his
clippings, many with underscoring, marginal notes, or the sketched
hand with index finger pointing to a key passage, which Stovall has
so carefully considered in his important study of the "foreground,"
in Emerson's term, of *Leaves of Grass.* Stovall reports from these
clippings that, while it is apparent that Whitman's primary interest
was literary, "his second greatest interest was in geography." In his
"huge atlas-scrapbook . . . articles on travel, geography, and history
predominate." As for the specific relation of this reading to
Whitman's poetry, Stovall concludes that "Whitman must have pored
many hours over these until he had built a solid foundation of fact
upon which his imagination could erect the vast structures of time
and space that we find in 'Song of Myself.' "[6]
   Whitman's excursions in geography were not all vicarious. In 1848
he traveled to New Orleans where he spent three months in newspaper work. Going by rail, coach, and steamboat, he traveled the
route of the Cumberland Gap and the Ohio and Mississippi rivers,
later to return by way of the Great Lakes and the Hudson River,
including a stop at Niagara Falls. His account of the journey, reported in his *Traveller's Note Book,* contains the eclectic observations
conventional in the genre, though noteworthy here is Whitman's dis-
appointment that the idealized Ohio River of "poetry and romance"
is not limpid but muddy. He took umbrage at the perils of steamboat
travel in an age supposedly of advanced technology, for when his

boat, the *St. Cloud,* scraped bottom while passing a "boiling-place" on the Ohio, Whitman wrote archly, "Does not the perfection to which engineering has been brought afford some means of remedying this ugly part of the river?"[7]

While Whitman's travel notes on the American landscape are conventional to their time, it seems that, as Miller observes, the journey to and from New Orleans permanently liberated Whitman's imagination "from the Provincialism of his small corner of the world." Miller observes, "His vision of America was enlarged to embrace its vast prairies, its treacherous and rapid rivers, its raw frontiers and its refined metropolises—and its melting pot of citizenry in the lively and bubbling processes of merging and fusing." Fussell remarks, moreover, that Whitman's firsthand impressions of American western geography enabled him to get rid of the sentimental strain in his writing in favor of a new "specificity and realism" and that ultimately "the only reasonable conclusion is that there was a direct and powerful relationship . . . between the 1848 Western tour and the gradual emergence of the developed poet."[8]

Stimulated to reportage of the American topography, Whitman simultaneously developed his interest in the American past, an interest virtually prerequisite to his poetic shaping of an American New Earth. His reading of world history and his absorption in Egyptology document his broadest engagement with the past, but it seems too that Whitman had a personal access to American history. After all, at a public ceremony on the Fourth of July 1825, little Walt had been picked up and carried by General Lafayette himself. Later, in 1842–43 Whitman drank toddies with Colonel Fellows and encouraged the old man to reminisce about his former friend Tom Paine, who had also been an associate of Whitman's father, and his father's confrere, the radical Quaker preacher Elias Hicks. Indicative too are the names of Walt's brothers: George Washington, Thomas Jefferson, Andrew Jackson. Not surprisingly, two of Whitman's earliest stories, in 1842, dealt with legends of the Revolution on Long Island. These biographical connections with American history suggest a fluidity between the personal and the national sense of the past. Temporal barriers surely dissolved as Whitman possessed American history in familiar anecdote. Gay Wilson Allen speaks of Whitman as a "time-binder," a mediator between past, present, and future. "Quite literally the poet conserves the wisdom of the race and brings it to bear upon the present and future. . . . The poet must be able to . . . live emotionally and imaginatively in an eternal present." As a mature poet, Whitman may have found it easy to live in the "eternal present" in part because he could summon to himself the American past he had lived over toddies on deal tables.[9]

As we shall see presently, Whitman's interest in American geography and history well served the New Earth of his mature poetry. But it is also relevant to notice here that among Whitman's quasi- or even nonliterary contemporaries the same materials of American space and history fostered continuing and vital imperatives of environmental reform in different areas of American thought. As Whitman came to embody the American New Earth in poems, others worked in complementary yet quite different directions. For the imagination of the engineer and the quantifier had not disappeared from American thinking on environmental reform. It is accurate to say, rather, that on this matter the poet and the pragmatist were separating at last, each in response to the topographical changes that were ineluctable in the latter one-half of the American nineteenth century.

Surrounding Whitman, these quasi-literary imperatives are to be found in diverse forms, and with new turns of emphasis. For instance, one figure whose writings possibly influenced Whitman, William Gilpin, turned his millennial expectations to the West, and over fifty years wrote prolifically on behalf of the expansion of the United States toward the Pacific. From a family of inventors and businessmen in the Brandywine area near Philadelphia, Gilpin at age sixteen had the extraordinary opportunity to assist Alexis de Tocqueville in collecting data on America in the libraries at Washington. The Frenchman, according to Gilpin, "taught me the importance and value of statistics and how to look into the future with a good deal of reliability from the data the present affords." [10] The writings of Gilpin's adult life prove how profoundly he took Tocqueville's lesson for his own mode of thought.

His biography shows Gilpin's attraction to the American West. Though he resigned from the United States Military Academy after one term, his military bent led him to Florida during the Seminole Wars, and later into the Rocky Mountains as he accompanied the first expedition of John Charles Frémont. Gilpin's western travels alerted him to the mineral resources ready for exploitation and furnished him as well the language in which he expressed his expectations of a western-based American Millennium. His literary credential was that of a journalist when, having settled in St. Louis as a young lawyer, he became in 1836 the editor of the Democratic *Missouri Argus.* Increasingly, he was involved in party politics as he endorsed the Jacksonian Van Buren and attacked Daniel Webster and Henry Clay as Federalists.[11] A strong partisan of Missouri's Sen. Thomas Hart Benton, Gilpin began to envision opportunities for the American acquisition of Oregon. He himself left St. Louis for the frontier settlement of Independence and in 1843 went with Frémont on his second expedition to explore and report on the Oregon Territory. A year later he served in the Missouri regiment in the Mexican War and finally, in 1861, achieved formal recognition of his commitment to the American West when President Lincoln appointed him governor of the Colorado Territory.

From his first government documents published in 1846 to his subsequent *The Central Gold Region: The Grain, Pastoral, and Gold Regions of North America* (1860) and *Mission of the North American People* (1874), William Gilpin wrote, in Henry Nash Smith's terms, as a bardic seer, a mystic expounding in apocalyptic language a theory of the imperial destiny of the United States in the West.[12] We hear in Gilpin the idea of geography as destiny as, from Alexander von Humboldt, he adopts the quasi-scientific proof that social progress followed an isothermal line westward over the globe. Gilpin wrote, "history chiefly occupies itself with the biography of empires . . . [that] lie along a serpentine zone of the north hemisphere of the globe, within an isothermal belt." And he lists chronologically "and upon the hereditary line of progress" the empires of China, India, Persia, Greece, Rome, Spain, Britain, and "last, the Republican Empire of North America." Congruently, the isothermal zone is exactly as wide as the "territory of the American people," and it occupies "the whole connecting space between Western Europe and Oriental Asia."[13] In an often quoted line, Gilpin wrote that the "untransacted destiny of the American people is to subdue the continent."[14]

As a propagandist Gilpin kept the evaluation of the American New

Earth in the offing because, in conceiving it to lie in the West, he kept it imminent in time. Not only did he think Europe to be in ruins, but the eastern seaboard of his family origins seemed to him antiquated and exhausted. He wrote in scorn of "salt water politics" of *"the old thirteen"* original states, urging instead a vital United States based upon "a new thirteen" of the West, itself allied with Asia by way of the Pacific.

Gilpin had in mind the utilitarian means of western development, specifically the exploitation of natural resources and the transcontinental railroad which he hoped would cross Asia and North America. He saw imperial ambition evident in the agriculture and manufacturing of the American interior, as when he wrote that there "nature has bountifully blended all her choicest gifts to locate the rural quintessence of America and of the World!" The crux of Gilpin's thinking is that "History is the journal of the geographic progress [of civilized society], its vicissitudes, its struggles, and its energies." It is therefore important that geography bear the stamp of civil progress. Thus American hemp, tobacco, flax, and so on, are made prestigious by those who "limned out the profile of our continental empire, and inaugurated the march of our destinies." Gilpin's limners are Daniel Boone and George Rogers Clark. But his pantheon of Americans whose souls were fired with "the divine instinct of progress and liberty" are "COLUMBUS, WASHINGTON, JEFFERSON, and JACKSON." In these convictions Gilpin is umnistakably consonant with George Bancroft.[15]

As a writer Gilpin tended to be repetitious, after the late 1840s using over and again the same phrases. He had one particularly significant figure of speech, that of the pioneer army comprising largely individuals, families, and whole communities from the United States and other nations. This is an army advancing inexorably, its outposts the new farms that "assail the wilderness." Doubtless adapted from his own military thinking, Gilpin's figure of the pioneer army conveys his imperative of western American destiny. It has recruits, platoons, ranks, flanks, and a "marine force" in the whaling fleet. More than that, the "vast *army* of pioneers" obeys "that mysterious and uncontrollable impulse which drives our nation to its goal." Gilpin goes on, "Thus *overland* sweeps this tide-wave of population, absorbing in its thundering march the glebe, the savages, and the wild beasts of the wilderness, scaling the mountains and debouching down upon the seaboard."[16] In all these phrases Gilpin encourages the idea of destined American empire. The westward movement is not one of national choice but one of "uncontrollable" impulse. He writes of it in mystic celebration, just as two centuries earlier Edward Johnson found the Christian army to be the agent of apocalyptic destiny.

We may notice in Gilpin's diction certain similarities to Whiman. His term "debouching," for instance, recurs in a similar expression in Whitman's *Pioneers! O Pioneers!* Gilpin's biographer notices that the two shared political views and attitudes toward the West. More intriguing, he speculates that Whitman discovered Gilpin from newspaper reprintings of Gilpin's 1846 report to the United States Senate, a document which contained the essence of Gilpin's thought on the West.[17] That point, however, remains as speculation. Of significance here is Gilpin's particularly western ideology of American environmental reform. For his vision projects upon some of the most intractable, formidable continental geography a people moved by libertarian spirit to civilize it and to locate in it the true, new site of the American New Earth.

It must be noted that Gilpin was not the only writer of the later nineteenth century to invoke military figures for millennial purposes. For we find the seventeenth-century military Millennium of Johnson revived in the *Memoirs* of Gen. William T. Sherman, who equated America with its Union of states and asserted

> the broad doctrine that as a nation the United States has the right . . . to penetrate to every part of our national domain, and that we will do it—that we will do it in our own time and in our own way . . . that we will remove every obstacle, if need be, take every life, every acre of land, every particle of property, every thing that to us seems proper; that we will not cease until the end is attained.

In 1864 he had written to Grant, "come out West [and] take to yourself the whole Mississippi Valley; let us make it dead-sure, and I tell you the Atlantic slope and Pacific shores will follow its destiny and as sure as the limbs of a tree live or die with the main trunk!" The survival of that "main trunk" is not really in question for Sherman. And though burning the landscape is a perverse variation on American environmental reform, Sherman evidently believed that scorching a swath of earth from Atlanta to the sea would insure Lincoln's reelection and thereby preserve the national destiny.[18]

Elsewhere, contrarily, it is not a scorched but a newly greened landscape that takes its place as one modern version of the American New Earth. In this sense reform of the landscape is reparative or corrective—not, as in the Enlightenment, of "rude nature" but of man's own blunders and errors vis-à-vis himself and the environment. Within Edward Bellamy's utopian system of Christian socialism in the fictional tract *Looking Backward* (1888) and its sequel *Equality* (1897), we find a millennial strain explicitly of a "kingdom of God on earth" which includes the familiar pattern of linked spiritual and environmental changes. With the American Revolution as a distant antecedent of his global socialist Revolution, Bellamy's twentieth century has attained "internal concord and mutuality" signified in a flag free of all military associations. Concurrently, his American landscape is reconverted from a wayward state of urban congestion to one of a verdant transcontinental suburb. From the slaughterhouses of Boston's outlying Brighton to the satanic mills and the denuded mountains of the interior, all of Bellamy's landmarks of capitalist oppression have vanished, to be now reformed by human effort. As Bellamy's nineteenth-century man, Julian West, observes in wonderment, "It seemed to me that I had stolen into the very laboratory of the Creator, and found him at the task of fashioning with invisible hands the dust of the earth and the viewless air into forms of life." Never named, Frederick Law Olmsted is the *genius loci* of Bellamy's American New Earth, for "parks, gardens, and roomy spaces" are an urban ideal modeled explicitly on Olmsted's Central Park. In Bellamy's novel they are projected over the entire continent, which, in a massive public effort, has been entirely reforested.[19]

Olmsted himself, the name preeminent in American landscape architecture, shows in his career the enactment of a certain programmatic version of the American New Earth. In some ways he was a man of letters, having been nurtured by writings of the Transcendentalists. Briefly he ventured with two friends to publish *Putnam's Monthly Magazine* (1855–56) and was an editor (1866) at the *Nation* at its beginnings. He authored two books, the first upon his return from a six-month sojourn in England, after which Olmsted prepared a book of travels and social observation entitled *Walks and Talks of an American Farmer in England*. Though in retrospect that work contains the germ of Olmsted's theories on the relation of people to their environment, *Walks and Talks* made little stir at the time, yet drew Olmsted to the attention of the editor of the *New York Daily News*, who commissioned the young man to go south and report personally on conditions there. Olmsted's subsequent book, *The Cotton Kingdom: A Traveller's Observations on Cotton and Slavery in the American Slave States* (1861), won the widespread approval of northern readers principally because it rejected slavery on economic grounds.

For all this, Olmsted is at best a quasi-literary figure. He confessed regularly (and justly) to his awkward rhetoric, and his biographer notices the labored style of his professional papers and remarks that graceful, clear prose ever eluded him.[20] His theories of landscape architecture sound sociological within a tradition of radical Protestantism, but his social criticism lacks the figurative language that is characteristically literary. Nevertheless, Olmsted deserves notice here because his career, like Whitman's, exemplifies a commitment to the reformed American environment.

Olmsted's New Earth is utterly secular. In 1884 he professed indifference to the sacred mysteries and declared that the most "horrible" mental waste in the world was theology. He repented his own youthful "sin in superstitious maundering."[21] Yet in 1846, at the age of twenty-four, he had written of his urge to be "useful in the world, to make others happy, to help to advance the condition of Society, and hasten the preparation for the Millennium."[22] The shape of his career suggests that Olmsted held to the tenor of that aspiration even as he repudiated the doctrinal Christianity of his Puritan lineage. In 1893 he spoke of landscape architecture in the Puritan sense of the word, as a "calling."[23]

Accordingly, he habitually attached moral purpose to his activities. Proposing his sojourn in England to his father, Olmsted rejected all sentimental reasons for travel, instead arguing for firsthand experience of the most advanced techniques in agriculture and manufacturing. Later, preparing *Walks and Talks,* he described his intention to interest "Farmers and men of small means and ordinary information" in the book, in order to engage them in ideas of good taste and improvement. Later still, as a Staten Island farmer experimenting in horticulture, he helped to found a county agricultural society whose constitution he authored, emphasizing "Moral and Intellectual Improvement" as the goal of agrarian life.[24]

Thus, despite a certain insouciant quality in Olmsted's youth, when by his own account he endlessly roamed the Connecticut hills with a fishing rod or gun, there is a salient moral motive in Olmsted's writings on landscape design. Fundamentally, he worked for a humane environment because he believed that man could be ennobled or degraded according to the quality of his surroundings. Like Whitman, he loved urban life in all its cultural diversity and complexity. Olmsted never subscribed to the idea that city and country stood in opposition or that urban America was the blight in a pastoral or edenic nation. Moreover, his visit in 1852 to the North American Phalanstery near Red Bank, New Jersey, convinced him that agrarian, utopian communities lacked a rich educational and cultural dimension. His faith lay in the nice balance of city and suburb in a technologically advanced age of rail and electricity.

Yet the urban scene as he perceived it troubled Olmsted deeply. For along with its crowding came the disease, misery, crime, and vice that Olmsted believed made people brutish. Turned thus selfish, insensitive to others, and incommunicative, these urban disaffected became for Olmsted the modern barbarians.

Olmsted's antidote to the trend toward barbarous cities was environmental design for humane purpose. Especially did Olmsted regard America as politically and socially susceptible to the advance of civilization. He saw an important distinction between democratic crudities and the pioneering conditions of a new culture. While in California drafting vast landscape plans for the Mariposa Company Estate in 1863, Olmsted saw beneath the abandonment of refinements and elegant manners a socially tolerant and even generous spirit that characterized "the chief *moral growth* of the pioneer state."[25] Though Olmsted never completed his planned book to justify the growth and structure of American society, he sustained his conviction of a progressing American culture. His landscape designs were intended to hasten that cultural progress, that is, to move forward the spiritual and environmental reform of America.

To a great extent Olmsted saw himself as a social engineer, though significantly his cohort paid tribute to the artist. Charles Eliot Norton called him "first in the production of great works which answer the needs . . . of our immense and miscellaneous democracy," and Daniel Burnham, the prominent Chicago architect of the late nineteenth century, spoke of Olmsted as an artist who "paints with lakes and wooded slopes; with lawns and banks and forest-covered hills; with mountain-sides and ocean views."[26] Significantly, these phrases complement those Olmsted himself had used when as a young man he thought about Eaton Park near Chester, England. Then he defined the landscape architect as one who "with far-reaching conception of beauty and designing power, sketches the outline, writes the colors, and directs the shadows of a picture so great that Nature shall be employed upon it for generations, before the work he has arranged for her shall realize his intentions."[27] This conception is of the landscape architect as artist posthumously creative, with the landscape itself as his kinetic sculpture. (It was a personally enduring definition which Olmsted paraphrased in a letter forty years later.) And he accepted the consensus of "a large body of men of influence" that he had elevated landscape design from a trade to an art.[28]

Yet he understood his to be a utilitarian, moral, and socially influential art. Importantly, he projected its societal fulfillment into the future. As he surveyed the extent of his work, he counted "scattered through the country, seventeen large public parks, many more smaller ones, many more public or semi-public works." After their creation, he notices, a majority of them have "been more or less barbarously treated." Undaunted, Olmsted sees them a century ahead of "spontaneous public demand" or that of the American cognoscenti. No matter, for Olmsted's deep pleasure is in the educative use of his parks, which he understood to be intrinsically civilizing.[29]

In his forty active years in landscape architecture, Olmsted created parks in urban and suburban Chicago, Buffalo, Cleveland, Baltimore, Montreal, Boston, and Brooklyn, to name only some prominent urban centers. Of course he remains most closely identified with Central Park, its New York City site originally one of slaughterhouses, pigsties, and bone-boiling works, its soil poor, its terrain altogether unpromising. To fulfill the aesthetic objective of the park, namely, the moral betterment of society, Olmsted and his partner, Calvert Vaux, had to superintend, design, defend, argue, and contend for a landscape virtually of the mind's eye alone. Their work expressed physically a kind of urban idealism as it brought together certain aspirations of the utopians, the liberal Christians, and the Transcendentalists. These groups hoped that Central Park would be central to human community, would alleviate the squalor of slum life, would help to change antisocial behavior in its recreational uses, and would embody "in natural forms the spirit of secular institutions."[30]

Olmsted's biography shows his continuous battles with politicians and editors on behalf of the integrity and realization of his desgns. Radically in America he changed the concept of landscape architecture from decoration to the practice of morality. His art was not conscious self-expression but an effort at social betterment. And it is here, at the question of motive, that Olmsted reveals himself as an ideological descendant of Edward Johnson, of Joel Barlow and Jedidiah Morse. For, like them, he was a social programmer for the New Earth. Olmsted's social engineering remains of course innovative in a context of urban planning and demographic development. But within the tradition of the New Earth in American literature, Frederick Law Olmsted is a logical, lineal descendant of writers whose social programs for environmental reform had been committed to print since the seventeenth century.

While looking briefly here at Whitman's contemporary nonpoetic proponents of the American New Earth, we can take another measure of these entrenched values of environmental reform by seeing their presence in a work considered to be a landmark of the conservationist movement. For that expansive strain of empiricism and pragmatism evident in *The Wonder-Working Providence* and in *The Columbiad* finds expression in the mid-nineteenth century in the work of George Perkins Marsh, the Vermonter whose *Man and Nature* (1863; subtitled *Physical Geography as Modified by Human Action*) earned him the title, father of the conservation movement.

Together with Whitman, Marsh adhered to this commonplace nineteenth-century view of man's relation to the environment:

The *terrestrial* Destiny of man is to oversee the globe, which is a vast domain confided to his care. This important trust supposes a general and perfect cultivation of its surface, the fertilizing of its deserts, the draining of its swamps and morasses, the covering of its mountains with forests, the regulating of its streams,—in short, the adorning and embellishing of it by every means in his strength and intelligence.[31]

Couched in an American Fourierist tract, these remarks echo from the Enlightenment, and in a strictly terrestrial sense they went unchallenged by Whitman, who was "not the least doubtful . . . on any prospects of their [that is, the United States'] *material* success." [32] Yet from within this, his sole realm of intellect and imagination, Marsh was not so confident. Chapter and verse, his *Man and Nature* offered what Marsh's recent editor calls an "exposé of the damage man has done to the earth," one "more graphic and comprehensive than any later work on conservation."[33] Marsh's is a running indictment of human destruction from ignorance and heedlessness of soils, waters, plant and animal life. It is a lament in statistics—in animal census and measurement of rainfall, of dune migration, temperature changes, stunted and sparse growth. The essence of his complaint is to be found in Marsh's remark that "with stationary life . . . man at once commences an almost indiscriminate warfare upon all the forms of animal and vegetable existence around him, and as he advances in civilization, he gradually eradicates or transforms every spontaneous product of the soil he occupies."[34] To Marsh such transformation was of course not relevant to the poetic rendering of environmental reform under discussion here. It meant instead relentless damage and destruction, empirical proof of which earned him his conservationist patronymic.

Yet not without irony, because Marsh's presuppositions make him the pragmatic counterpart of the poet and show as well a cultural debt reaching back to Edward Johnson. For Marsh's deepest conviction in *Man and Nature* is that, having recognized the extent of environmental damage caused by man, man himself can proceed rationally to correct his own mistakes. He is confident that in the natural world science and technology enable reparation or *human* error. To Marsh, man's power before an "impotent" nature "tends to prove that . . . he is not of her, that he is of more exalted parentage, and belongs to a higher order of existence than those born of her womb and submissive to her dictates." On a plane exalted beyond the natural world, man's "utmost ingenuity and energy must be

tasked to renovate a nature drained by his improvidence, of fountains which a wise economy would have made plenteous and perennial sources of beauty, health, and wealth."[35]

Importantly, Marsh recognizes the aesthetic dimension in human
change to the environment. His own intermittent efforts at literary
description are pompous and sentimental (e. g., "Flora is already
plaiting her sylvan wreath before the corn flowers which are to deck
the garland of Ceres have waked from their winter's sleep"), but
Marsh's vision of desirable environmental change includes aesthetics
as well as utility. He may find it pointless ("rash and unphilo-
sophical . . . unprofitable") to speculate on future technology or on
the limits of man's power over the earth, but developments in steam,
telegraphy, and explosives encourage this son of Vermont's Green
Mountains to anticipate the day when man can make the most craggy
of the alps "support a vegetable covering" or plant for forest "large
extents of denuded rock."[36] His ideal is that man, guided by science,
"make himself, on a grand scale, a geographical power." As his
editor, David Lowenthal, says of his thinking, "Increasingly dubious
about political and social progress, Marsh never abandoned his faith
in science. . . . Marsh reiterates his belief that man can control the
environment for good as well as for ill."[37] At base, Marsh is
optimistic in his belief that man can engineer the New Earth after all.

As an exponent of nineteenth-century American science (if lacking
its academic credential), Marsh warrants brief attention here because
Man and Nature proves that imperatives of environmental reform did
not endure solely in belles lettres but flourished as well in writing
that furthered the quantification and the blueprinting which Johnson
and Barlow needed as indices of progress and guides for continuity
and which sustained both of those writers ideologically as it
weakened them aesthetically. Marsh proves the endurance of their
engineering mentality in the mid-nineteenth century, and *Man and
Nature* takes its place as the materialistic obverse of *Leaves of Grass.*
It is with careful qualification that Marsh and Whitman would agree
to the view of William Dean Howells's fictional Silas Lapham, who
recounts the hard work of land clearance and concludes, "I say, the
landscape was made for man, and not man for the landscape."[38]

Whitman of course had the problem of inventing a poetic landscape, one sustained in language alone. And like Gilpin, Olmsted, and

Marsh, he needed some philosophy or idea on which to build his poetic themes or convictions on America. He needed a principle of coherence beyond chauvinism, one that could enable him to integrate history, geography, and art. Stovall, once again, suggests the specific sources for Whitman's philosophy, which points in turn to his poetic representation of the American New Earth. Of particular importance was the epochal interpretation of history in Victor Cousin's *History of Modern Philosophy*, which, based upon a historical structure, derived theoretically from Hegel's dialectic. It emphasized that history is the " 'manifestation of God's supervision of humanity' " and that in the third of the three epochs comprising all of history, the *infinite* (geographically centered in Asia) and the *finite* (located in Europe) would fuse in America, which geographically combines characteristics of the other two. This third epoch is the focus of a different book which Stovall believes may have had "great influence" on *Leaves of Grass*. It is Arnold Guyot's *The Earth and Man* (1849), based upon a series of Boston lectures endorsed by Louis Agassiz, George Ticknor, Charles Sumner, and Benjamin Pierce, among others. Originally published in 1849, the work was revised in the following year and went through four printings. There was a copy of *The Earth and Man* available for Whitman's use in the Brooklyn Public Library.[39]

Guyot describes the destined steps by which the civilized European seeks out the New World, transplants to it his domestic animals, and begins to exploit the incredible fertility of an America "glutted with its vegetable wealth." Even in its English translation the geographer's rhetoric is taut with the suspense of the present progressive. Of the Revolution he says, "The hour of independence has struck; the fruit is ripe; it drops from the tree." In the present the Americans' "appointed task . . . is to work the virgin soil, and the wealth of the land Providence has granted to him, for his own benefit and that of the whole world." He predicts cosmic unity ("Steam will soon join the shores of the Atlantic and the Pacific, and place the United States on a great highway from Europe to China"), and he calls America "the young man, full of fire and energy," at once practical, shrewd, and active. Though America cannot, says Guyot, fulfill "her destinies" without the stimulus of European intelligence, the imminent epoch will reveal the immensity of "the importance of America to the entire race of man." He concludes his work with a peroration ringing with the millennial fervor we have seen in writings onward from the seventeenth century:

> A new work is preparing. . . . To what people shall it belong to carry out this work into reality? The law of history replies, to a new people. And to what continent? The geographical march of civilization tells us, to a new continent west of the Old World—to America.

Because he believes that scientifically verifiable events indicate the future, Guyot boldly predicts that racial distinctions will disappear in an emancipated and libertarian America and that "every language" and "every character" will blend into "one nationality." He reiterates the idea of the American Enlightenment that the immigrant sheds his social and political past at the threshold of the New World. Then he moves to validate his scientific predictions with Christian eschatology. "And what is the vital principle which we find at the very root of this nation?" he asks. "It is the gospel. . . . Luther drew the Bible forth from the dust of libraries, where it lay forgotten, at the moment when Columbus discovered the New World; will any one believe that here was only an accidental coincidence?" Guyot concludes, not with the possibility of human invulnerability to American geographical problems, but with assertion of achieved human mastery over that environment. His "last characteristic" of the United States is its

> greater emancipation from the dominion of nature. . . . Man, the master, now explores its vast territory. A perpetual movement, a fever of locomotion, rages from one end of the continent to the other. The American uses things without allowing himself to be taken captive by them. We behold everywhere the free will of man over-mastering nature. . . . The great social country wins all interest, and all affection; it overmatches entirely geographical country.[40]

In Guyot we see a very familiar composite of ideas present in the American literature we have reviewed from the seventeenth century onward, and immediately familiar from Barlow's *Columbiad*. Seen in its historical context, the popularity of *The Earth and Man* at mid-century shows the continuing embedding in American culture of these ideas on the New Earth. Guyot's is only the modern, nineteenth-century method of its proof, a scientific rationale based in his successive chapters on geography, geology, botany, zoology, and climatology.

What Guyot, together with contemporary lecturers in astronomy and geology, especially may have provided for Whitman is, first, the idea of geographical and historical coherence with particular emphasis on America. Guyot's is one printed study that worked at the level of philosophy rather than on a journalistic plane of chauvinism and cant. Moreover, a scholar like Guyot invoked the terminology of the sciences (accompanied, of course, by measurements of time and space in the "——illions") and thus so expanded Whitman's own lexicon and conception of time and space that his thought, as Gay Wilson Allen writes, "carried him both emotionally and intellectually almost the whole distance to his emancipation from both human and finite time, for he assumed that the creative process in the universe (or plurality of universes) is eternal." What's more, Guyot (or the synopsis of his work which appeared in the *Whig Review* for September 1851) may have provided Whitman the basis for acceptance of unity in the diversity and multiplicity in the cosmos. Stovall reads Guyot's "mode of progress" as "diversity, the establishment of difference" whose "end is a new and harmonious organic unit." Whitman himself thus speaks theoretically of a United States in which "history and humanity seem to seek to culminate," which is definitely "the grand producing land of nobler men and women" and "the modern composite nation . . . welcoming all immigrants—accepting the work of our own interior development, as the work fitly filling ages to come."[41]

Thus far in this Americanist education Whitman is really consonant with his predecessors Joel Barlow and Edward Johnson, both of whom understood a religiophilosophical coherence in the cosmos just as they believed in America's cosmic destiny through time. Whitman's radical departure from them, and from Cooper and Bancroft as well, lies not in his philosophical differences but in his methods of mimesis of the New Earth. For as social programmers, all these others were obligated to chronicle and interpret the transitory phenomena of the material world, which Emerson well understood to be a literary trap because he saw the constraints upon a writer caught up in these ephemera, no matter how epochally auspicious they might appear to be. "Soon these improvements and mechanical inventions will be superseded," he wrote, "these modes of living lost out of memory; the cities rotted, ruined by war, by new inventions, by new seats of trade, or the geologic changes; all gone." [42] Emerson's is no futuristic version of the *ubi sunt* motif but a call for recognition that the literary voice alone can transcend material flux. Within this discussion his comment goes far toward explaining the achievement of Whitman's New Earth in poetry, for Whitman understood and believed in—and risked the creation of—a world autonomous in language alone.

Whitman urges us toward that edifice of the mind as he conceives it. In 1852, when he clipped from *Graham's Magazine* the reprinted essay, "Imagination and Fact," Whitman bracketed and underlined this sentence: "The mountains, rivers, forests, and the elements that gird them round about, would be only blank conditions of matter, if the mind did not fling its own divinity around them." Stovall reports that Whitman "drew a line to the bottom of the page where he wrote in ink: 'This I think is one of the most indicative sentences I ever read.' " Stovall remarks on the newness of the idea to Whitman, who just a few years later would not have found the idea of poetic transformation of matter to be particularly striking. [43] It makes the obvious explicit to say that Whitman's New Earth can succeed in poetry because he grasped early-on in his career this elemental function of literature. But it is a function that neither Joel Barlow nor Edward Johnson could have understood. Aesthetically constrained by their programs and doctrines on environmental reform in America, they took on the literary task to edify a national scheme, especially when it was (in Johnson) God's own. Their approach was in part that of the engineer. As for the process of poetry, they understood it principally as embellishment or as a vehicle of social planning.

For Whitman, of course, poetry was not decorative (much less artifactual), and his New Earth would be vindicated as a construct solely of the imagination. In *Calamus* he says outright that he leaves no "labor-saving machine," "discovery," "wealthy bequest," record

of public heroism, or bookish monument of the intellect or of literature presumed to be precious, recondite, arcane. "But a few carols
vibrating through the air I leave."[44]

Of course he acknowledges nationalistically that the matter of
America is compelling and inspiring to its writers. And in his survey
of this literary matter we find history and geography intertwined
when Whitman lists as poetically useful the origin of "these States,"
"Washington, '76, the picturesqueness of old times, the war of 1812
and the sea-fights; the incredible rapidity of movement and breadth
of area." To the American litterateurs comes the opportunity to
"fuse and compact the South and North, the East and West, to
express the native forms, situations, scenes, from Montauk to California, and from the Saguenay to the Rio Grande." But when
Whitman boasts, "I skirt sierras, my palms cover continents," we are
alert to the boast of geographic comprehension in the imagination
alone. His is the mind's grasp of America, a point verified when in
Song of Myself he says, "I am afoot with my vision." Charles
Feidelson remarks that along with other American romantics
Whitman inherits the basic problem of romanticism: the vindication
of imaginative thought in a world grown abstract and material." It
may be fair to say that Whitman achieves that sense of an ineffable
reality beyond the bourn of language through a diction strikingly
materialistic. But unlike those other writers confronting the
American environment with reformist motives, he understood the
necessity of the imagination to transcend the sociopolitical plane of
experience. As Fussell says, "Whitman's new world is the world of the
imagination, a poetic world of rhythm, language, metaphor, syntax."
Whitman himself said in his 1855 preface to *Leaves of Grass,* "the
land and sea, the animals, fishes and birds, the sky of heaven and the
orbs, the forests, mountains and rivers, are not small themes—but
folks expect of the poet to indicate more than the beauty and dignity which always attach to dumb real objects—they expect him to
indicate the path between reality and their souls."[45]

Whitman's well-documented engagement with the entity of language bears especially on his representation of an ideographic
America, this "permanent edifice" of the mind alone. In this short
passage, wisely omitted from all but the first version of *By Blue
Ontario's Shore* (1856), Whitman announced his attempt to develop

a theory of language for poetry and to define a truly national language, one distinctly modern. Such language must also capture the ineffable even as it encompasses all human emotions.

> Language-using controls the rest;
> Wonderful is language!
> Wondrous the English language, language of live men,
> Language of ensemble, powerful language of resistance,
> Language of a proud and melancholy stock, and of all who aspire,
> Language of growth, faith, self-esteem, rudeness, justice,
>   friendliness, amplitude, prudence, decision, exactitude,
>   courage,
> Language to well-nigh express the inexpressible,
> Language for the modern, language for America.[46]

The dreariness of celebration decreed but not rendered ought not to mask the importance of these lines as a statement of intention, in fact of poetic theory. Whitman's America reverts to John Winthrop's City upon a Hill in its metaphoric reality, but unlike the sectarian who can be comforted by doctrinal truth when his own powers of language are exhausted, Whitman sustains his America only as long as his own verbal powers remain intact and vital. It is the continuous "language-using" the keeps him in control of (i.e., in creation of) his America. It is the key to his success as well as the necessity for his survival. Continuously he must reinvent America in words. He puts his case in *Thou Mother with Thy Equal Blood:*

> Brain of the New World, what a task is thine,
> To formulate the Modern—out of the peerless grandeur of
>   the modern,
> Out of thyself, comprising science, to recast poems, churches,
>   art,
> (Recast, may-be discard them, end them—may-be their work
>   is done, who knows?)
> By vision, hand, conception, on the background of the mighty
>   past, the dead,
> To limn with absolute faith the mighty living present.[47]

Immediately Whitman acknowledges that what is modern contains "the essence of the by-gone time." Of particular importance here, however, is his vow to "limn with absolute faith," to sustain the poetic America from a necessary confidence. The mind may build the permanent edifice that is America, but only by an unremitting inventiveness, a quality Feidelson identifies in Whitman as "exploration as a mode of existence."[48]

Of course Whitman arrogates to himself the powers of genesis. Only the poet as maker can boast of this promise to "make the continent indissoluble," and only the cosmic "I" can invoke phrases of national procreation ("This day I am jetting the stuff of far more arrogant republics. . . . Every hour the semen of centuries, and still of centuries . . . I pour the stuff to start sons and daughters to fit these States"). The begetting of America in "carols," in "songs," self-consciously in immaterial entities tasks the poet endlessly. His is no social program but a "programme of chants . . . shooting in pulses of fire ceaselessly to vivify all." Astonishing is his brief meditation in *Starting from Paumanok* on those who were the foci of spiritual vitality in the past (poets, priests, martyrs, artists, and others). All have his respect, including the "language-shapers on other shores," but "dismissing it/I stand in my place with my own day here."[49]

His poetic declaration of independence from the past, discursive as it is, forces readers to anticipate the supranational, the modern, the full compass of human feeling in his singular poetic world. Whitman's own anxiety can be inferred in his musings on the endurance of aesthetic experience, which is to say, the reforming of the inner life:

> The gist of histories and statistics as far back as the records
>   reach is in you this hour, and myths and tales the same,
> If you were not breathing and walking here, where would they
>   all be?
> The most renown'd poems would be ashes, orations and plays
>   would be vacuums.
> All architecture is what you do to it when you look upon it.[50]

Though Whitman throws to the reader, to his "scholars dear," the problem of continuously enlivening literature, this problem reverts to him in two ways. For poetry must begin with him, with the maker as architect. The breathing, walking respondent to poetry only becomes so from Whitman's own tutelage. Thus the poet is both architect and shaper of responses to it. "Ashes" and "vacuums" are the specter of his own failure.

Without doctrine, then, and repudiating ideology, Whitman assumes the creation of America and promises its embodiment in words: "See, in my poems, cities, solid, vast, inland, with paved streets, with iron and stone edifices, ceaseless vehicles, and commerce."[51] His will be the real city "where no monuments exist to heroes but in the common words and deeds." "One with the rest," this poet-democrat has his modern banner of the vernacular, En Masse, and his are "exulting words, words to Democracy's lands." The words of poetry, of "the real poems" as distinct from spurious ones ("merely pictures"), are not suggestions or symptoms or approaches to essence but are qualitatively the essence itself:

> The words of the singers are the hours or minutes of the light or
>   dark, but the words of the maker of poems are the general,
>   light or dark.
> . . . .
> The singers do not beget, only the Poet begets.[52]

The Whitman who late in life confided to Horace Traubel that he sometimes considered *Leaves of Grass* to be "only a language experiment" confirms what his musings on words have suggested all along: that the "words of true poems" comprise a cosmos all by themselves.[53] He adopted this idea early, in 1856, when in the margin of a review he clipped and saved Whitman wrote, "Every first-rate poet is felt to be the regent of a separate sphere, and the master of a complete poetic world of his own."[54] We must look for Whitman's American New Earth, then, as a "heart's geography's map" made and validated solely in the words that are respirant from the poet's mind.

II

The Song of the Broad-Axe, which is just such a "map," has been examined for its political, religious, and psychoanalytic meanings but interests us here for the successful rendering of the American New Earth within a self-enclosed poetic world. Among the *Chants Democratic*, which few readers find to represent Whitman at his best, *The Song of the Broad-Axe* embodies ideas on environmental reform in a

millennial America in ways that encourage acclaim for aesthetic
achievement. In context of *Leaves of Grass,* the *Song* is an elaboration upon and companion piece to Whitman's masterpiece, *Song of
Myself.* Evidently Whitman cared to realize from the *Broad-Axe* a
new national symbol, for in a preparatory note he wrote, "Make it
the American emblem preferent to the eagle," his sense of that
official bird probably like Hawthorne's—of an "unhappy fowl."[55]

Whitman means instead to realize the axe as "the mighty and
friendly emblem of the power of my own race, the newest, largest
race" (83). His attentive revisions of his *Song* between 1856 and
1881 suggest continuous connection with the poem and may indicate
serious political intention to supplant the bird of prey with the artifact symbolic of human creativity in the new continent. Intentions
notwithstanding, our concern here is to recognize those poetic
powers by which Whitman embodies themes of environmental
reform with the aesthetic success that eluded American writers for
some two centuries.

First, his literary relation to the America of his vision is very different from those of his predecessors concerned with the New Earth.
They maintain a discursive distance, while he speaks intimately. It is
significant that Whitman does not immediately present his credential
as speaker in the poem. We meet him obliquely in the second stanza;
only after he has dazzlingly transformed the broad-axe into a symbol
does he announce his poetic intention and begin to reveal his own
identity:

> Long varied train of an emblem, dabs of music,
> Fingers of the organist skipping staccato over the keys of the
>   great organ.   [8–9]

His design is deliberately improvesational. As the maker of music, his
fingers will skip staccato over the banks of keys; the music will come
in "dabs." (Later he will remind readers that the "loose drift of
character, the inkling through random types" is his way to work.)
Refusing familiar set forms, he yet promises desultorily a complete-
ness and focus: shapes of strength and its attributes, masculinity. But
the speaker of this poeem is present here only as the fingers of the
musician, not even as the whole man, much less the composer. In a
pattern typical of the poem, Whitman states his relation to the world

of his poem only after he has demonstrated it. He withholds himself until he has proven his powers.

Accordingly, when next the persona comes before us he has metamorphosed into the blacksmith, a perfectly democratic self claiming manufacture of the axe and, metaphorically, authorship of the American panorama which he has put before us (and to which we shall turn presently). Here he pauses to define the poet in the metaphor of the smith:

> The forger at his forge-furnace and the user of iron after him,
> The maker of the axe large and small, and the welder and temperer,
> The chooser breathing his breath on the cold steel and trying the
>   edge with his thumb,
> The one who clean-shapes the handle and sets it firmly in the
>   socket.   [73–76]

It is of course the poet as forger, maker, welder, temperer—and now as chooser, governing the poem and confident of his symbol, which is strengthened as the poem has proceeded. Directly Whitman will use it even more strenuously, to cleave deep into history. And only after we have participated in Whitman's scenes of the imagined past and taken his lesson in what is the specious and the valid America does he come forward in the persona of the Literatus to speak of the transforming power of poetry. He does so with a certain indirection born not of coyness but of invitation to readers to crystallize into thought the experience of this poem:

> All waits or goes by default till a strong being appears;
> A strong being is the proof of the race and of the ability of the
>   universe,
> When he or she appears materials are overaw'd,
> The dispute on the soul stops,
> The old customs and phrases are confronted, turn'd back, or laid
>   away.   [137–141]

In these lines converge the persona, the "strong being" or Literatus, and the experience of poetry itself as creation, renewal, and transformation. Since there can be no more powerful claim for the poet, Whitman risks that readers' own experience of the *Song* up to this point corroborates him. Then, assured that this is a convocative poem and that the persona has proven himself, Whitman comes boldly forward in the role of the visionary embodiment of America, the "I" who celebrates the ascendance of the nation repeatedly in the oft-cited line, "The shapes arise!"

In careful stages Whitman has traveled the distance from the organist's fingers to the ego of the nation, along the way revealing an artful closeness to the American New Earth not shared by those of his predecessors who cared as fervently as he to celebrate it. For the others had kept a distinct literary distance from their subject while asserting their authority on it—Edward Johnson as the spokesman for God's truth, Joel Barlow as the Homeric genius of the Western Hemisphere, Cooper as the American gentleman, and George Bancroft as the genteel Miltonic high priest. All of these writers mistook Olympian perspectives for personae of authority. Theirs were the assertions of understanding of America but not the renderings of it. As speakers they remain consequently aloof from the America of their conceptions. Theirs are programs to impose, Whitman's a personal vision to evoke. The fingers of the organist, the blacksmith, and finally the "I" who is "the proof of the race" and not its spiritual aristocrat form together the democratic identity of the writer who takes personal responsibility not only to represent but to embody the New Earth of his vision.

The Song of the Broad-Axe is, however, a vision realized from the materials of American culture, which brings Whitman potentially to the problem which his predecessors never solved, namely, the aesthetic limitations of materialism. As futurists, both Joel Barlow and George Bancroft failed miserably to evoke the apotheosis of human happiness which is the ideological culmination of environmental reform. Barlow, his vocabulary exhausted, his technological visions all set forth, his invention done, gives us the mimesis of the blocked imagination when he offers readers a statuary garden to represent the fulfillment of material and moral progress. Intending to represent apotheosis, he instead suggests terminus. He, together with the other writers we have reviewed, tries to represent the American New Earth through the quantifying and amplifying of materials, as a consequence of which it is static, crowded, and airless. Apart from Edward Johnson, whose prose is fiercely energetic, these celebrants of the New Earth gloss their lack of literary vitality with words of motion.

In the *Broad-Axe* Whitman overcomes the airless fixity of a materialistic New Earth. From the grand embrace of his setting (at the conclusion of which Whitman anchors us in "lands of the make of the axe"), the poet begins "skipping staccato" in associational images, which may pose problems in reading, since in every line are several figures, only one of which (and often a tangential one) is the pivot to the next complete image. We move, for instance, from the "sylvan hut" and cleared garden plot to the leaves on which rain-drops are tapping after a storm—which calls up private, presumably inner, storms (the "wailing and moaning at intervals") before the poet brings to mind those elsewhere, at sea, and the desperate cutting of the masts under threat of capsizing. The imperiled ships "on their beam end" call up other beams, the timbers of "old-fashion'd houses and barns"; and both the "sentiment" and the "old-fashion'd" nature of them elicit qualities of remembrance and thus of the past itself, a time of beginnings, of the "voyage at a venture" of men, families, whole communities.

So from "the log at the wood-pile" which begins this section of the poem, we move in resonance of the wood and steel of the axe to reach national origins and the continuing process of settlement:

> The voyage of those who sought a New England and found it, the
>   outset anywhere,
> The settlements of the Arkansas, Colorado, Ottawa, Willamette,
> The slow progress, the scant fare, the axe, rifle, saddle-bags.
>   [33–35]

Here Whitman names some of those lands he had earlier welcomed and immediately begins the panorama of Americans creating their culture. Principally we see them at work, though some seem too fixed, like carved figures in a model of America ("The butcher in the slaughter-house, the hands aboard schooners and sloops, the rafts-man, the pioneer,/Lumbermen in their winter camp"). Perhaps sensing this, Whitman enlivens the figures with particular detail ("stripes of snow on the limbs of trees, the occasional snapping"). He must do so, which is to say he must sustain belief in the authority of his imagination, because he aspires to be the "strong being" to overawe matter, to grasp the "long varied train of an emblem." He aspires to nothing less than the embodiment of the nation.

Vitally important to Whitman's diminishment of material early in the *Song* is his exaltation of "actions that rely on themselves" (38). It is a phrase apparently offered in passing, its import for the poem unclear as it comes sandwiched between hirsute woodmen and "the American contempt for statutes and ceremonies." In fact, the reader may not at first notice Whitman's short phrase on self-relying actions because it sounds most like a mental jotting to himself (and may subconsciously elide "axe" with "action"). The rest of the poem, however, makes clear the importance of self-relying actions—and reveals the difference between the reformed environment of the real poet and that of the social programmer, versifier though he be.

For we are to see throughout the *Song* the constructive use of the broad-axe in America (in contrast to its destructive use in a benighted European past). The results, however, of the axe-work, namely, the objects constructed, threaten to take precedence over the actions of the building. The poet who in *Birds of Passage* said, "I believe materialism is true and spiritualism is true, I reject no part," ran the risk in *The Song of the Broad-Axe* of leaving readers principally with the materials of American culture. If "objects gross and unseen soul are one," Whitman nonetheless has a potential problem of America's emerging as an aggregation of "chef-d'oeuvres of engineering, forts, armaments."[56] No matter how splendid might be such a four-gated city of millennial America, the entity is per se inimical to his rendering of the experience of America. (It may be for this reason that Whitman avoids reference to the axe as a tool, that term emphatic of means to something else, and instead twice speaks of it as a weapon.) For to indicate America in its axe-work, that is, to locate its essence in the building of its material culture, is to risk obscuring the preeminence of "actions that rely upon themselves." Whitman must downplay the concrete results of those actions.

In part he does so with an emphasis upon the qualitative and the personal. Before plunging to the midst of the building trades, even before "the preparatory jointing, squaring, sawing, mortising," we hear

> The glad clear sound of one's own voice, the merry song, the
>   natural life of the woods, the strong day's work,
> The blazing fire at night, the sweet taste of supper, the talk, the
>   bed of hemlock-boughs and the bear-skin.   [43–44]

Whitman's emphasis in the *Broad-Axe* on personal qualities, his re-

mark that "nothing endures but personal qualities" and that "the
floridness of the materials of cities shrivels before a man's or a
woman's look" (99, 136), directs readers preferentially toward what
is intrinsic to the self, a vitality adduced in the savoring of intimate,
casual experiences fully sufficient to life. His readers are to understand the supremacy of this vitality through all time:

> What always served and always serves is at hand.
> Than this nothing has better served, it has served all.
> . . . .
> Served not the living only then as now, but served the dead.
> [150–151, 165]

These lines, which conclude one stanza and frame another, open
cosmically what otherwise might be parochial. From such expan-
siveness in the *Broad-Axe* and elsewhere, Richard Chase says of
Whitman's view of history, "Despite all his appeals to the future
greatness of America there is nothing in this future which is not
merely a further revelation of the totally adequate dispensation
vouchsafed to Americans at the birth of the Republic." Chase goes
on, "Change is understood as a progressive discovery of something
already given, though not at first correctly or clearly perceived in its
entirety."[57] In the *Broad-Axe* Whitman distinguishes from
ephemeral material culture the enduring personal sufficiency
vouchsafed to all humankind forever.

Even so, the poet of the *Broad-Axe* must traffic in materials lest he
compromise his vision. Here are his scenes of a carpentered America:

> The house-builder at work in cities or anywhere,
> The preparatory jointing, squaring, sawing, mortising,
> The hoist-up of beams, the push of them in their places, laying
>   them regular,
> Setting the studs by their tenons in the mortises according as they
>   were prepared,
> The blows of mallets and hammers, the attitudes of the men,
>   their curv'd limbs,
> Bending, standing, astride the beams, driving in pins, holding on
>   by posts and braces,
> The hook'd arm over the plate, the other arm wielding the axe,

The floor-men forcing the planks close to be nail'd,
Their postures bringing their weapons downward on the bearers,
The echoes resounding through the vacant building;
The huge storehouse carried up in the city well under way,
The six framing-men, two in the middle and two at each end,
  carefully bearing on their shoulders a heavy stick for a
  cross-beam,
The crowded line of masons with trowels in their right hands
  rapidly laying the long side-wall, two hundred feet from
  front to rear,
The flexible rise and fall of backs, the continual click of the
  trowels striking the bricks,
The bricks one after another each laid so workmanlike in its
  place, and set with a knock of the trowel-handle,
The piles of materials, the mortar on the mortar-boards, and the
  steady replenishing by the hod-men.   [45–60]

We notice Whitman constantly pointing, not to the structures but to actions, as in the verbs of progression (bending, driving, holding, wielding, bringing) and in the pictorial details or "dabs" of vision ("the hook'd arm," "the flexible rise and fall of backs," the "knock of the trowel-handle," "the butter-colored chips flying off").

But finally the shapes are ineluctable. In the background, as through a screen, stands the house, while at the waterfront are "wharves, bridges, piers, bulk-heads, floats." These shapes are before us, fixed and finite. As Whitman put them there, he must contend with them, though potentially the poet has reached a cul-de-sac because the material culture of America seems preeminent after all. Focused, the aggregation of buildings seems to represent America despite his contrary emphasis on self-relying actions. Only later in the poem will he say of himself as Literatus, "When he or she appears materials are overaw'd" (139). The question at this point is how. It is crucial that Whitman mimetically reassert the axe-work so as to diminish the powerful presence of material symbols of America.

He does it with creative axing—fire-axing—of the very houses in whose construction we have engaged as readers. The abrupt entry of city firemen to a scene in want of one preparatory wisp of smoke has seemed to some to indicate Whitman's lack of control of his poem. [58]

But it does so only if *The Song of the Broad-Axe* is read as a narrative rather than an associative, structurally improvisational poem. Viewed as a reemphasis of the ineffable America of self-relying actions, the firemen with their "crash and cut away of connecting wood-work" are a brilliant strategic image at this point. For Whitman gives them parity with the carpenters who first worked that wood, just as the sailors "cutting away masts" in the storm are as welcome as the shipwrights who swing "their axes on the square-hew'd log shaping it toward the shape of a mast" (62). Shipyard or housing site, firestorm or storm at sea—all occasion the actions representative of the essential America, to which "hotels of granite and iron" or "the best-built steamships" are irrelevant. The material structures only refer to enacted energy as Whitman's America is proven in "muscle and pluck forever" (94) and not in its engineering.

Dauntless animal spirits, however, cannot by themselves constitute the American New Earth, which to Whitman is attainable by the very nexus of environmental and spiritual reforms that had been stanchions of faith for his predecessors. In *The Song of the Broad-Axe* Whitman's New Earth ("where a great city stands") is a collective state of mind expressed in human relationships to be found in the here and now and made plausibly exemplary because these relationships are selected "dabs" from life and do not pretend to be all of it. Refusing to confine his exemplary city in American space or to bind it to a calendric schedule, Whitman manifests it in the present, insisting all the while that it exists in the past and is vouchsafed to the future. In an excruciatingly long periodic sentence that holds readers half-tantalized to think the poet will, after all, place that city in time and space, we see instead a parade of virtues in a qualitative City upon a Hill. It is one where the brawniest orators and bards are beloved, where "common words and deeds" form the monuments to heroes, where thrift, prudence, equanimity, spiritual speculation, sexual equality, fidelity, health, and cleanliness all inhere in human community (115–34).

Whitman's spiritually regenerate city emerges in a lesson alternately of affirmation and repudiation—of what the city, America, is and is not. With enduring humanity as his defining criterion, Whitman rejects "teeming manufacturing," "a prepared constitution," and "the best-built steamships. Located not in tall buildings, cosmopolitan marketplaces, or in "the best libraries and schools," nor bound in "respectability," "theology," "tuition," "society," "traditions," "statute-books," the greatest city is paradoxically ideographic and self-renewing, yet fully embedded in the America that exists now and is therefore accessible in the present. In this respect Whitman parts company from Johnson and Barlow, from Bancroft and Cooper. For his millennial "great city" need not, like theirs, be yearned for in grammar of the subjunctive. It does not teeter on conditions to be met. Nor is it predicated upon moral evolution or by that now-debased doctrine of the perfectibility of man. Whitman's millennial America exists, rather, as a spiritual intaglio present in the continent. It is irrefutable, irrefragable, and endlessly durable.

Now we can see what larger poetic opportunities Whitman enables for himself. Since his America of the spirit is unassailable, it can coexist without threat or taint along with the tawdry, the disreputable, the craven, the murderous:

> The shape of the sly settee, and the adulterous unwholesome
>   couple,
> The shape of the gambling-board with its devilish winnings and
>   losings,
> The shape of the step-ladder for the convicted and sentenced
>   murderer, the murderer with haggard face and pinion'd arms,
> The sheriff at hand with his deputies, the silent and white-lipp'd
>   crowd, the dangling of the rope.
>
> [228–32]

In such figures as these Whitman can, without diatribe or invective, encompass the tensions and polarities of the individual psyche (magnified in those of the culture) and avoid the sentimentality and one-sidedness that beset Bancroft and Cooper in their representations of America's spiritual biography. They (and Barlow before them) mistook the refinement of sensibility for moral progress and urged social evolution as an escape from the baseness of human nature. In a sense they suppressed or repudiated those very qualities that create rich tension in literature. Whitman well understood how confining was the programmatic and exclusive approach. As Tony Tanner reminds us, Whitman's "quarrel with existing conventions was that they did not allow enough of America into literature." The New England tradition, as Tanner remarks, "tended to extol a cultivated dignity of demeanor and a social formality which had no place in it for rough nonchalance."[59] If along with rough nonchalance we include the vernacular and an unflinching acknowledgment of human predations, of death, dark impulses, and violence, then Whitman's achievement in *The Song of the Broad-Axe* becomes even clearer. By embedding his atemporal millennial City of America in its larger social context (in fact, in creating his "greatest city" from the best parts or "dabs" of ambient America), Whitman follows his drive to "know all and expose it" without compromising his belief that the democratic principle had brought forth "a new earth and a new man."[60]

It remains to be said how Whitman uses themes explicitly of environmental reform without sounding like a social programmer, how within the world of the poem he can measure the New Earth in its conversion from "the solid forest" and can resort to his characteristic catalogs without seeming to present an inventory of the natural resources and the wood manufactory of the continent.

The essence of his success is Whitman's symbolic understanding of the broad-axe. For the implement which Cooper took to be a sign of political power and legitimacy in the process of civilization becomes in Whitman a fundamental symbol of life and of creation. Even those who interpret Whitman's reworking of *The Song of the Broad-Axe* as a sign of ongoing confusion must consider the aesthetic integrity of these first six lines, which Whitman never revised:

> Weapon shapely, naked, wan,
> Head from the mother's bowels drawn,
> Wooded flesh and metal bone, limb only one and lip only one,
> Gray-blue leaf by red-heat grown, helve produced from a little
>   seed sown,
> Resting the grass amid and upon,
> To be lean'd and to lean on.

Through these lines we move away from the axe-as-weapon and into the axe-as-newborn, at each step giving up the conventional denotative broad-axe as simultaneously we accept the figures of life.

Anatomically the flesh, bone, limb, and lip suffice; from closer human analogy we could rebel. More than superimposition, Whitman has caused a melding of the axe with the newborn so that they stand in mind, not as a metaphysical conceit but as a fusion of two figures. The axe *is* the newborn. When as leaf from seed Whitman rests the axe amid and upon the grass, we reassert in memory the context of a conventional axe, though in the mind's eye it is now realized as life. Throughout the poem the axe can revert to the lesser status of a sign, in fact to the *leitmotiv* in pioneering; but from that first stanza it is a fully realized symbol and can be summoned again to its organic office.[61]

Associationally, of course, Whitman can play freely on the ramifications of the axe, on metals and woods, on related tools, on such weaponry as the halberd and the ceremonial axe in the fasces of the Roman lictors. He saturates the past and all global space with the implicit presence of the axe. Yet this poet so often criticized (justly so) for stalling in endless catalogs shows in the *Broad-Axe* a fine restraint in letting the axe only be inferred in those contexts of its obvious use, for instance, in the scene of the firemen at work, in which the cutting tool is never named.

Throughout, the poet keeps alive the symbolic possibilities which he will realize later on in celebration of American environmental reform. The *symbolic* broad-axe even allows the poem to remain above political polemic when, looking into the benighted European past, the poet sees the headsman "wet and sticky" with blood and leaning "on a ponderous axe" since washed clean, indeed retired in disuse in the poet's beloved America. That European executioner's death-axe, no symbol of life or of creation, is instead but a sign of epochal transition into the New Earth wrought by the symbolic broad-axe, and evoked here as we see "the solid forest" transformed into arising shapes:

> The axe leaps!
> The solid forest gives fluid utterances,
> They tumble forth, they rise and form,
> Hut, tent, landing, survey,
> Flail, plough, pick, crowbar, spade,
> Shingle, rail, prop, wainscot, jamb, lath, panel, gable,

Citadel, ceiling, saloon, academy, organ, exhibition-house, library,
Cornice, trellis, pilaster, balcony, window, turret, porch,
Hoe, rake, pitchfork, pencil, wagon, staff, saw, jack-plane, mallet,
  wedge, rounce,
Chair, tub, hoop, table, wicket, vane, sash, floor,
Work-box, chest, string'd instrument, boat, frame, and what not,
Capitols of States, and capitol of the nation of States,
Long stately rows in avenues, hospitals for orphans or for the poor
  or sick,
Manhattan steamboats and clippers taking the measure of all seas.

[186–99]

This is one of the two places in the poem in which, in a manner of speaking, Whitman himself tumbles forth a seemingly endless list of things American. Here the objects are artifacts; earlier in the poem they were agricultural and metallic resources. For having been engaged in the making of a symbol and promised that "long varied train of an emblem," readers were at the outset launched in Whitman's litany of "all the earth's lands," both those fecund and "more hard-faced." Removed from the poetic context, Whitman's list of fruits and grains and metals is similar to that of Edward Johnson, Joel Barlow, or the geographer Jedidiah Morse. Too, his catalog of products manufactured principally of wood is not by itself easily distinguishable from theirs. Importantly, however, Whitman's shapes in wood and his list of food and fiber and of "manly and rugged ores" are not a utilitarian invoice for the nation. Nor are they an economic promise for the future. Rather, they form in the aggregate the sensuous character of his "heart's geography's map." The wainscot and workbox, the sugar and rice, flax and tin are not merchandise or commodity futures but qualitative images that furnish the imagined landscape of the poem. Further, they serve the purpose which Lawrence Buell finds to be central in Transcendental catalog rhetoric, namely, the manifestation of divine plentitude evincing a "cosmic unity in diversity."[62] Those readers who in the opening stanza of *The Song of the Broad-Axe* do the hard, responsive work of transforming axe to newborn are readied to move *from* literal meanings of the poet's words, and thus to recognize in both catalogs Whitman's geographic convocation.

We cannot but notice the easy transition from "solid forest" to the panoramic New Earth of a predominantly urban America. The forest gives its "fluid utterances" as its trees "tumble forth" only to "rise and form" in all the versatile shapes that bespeak the reformed environment of a millennial America. As the poet, Whitman has the prerogative not available to those of his predecessors attempting a mimetic correlate of a changing American landscape. His broad-axe, symbolic of life and of creativity, at once reforms the American environment and binds together the life of the nation. Whitman will close his poem with these millennial effusions:

> The main shapes arise!
> Shapes of Democracy total, result of centuries,
> Shapes ever projecting other shapes,
> Shapes of turbulent manly cities,
> Shapes of the friends and home-givers of the whole earth,
> Shapes bracing the earth and braced with the whole earth.
>
> [250–55]

Dynamic, communal, energetic, embraced and fortified, Whitman's New Earth lives within *The Song of the Broad-Axe* without obligation to sociopolitical or economic considerations. Within the symbolic realm of the work of art Whitman is free to omit searching questions on the value of wilderness. He is free of an obligatory reckoning on forest acreage lost. In fact, in the simple exchange of tree trunk for cornice, porch, tub, and so on, there is no diminishment but only augmentation as the poem makes its own economics.

Unsurprising, therefore, is Whitman's elaboration on this bounty of shapes as he begins to celebrate huge feats of American engineering and construction, thus showing one solution to the literary problem which James Russell Lowell thought the new technology posed, namely, to "find out what there is imaginative in steam and iron and telegraph wires":[63]

The shapes arise!
Shapes of factories, arsenals, foundries, markets,
Shapes of the two-threaded tracks of railroads,
Shapes of the sleepers of bridges, vast frameworks, girders, arches,

Shapes of the fleets of barges, tows, lake and canal craft, river craft,
Ship-yards and dry-docks along the Eastern and Western seas, and
   in many a bay and by-place,
The live-oak kelsons, the pine planks, the spars, the hackmatack-
   roots for knees,
The ships themselves on their ways, the tiers of scaffolds, the
   workmen busy outside and inside,
The tools lying around, the great auger and little augur, the adze,
   bolt, line, square, gouge, and bead-plane.

[207–15]

It is significant that after a great crescendo Whitman reverts to those hand tools that are kin to the axe. For now the poem becomes deeply personal as he fuses themes of environmental reform and of the spiritual vitality of America. Again, it is the symbolic mode that enables an aesthetic success that Whitman's predecessors never achieved. For their realms of American matter and spirit, precisely of the reformative environment and of the ineffable vitality of the nation, were conjoint but never merged. In the work of Edward Johnson, of Joel Barlow, of Bancroft and Cooper (not to mention related writers of the Puritan, Early National, and Romantic periods), convictions on environmental reform and social-spiritual regeneration in America form a nexus of themes mutually strengthening, interdependent, and verifiable one from another. But they reach only thematic conjunction and not fusion. When those writers confronted environmental modification or religiopolitical advances toward the millennial New Earth, they did so in alternating address. By turns they focused upon the American environment or upon the quality of the national spirit but within their work brought the two together only as coexisting but discreet parts of one ideology. It need hardly be said that aesthetic unity makes demands separate from those of ideological coherence, but these writers paid a price for not transcending a rhetoric of ideology.

Not Whitman. As a symbol his broad-axe can insinuate itself in fundamental, deeply personal parts of American life, because within the poem Whitman celebrates "shapes of the using of axes anyhow, and the users and all that neighbors them" (200). By extension the broad-axe brings to itself its total ambience, both terrestrial and human; its wielders and recipients alike:

Cutters down of wood and haulers of it to
    the Penobscot of Kennebec,
Dwellers in cabins among the Californian mountains or by the
    little lakes, or on the Columbia,
Dwellers south on the banks of the Gila or Rio Grande, friendly
    gatherings, the characters and fun,
Dwellers along the St. Lawrence, or north in Kanada, or down by
    the Yellowstone, dwellers on coasts and off coasts,
Seal-fishers, whalers, arctic seamen breaking passages through the
    ice.

[202–06]

Then can the poet extend the symbolic axe-work into the life cycle
in these images implicitly replicable throughout America:

The shapes arise!
The shape measur'd, saw'd, jack'd, join'd, stain'd,
The coffin-shape for the dead to lie within in his shroud,
The shape got out in posts, in the bedstead posts, in the posts of
    the bride's bed,
The shape of the little trough, the shape of the rockers beneath,
    the shape of the babe's cradle,
The shape of the floor-planks, the floor-planks for dancers' feet,
The shape of the planks of the family home, the home of the
    friendly parents and children,
The shape of the roof of the home of the happy young man and
    woman, the roof over the well-married young man and woman,
The roof over the supper joyously cook'd by the chaste wife, and
    joyously eaten by the chaste husband, content after his day's work.

[216–24]

Of course they are idealized tableaux, but that is exactly the point.
Immediately Whitman will counterbalance with figures of base acts
and feelings, of prodigality and shame; but at this moment he returns
to his "greatest city" of the exemplary America. This elaboration of
domestic images brings us back again to the quintessential America
of the spirit and to the "main shapes . . . of the friends and home-
givers of the whole earth" (249, 253) with which he will conclude his
poem. The coffin, the bridal bedposts, the cradle, and "planks of the

family home" are more than furnishings in a domestic emblem of America. And their fashioning from wood by the axe suggests much more than the poet's own carpentry. In the world of the symbolic broad-axe—of life and of creation—the symbol itself vivifies these artifacts. At the same time the insistent life cycle suffuses with vitality those objects that identify distinct stages of life. We thus have a true fusion, beginning with the America shaped from the "solid forest" and represented in the useful and unmistakable artifacts of death, of marriage, birth, and family life. The material America, wrought from "all the earth's lands," fuses with the millennial idea of the "greatest city," one embodied in a spiritualized (or, if one will, idealized) domestic life. Here Whitman's life cycle, begun with death in order to affirm life and in each image personal and communal, in turn imparts meaning to the wood forms of posts and rockers and planks. Life and creation resound as readers move back and forth between bedposts and marriage, between cradle and birth, between friends and family and floor-planks and roof. The personal qualities, the greatest city, and the arisen shapes whose meanings have been the experience of the poem—all converge at this point. It is one of integrated experience, and no component can be factored out. Here in poetry Whitman's New Earth is complete, dynamic in repose, at once attained yet ever imminent. In symbol, in his "hearts geography's map," Whitman locates the American New Earth.

III

In recognition of Whitman's achievement in elevating ideology to art, it is important to understand too the inverse relation of the poet to his source material. Specifically, in *The Song of the Redwood-Tree* (1873) Whitman's persona—that of the giant sequoia willing to be felled for the new race of Americans—is explicable only within the two-centuries-long ideology on the American New Earth. The speaker of this poem is the sequoia soon to be felled by the broad-axe of the lumbermen, and the poem is itself the "death-chant" of the redwood, albeit a celebratory one filled with the millennial themes we have examined in *The Song of the Broad-Axe*. The tree bids

Farewell my brethren,
Farewell O earth and sky, farewell ye neighboring waters,
My time has ended, my term has come.

[6–8]

But then the redwood proclaims faith in the millennial America long evolving geologically and humanistically. His is a chant "not of the past only but the future" (23).[64]

Readers have paired this poem with *The Prayer of Columbus* (1871), which was published in *Harper's Magazine* just one month after *The Song of the Redwood-Tree* in 1874. Frederik Schyberg particularly recognizes that the two belong in the Camden poems, those of an aging man in ill health, impaired and, in Allen's phrase, needing "to believe that what he had struggled in the past to accomplish would not be lost in the future."[65] Whitman's self-identification with Columbus suggests an act of faith in the enduring recognition of his own accomplishment. Pointing toward the future, the title vindicates the anguished speaker. In *The Song of the Redwood-Tree,* however, the choice of a seemingly doomed sequoia as a persona is less easily comprehensible. And when the hearer of the "death-chant" reports in the poem that in the echo of the teamsters' chains and axes he hears "the falling trunk and limbs, the crash, the muffled shriek, the groan" (75), the reader may well agree with the critic who writes that Whitman, like the tree, felt "doomed to a senseless extinction."[66]

Far from senseless, however, the felling of this sequoia is the moment of destiny fulfilled after a preparatory evolution:

The fields of nature long prepared and fallow, the silent, cyclic
    chemistry,
The slow and steady ages plodding, the unoccupied surface ripening,
    the rich ores forming beneath;
At last the New arriving, assuming, taking possession,
A swarming and busy race settling and organizing everywhere.
                                        [87–90]

As for the redwoods, they themselves "pledge" and "dedicate"

    To the new culminating man, to you, the empire new,
    You promis'd long . . .   [53–54]

This poem, it is true, lacks the compelling lyric depths of *Columbus,* largely because of Whitman's operatic structure of speakers and listeners and because of a certain sententiousness of syntax. But even as a public statement of faith in the nation's future, the demise of the redwood is not a loss. At the very least it signifies a destined transition long encoded in the cosmos. It is Gilpin's American destiny transacted at last.

Central to the poem is Whitman's effort to fuse American geography and humanity into one organic identity. To this end the redwood recounts as a personal narration the natural history of pre-colonial America:

You untold life of me,
And all you venerable and innocent joys,
Perennial hardy life of me with joys 'mid rain and many a
    summer sun,
And the white snows and night and the wild winds;
O the great patient rugged joys, my soul's strong joys unreck'd by
    man,
(For know I bear the soul befitting me, I too have consciousness,
    identity,
And all the rocks and mountains have, and all the earth,)
Joys of the life befitting me and brothers mine,
Our time, our term has come.

                                                    [24–32]

Whitman's meshing of geologic time with that of human history instances a theory of history philosophically discredited by R. G. Collingwood, though of course the poet works in a symbolic and not a philosophical mode. Here Whitman tries to resolve the problem of the representation of the true relation of Americans with their land. For since the seventeenth century the idea of an intrinsically regenerative American geography had abutted the idea that the New World itself was somehow exalted by the very presence of these chosen people, the Americans. In literature these ideas had been complicated by the chauvinism of critics who, as of the Early National period, anticipated a national literature as ample as the continent or as sublime as Niagara Falls—similes that asserted, without explanation, some qualitative parity of imaginative expression with geophysical phenomena. As we have noticed, Joel Barlow tried to use causality to clarify the relation between Americans, their geography, and spiritual-political regeneration; but he so muddled cause and effect that the issue was altogether confused.

Whitman tries another way, that of a mutual assimilation of qualities he believes to be indigenous to the geography with those he finds inherent to the new race of Americans. Thus his symbol of

American geography through time is his speaker, the sequoia with "foot-thick bark," "Down from its lofty top rising two hundred feet high" (21). Allen suggests that Whitman may have got the idea for the symbol from reading of recently felled sequoias, though, as a reader of Cooper's fiction, Whitman had a splendid antecedent in the towering pine by Lake Otsego in *Home as Found*. The pine's "Mass of green waved there in the fierce light when Columbus first ventured into the unknown sea." As Cooper's Eve Effingham exclaims, "When the Conqueror first landed in England this tree stood on the spot where it now stands!" Most important for Whitman, "Here is at last an American antiquity," and one which "tells the same glowing tale to all who approach it—a tale fraught with feeling and recollections."[67] As we know, this is the very kind of tale which Whitman's own redwood tells.

As for the symbol of American natural history, the redwood endows the new race of Americans with those qualities Whitman believes to be essential to the continental, expecially western, geography:

In them these skies and airs, these mountain peaks, Shasta, Nevadas,
These huge precipitous cliffs, this amplitude, these valleys,
* far Yosemite*
To be in them absorb'd, assimilated.

[41–43]

The assimilation of geography and the new race, however, is mutual, and Whitman uses the persona of the redwood to characterize the Americans in phrases suitable to describe the tree itself:

Here may he hardy, sweet, gigantic grow, here tower
  proportionate to Nature,
Here climb the vast pure spaces unconfined, uncheck'd by
  wall or roof,
Here laugh with storm or sun, here joy, here patiently inure,
Here heed himself, unfold himself, (not others' formulas heed,)
  here fill his time,
To duty fall, to aid, unreck'd at last,
To disappear, to serve.

[67–72]

Through the sensate and conscious sequoia Whitman characterizes the ascendant Americans as "The new society at last, proportionate to Nature" (99).

None of this, however, begins to explain why the redwoods must succumb or in Whitman's term, "abdicate," why they cannot in fact coexist with this "superber race." Significantly, when Whitman wrote *The Song of the Redwood-Tree* the public valuation of the American wilderness had never been higher, and politically as well as aesthetically the preservation of the wilds was being publicized as advantageous to the nation.[68] Within the poem itself there is no plea for necessary additional space for settlement, and Whitman's own deep reverence for the wondrous sequoia is never in doubt. To understand the poet's motives for the abdication of the tree, then, readers usually have reverted to the biography of an aging, ailing Whitman, his poetic power failing, his sense of his death heavy upon him. In this light *The Song of the Redwood-Tree* is seen as a projection of Whitman's own state of mind in the 1870s.

Yet within the poem the demise of the redwood is not treated poignantly or with pity. No aura of regret, ambiguity, or even sadness settles from Whitman's tone. Instead the sequoia addressed the ascendant *"culminating man"* in a sonorous and sapient voice:

> You unseen moral essence of all the vast materials of America,
>   (age upon age working in death the same as life,)
> You that, sometimes known, oftener unknown, really shape and
>   mould the New World, adjusting it to Time and Space,
> You hidden national will lying in your abysms, conceal'd but
>   ever alert,
> You past and present purposes tenaciously pursued, may-be
>   unconscious of yourselves,
> Unswerv'd by all the passing errors, perturbations of the surface;
> You vital, universal, deathless germs, beneath all creeds, arts,
>   statutes, literatures,
> Here build you homes for good, establish here, these areas entire,
>   lands of the Western shore,
> We pledge, we dedicate to you.
>
>   [58–65]

Decidedly this is not the voice of infirmity—which is not to doubt Whitman's personal fears and anxieties in his later years.

It is to say that in drawing upon the American ideology of environmental reform, Whitman may have found a symbol that satisfied his need to authenticate his life's work. From the idea of an American New Earth contingent upon reforms of the spirit as well as of the environment, Whitman could find in the abdication of the redwood the noblest act of such reform. He could transform his inevitable death into a volitional act of transcendent national meaning, for symbolically the felling of that sequoia is the rite of passage to the Millennium. By it Whitman may have sought the solace that he was "clearing the ground for broad humanity, the true America, heir of the past so grand" (104). This self-affirming identification with the fallen redwood—certainly a conservationist's horror—is evidently Whitman's act of faith both in the endurance of his work and in the American democratic apotheosis of "a new earth and a new man."

Epilogue

The American New Earth, once realized successfully in the poems of Walt Whitman, has not again been wrought with aesthetic power in our literature. True, there are some twentieth-century echoes of Whitman's New Earth, for instance in Charles Olson, whose persona, Maximus, expounds an American and worldwide cosmography centered especially in Gloucester, Massachusetts, an emblem of all America. Maximus says "that forever the geography/which leans in/on me I compell/backwards I compell Gloucester/to yield, to/ change."[1] In such lines one is reminded of Whitman's "heart's geography's map," the conceptual source of his American New Earth. Too, Ezra Pound departs explicitly from Whitman, whom he understood as a kind of elemental fact of America. In 1912 Pound believed the nation to be on the verge of yet one more renewal of its mission, which he named an "American Risorgimento." In the "surging," "eager," "careless" crowds on New York's Seventh Avenue Pound saw distinctly American "animal vigour" that augured an awakening "in the arts, in life, in politics, and in economics," together with a new liberation from "ideas, from stupidities, from conditions and from tyrannies of wealth or of army."[2] In this imminent American Renaissance, Pound saw "lines of force [that] run from New York, Cincinnati, Chicago, St. Louis, San Francisco."[3] Again, in such phrases as these we hear Whitman's voice brought forward into the new century.

Yet for the most part the major American literary voices of the twentieth century have not confirmed Pound's hopes and expectations. Thus they have not continued from Whitman the American literary tradition of the New Earth. It is as if the two-centuries-old ideology of environmental reform at last found full aesthetic expression in Romantic poetry, only to be repudiated in this century by writers unable to share the commitment to a millennial America. Twentieth-century writers who confront the American landscape in

fiction and poems offer very little hope for the spiritual and environmental redemption of the nation and decry the spoliation of the
landscape. In this way Sinclair Lewis, John Dos Passos, John
Steinbeck, Nathanael West, F. Scott Fitzgerald, William Faulkner,
Thomas Pynchon, and even William Carlos Williams align themselves
historically with the cataclysmic visions of Joel Barlow's *Columbiad*
and with Cooper's *Crater*. Their works thus confirm the fears and
despair of the earlier writers and in this century belie the millennial
splendor of Whitman, Bancroft, and even Cotton Mather.

In large part the skepticism of twentieth-century American writers
seems traceable to contemporary events of American and world
history. The two world wars with their horrendous technologies, the
failed League of Nations, fascism, death camps, the atom bomb, and
within the United States the collapse of the so-called age of reform
(1913–21), the Great Depression, the political hysteria of Sacco-
Vanzetti and later McCarthy, the internment of the Japanese,
flagrant racism—all in the public sphere work against the idea of an
imminent or progressing Millennium.

Yet even these horrific events might not have turned American
writers away from the tradition of the New Earth had they not
embraced the ethos of modernism exemplified by T. S. Eliot's *The
Waste Land*. In a turn-of-the-century literary climate which Pound
thought dry-rotted, pornographic, stylistically effulgent, and fraudu-
lent in its parade of sociology as literature, it was Eliot who put
forward a cogent aesthetic of pervasive spiritual enervation. Importantly, it was in a voice of disaffection and alienation from the
American mainstream that Eliot and others developed an adversary
cultural relation to America. This point is crucial to the demise of
the American New Earth in the literature of this century. For in
addressing the subject of the national spirit and the actual environment, the major American writers of this century have not identified
themselves with the nation. in fact, they have rejected such identification. And their alienation proclaims a radical change from the personal nationalism of their literary predecessors. In Cotton Mather and
Edward Johnson, in Barlow and his confreres of the Enlightenment,
in Cooper and Bancroft, and finally in Whitman we have seen how
closely identified with the American nation were literary proponents

of environmental reform. Only Whitman, it is true, found a voice at once intimate and at ease with his audience and with his American materials. His is a voice which in and of itself distinguishes art from the ideological rhetoric of his predecessors. Yet whether speaking as militarist, schoolmaster, founder, prophet, high priest, or, in Whitman, as "one with the rest," the writers in the tradition of the American New Earth ally themselves personally with the nation. Essentially, their personae are integral to it.

But when this self-identification with the American nation disappears in the twentieth century, writers on the subject of environmental change offer sidelong, intermittent, ironic, often scathing glances at an American ruin. Together they suggest that environmental havoc or spoliation is the just manifestation of an immoral or corrupted—or imaginatively bereft—America. While their judgments descend directly in kind from the Puritans, they find no solace in the possibilities for spiritual renewal, let alone satisfaction in the idea of a destined millennial apotheosis for America. At the beginning of *Babbitt* (1922), for instance, Sinclair Lewis represents the modern American urban aesthetic in the "towers of Zenith . . . austere towers of steel and cement and limestone, sturdy as cliffs and delicate as silver rods . . . frankly and beautifully office-buildings."[4] Lewis, however, repudiates this man-made environment in corrosive and unremitting satire throughout the novel, while for his part, Nathanael West achieves as thorough a demolition in just a few lines when his suffering protagonist, the lovelorn columnist Miss Lonelyhearts, turns "his trained eye on the skyscrapers . . . [of] forced rock and tortured steel." Miss Lonelyhearts speaks, it seems, for West when he goes on to say of the nation's environmental change, "Americans have dissipated their racial energy in an orgy of stone breaking"; "they have done their work hysterically, desperately, almost as if they knew that the stones would some day break them."[5] Such hysteria and desperation of course can form no part of the millennial New Earth.

West is not alone. John Dos Passos joins him in denouncing these qualities as spiritually definitive (and destructive) of America. Dos Passos's vignette of Luther Burbank in *The 42nd Parallel* presented an American who, in the tradition of Edward Bellamy and Frederick Law Olmsted, has "his apocalyptic dream of green grass in winter/

and seedless berries and stoneless plums and thornless roses brambles cactus." But as a Darwinian "infidel" Burbank provokes the middle-American "congregations" who kill him in volcanic fury, implicitly ruining the sweet apocalyptic dream for America as well.[6] Elsewhere, in John Steinbeck's *The Grapes of Wrath,* there is another version of the ruined American New Earth. For in Steinbeck the Luther Bur-banks—horticulturists, botanists, chemists—perfect seeds and roots until the California fruit swells on tree and vine. These men "have transformed the world with their knowledge." Yet an inhumane and wasteful economic system turns this world into a scene of rot, poisoning the very air. Rather than give away the unmarketable car-loads of oranges to the hungry, the owners destroy the crop. "A million people hungry, needing the fruit, and kerosene sprayed over the golden mountains." As Steinbeck concludes, "There is a failure here that topples all our success," and he signals a forthcoming holocaust as "in the souls of the people the grapes of wrath are fulling and growing heavy, growing heavy for the vintage."[7]

Perhaps the most haunting image of the completely subverted agrarian New Earth in twentieth-century American literature is that "valley of ashes" in Fitzgerald's *The Great Gatsby.* This is "a fantas-tic farm where ashes grow like wheat into ridges and hills and gro-tesque gardens; where ashes take the forms of houses and chimneys and rising smoke and, finally, with a transcendent effort, of ash-gray men."[8] Here of course the human spirit and the American environ-ment are jointly deadened, even incinerated. It is common know-ledge that the valley of ashes (and its presiding deity, the optometrist T. J. Eckleberg staring vacantly from his billboard) comes from Eliot's *Waste Land.* But within the literary tradition of the New Earth, Fitzgerald confronts the quality of environmental change and the spiritual quality of the American populace, only to declare them both ruined. Here in Fitzgerald we see confounded Crèvecoeur's agrarian America, as well as a repudiation of George Bancroft's proud vision of the Hudson valley civilized from its loathesome wilderness.

William Faulkner, too, joins the literary chorus decrying the twentieth-century destruction of the American earth. The very saw-mill that Whitman celebrated and which in the seventeenth century heralded the Puritan Edward Johnson's technological New Earth becomes, in Faulkner's *Light in August,* the means of desecration of the land and of the uprooting of its people. In a span of fourteen years the mill will "destroy all the timber within its reach," after which "some of the machinery and most of the men who ran it and existed because of it and for it would be loaded into freight cars and moved away." Even as men and equipment are freighted off, the economically profligate installment plan encourages the junking of machinery on the mill site. Like Steinbeck, Faulkner implies that perverse economics encourages waste and ruin, for the scene is of "gaunt, staring, motionless wheels rising from mounds of brick rubble and ragged weeds with a quality profoundly astonishing, and gutted boilers lifting their rusted and unsmoking stacks with an air stubborn, baffled and bemused." Here is not simply industrial litter but environmental wreckage "upon a stumppocked scene of profound and peaceful desolation, unplowed, untilled, gutting slovenly into red and choked ravines." The inheritors of this environment are not redeeming farmers but the "the hookwormridden" who pull down the abandoned mill buildings for fuel.[9] Faulkner's emphasis is, of course, upon transience, ruin, and rubble.

There is a strong suggestion on the part of these twentieth-century American writers that the collapse of the American spirit (correlatively of the shaped environment) is rooted in the failure of the national imagination. This problem of imaginative vitality, a direct legacy of romanticism, surfaces in Whitman's remarks about "language-using," about his continuous invention of America in words. Embodying the nation, he speaks for all its people in the act of bringing forth a new earth and new man. But Ezra Pound saw qualitative change in the American imagination both in and out of poetry since Whitman's time. Whitman's worldly counterpart, "the type of man who built railways, cleared the forest, planned irrigation," is for Pound "a man of dreams, in a time when dreams paid." This man is the worldly twin of the visionary poet. Yet the successors of such visionaries are in 1910 but "acquisitive, rapacious, tenacious," and deal not with human beings but "with paper." Pound, together with others, pronounces the American environment impoverished because the national spiritual life, centered in its imagination, is warped or deadened. We can recognize implicit indictments of the American imagination in Steinbeck's and Faulkner's juggernaut of man-made economic systems, and in Lewis's Babbittry of enslavement to a mindless material progress. In the novel *The Crying of Lot 49* Thomas Pynchon too offers an example of the debased imagination when he portrays his San Narciso, "like many named places in California, . . . less an identifiable city than a grouping of concepts—census tracts, special purpose bond-issue districts, shopping nuclei, all overlaid with access roads to its own freeway."[10] The area is, we learn, the corporate headquarters for a twentieth-century business mogul.

Fitzgerald and West, too, suggest that the failure of the American New Earth is consequent of the failure of the national imagination. In *The Great Gatsby* and *The Day of the Locust* both writers satirize the imitative architecture that debases the environment and reveals (in Pound's term) that "the [American] plutocrat . . . has lacked and lacks imagination, and especially originality in imagination."[11] As had Cooper one century earlier, Fitzgerald and West deplore the tawdriness of imitative buildings in a farrago of styles and (in West) of cheap materials. More important, these fake Norman, Spanish, even New England buildings reveal the counterfeit lives of a people desperate for inner fulfillment, feeding upon vulgar fantasy, imaginatively unresourceful amid material sufficiency, and in the anger of betrayal driven toward holocaust.

Fitzgerald further sees a fated and tragic dimension to this debased American imagination when he writes that the Dutch explorers who first saw "the fresh, green breast of the New World" were "face to face for the last time in history with something commensurate to [man's] capacity for wonder." Tragic doom therefore hangs necessarily over all the human energies of settlement and of American life thereafter. Never again can there be that transcendent moment of the imagination engaged with America. In fact, Fitzgerald suggests that maturity means a recognition of the proper limits of imagination. From the Queensborough Bridge the young and hopeful Nick Carroway in quest of a new eastern life sees a New York City of "white heaps and sugar lumps" embodying the "first wild promise of all the mystery and the beauty in the world."[12] But late in the novel Nick symbolically has turned thirty and remarked that he is too old to lie to himself and call it honor. He retreats in mature experience back to the Middle West, far from the delusive, dangerous sugarplum vision of the America which New York symbolizes.

There is literary consensus but not unanimity on the failings of the American imagination. True, this bleak survey shows a dilemma: imagination to excess (in Fitzgerald) is dangerously delusory, but the dearth of it (in West, Dos Passos, and Steinbeck) leads to holocaust. And the result of this failure of the American imagination is the betrayal of the millennial New Earth. While no writer to date has seriously challenged this point, Wallace Stevens's "Anecdote of a Jar" (from *Harmonium,* 1931) does remind us of the poetic primacy of the imagination to order experience, including the experience of the environment. Stevens's much discussed jar, an artifact symbolic of the artistic imagination, "made the slovenly wilderness/Surround that hill" on which it was placed in Tennessee. "The wilderness rose up to it,/and sprawled around, no longer wild." In reordering the landscape, the imagination imposes form and rightfully takes "dominion."[13] The mind itself, individual and subjective, reorders the American experience, including that of the landscape.

Within the tradition of environmental reform in American literature, Stevens really restates Whitman's poetics. To the mind belongs the power to transform matter, even that of an entire environment. Stevens, however, does not take up the complicated question of how the individual imagination may transform an environment made slovenly—or perhaps conceived of as ruined—by men. One writer who does confront this problem, William Carlos Williams, understands a personally vibrant American spirit and a renovated earth to be possible within the imaginative consciousness of the individual. Williams's *Paterson* suggests that on a personal basis the poetic imagination may yet take dominion over a crazed American environment.

Paterson (1946), which is a poet's autobiography schematized in symbols, represents America in the urban contemporary scene of Paterson, New Jersey, near the poet's lifelong home. In this poem Williams's urgent search for a language for the experience of America is comparable to that of Whitman. But the cultural attitudes underlying *Paterson* differ greatly from those of Whitman or any of the other writers in the literary tradition of the millennial New Earth. In his earlier *In the American Grain* (1925) Williams had emphasized the destruction of American native cultures by transplanted Europeans whose own civilization was profoundly unsuited to the

New World. Far from millennial ideas of progress, Williams believed
the colonial legacy to be one of dispossession, both of the Indians
and of the Europeans who, through three centuries, never found
ways of life congenial to the New World. Settlement and landscape
continued to be in perennial contention or, in Williams's word, in
divorce. He likened the contemporary average American to an Indian
wandering in a forest of machines.[14] In Williams's view, man's environmental change to America has degraded and damaged it. On this
point, of course, he joins Faulkner, Fitzgerald, West, and Steinbeck.

But Williams sees possibilities for the redemption of this fallen
world, America, in the imagination of the poet. As Williams wrote,
Paterson "is an attempt, an experiment, a failing experiment, toward
assertion ... of a new and total culture, the lifting of an environment to expression."[15] Thematically, the poet's task is to marry
Americans with America, to integrate the culture with the land. In
symbol he converts the topography of Paterson into the male giant
(in part the industrial city) at rest beside the mountainous and floral
female giant. Thus the male city and womanly nature must be
brought to marriage if the poet is to succeed in redeeming a fallen
America. The poet is both marriage broker and priest, his sacraments
language itself. And Williams is constantly aware of how risky is his
mythic, epic mission. His text is riddled with metaphors of the
treachery of his poetic task. Falling (including the Passaic Falls of
Paterson), leaping, speechless plunges—all revert to the poet's own
sense of struggle to sustain the poem. As one writer concludes,
"*Paterson* is an attempt to tell the story of Williams's search (in the
past, in his own mind) for the new form by which to master the
specifically American experience."[16]

Paterson, however, may mark the great distance of twentieth-
century writers from those who, from the Puritans through Whitman,
espoused environmental reform as a grand part of the American millennial destiny. Cotton Mather, Edward Johnson, Barlow and
Bancroft, Whitman—all looked into the American experience for
good omens of the millennial future. But Williams looks back into a
violent, oppressively industrial, greedy, soulless, alienating American
past to see how he might find for himself some explanation and
acceptance of his present. He speaks, not as a poetic self embodying
America, but as one imagination trying to make coherence in his own

life by shaping a conciliatory, nuptial cohesiveness in American history enacted on New World soil. For himself he works to redeem the Waste Land and not (in the prophetic tradition of the jeremiad) to prophesy the national destiny.

Paterson may be, as he called it, a "social instrument," but the poem does not insinuate itself as a document of American social change. Williams, rather, hearkens heuristically to Mather's visionary America declared vibrant in the *Magnalia* if not in the world at large, and to Thoreau's individuated American life in *Walden*. Late in the nineteenth century Whitman had embodied the nation in himself and affirmed the American New Earth. Williams, working in reverse, sought to locate himself in the history and geography of America. In a century whose writers repudiate the millennial New Earth, Williams suggests that the American literary imagination best takes dominion in engagement with American beginnings. He implies that the contemporary imagination must seek an original relation, not to the degraded and repudiated New Earth but to that first America of the New World.

Notes

PREFACE

1 Gene Marine, *America the Raped* (New York: Simon and Schuster, 1969); and Robert J. Gangewere, ed., *The Exploited Eden: Literature on the American Environment* (New York: Harper and Row, 1972). See also John Muir, *Our National Parks* (Cambridge, Mass.: Riverside Press, 1901), p. 336; and Perry Miller, "Nature and the National Ego," in *Errand into the Wilderness* (New York: Harper and Row, 1956), p. 212.
2 John Seelye, "Ugh! Richard Slotkin, *Regeneration through Violence: The Mythology of the American Frontier, 1600–1860*. A Review-Essay," *Seventeenth-Century News* 34, nos. 2-3 (Summer-Fall 1976): 38.

CHAPTER 1

1 William Gass, "Gertrude Stein, Geographer: I," *New York Review of Books*, 3 May 1973, p. 7, col. 1.
2 Richard Goodwin, "Reflections (The American Social Process—II),"*New Yorker*, 28 April 1974, p. 40.
3 See D. H. Lawrence, "Fenimore Cooper's White Novels" and "Fenimore Cooper's Leatherstocking Novels," in *Studies in Classical American Literature* (1923; rpt., Garden City, N.Y.: Doubleday, 1953), pp. 43–73.
4 Lynn White, Jr., "The Historical Roots of Our Ecological Crisis," *Science*, 10 March 1967, pp. 1203–07.
5 John Updike, "Packing Dirt, Churchgoing, a Dying Cat, a Traded Car," in *Pigeon Feathers* (1959; rpt., New York: Fawcett, 1963), p. 169. I am thankful to Sayre Sheldon for calling this passage to my attention.
6 Colman McCarthy, "It's the Keepers vs. the Spoilers," *Boston Sunday Globe*, 4 July 1976, p. A2, cols. 1–3.
7 "A New Land Like unto That of the Golden Age," in *The Elizabethans' America: A Collection of Early Reports by Englishmen on the New World*, ed. Louis B. Wright (Cambridge: Harvard University Press, 1966), pp. 104–05.
8 See Leo Marx, *The Machine in the Garden: Technology and Pastoral* (New York: Oxford University Press, 1964); Charles L. Sanford, *The Quest for Paradise* (Urbana: University of Illinois Press, 1961). In *Prophetic Waters* (New York: Oxford University Press, 1977), John Seelye examines the national, epic implications of the edenic South.

9 "To the Virginian Voyage," in *The Elizabethans' America,* pp. 160–62. Other promotional, edenic accounts of the South in this anthology include "Harriot Tells of the Goodness of Virginia (1588)," pp. 115–33.

10 "A Promising Description of New England (1602)," in *The Elizabethans' America* pp. 137–44. See also "Captain Waymouth Explores the New England Coast (1605)," pp. 144–54.

11 "Fish, Furs, and Timber Better Than Gold," in *The Elizabethans' America,* pp. 258–63.

12 George Perkins Marsh, *Man and Nature; or, Physical Geography as Modified by Human Action,* ed. David Lowenthal (1864; rpt., Cambridge: Harvard University Press, 1965), p. 15.

13 John Cotton, *God's Promise to His Plantation* (London, 1630), p. 4.

14 John White, *The Planter's Plea,* in Peter Force, *Tracts* 2 (Washington, D.C., 1838): 1-2.

15 Thomas Tillam, "Uppon the First Sight of New-England, June 29, 1638" in *Seventeenth-Century American Poetry,* ed. Harrison T. Meserole (Garden City, N.Y.: Doubleday, 1968), p. 397.

16 Michael Wigglesworth, "God's Controversy with New-England," in *Seventeenth-Century American Poetry,* p. 45.

17 Richard Steere, *"Earth Felicities, Heavens Allowances,"* in *Seventeenth-Century American Poetry,* p. 259.

18 John Cotton, *God's Promise,* p. 19.

19 William Hubbard, "From Pascataqua to Pemmaquid," in *The Present State of New-England, Being a Narrative of the Troubles with the Indians* (1677; facs. rpt., Bainbridge, N.Y.: York Mail-Print, 1972), pp. 80–81.

20 Increase Mather, Preface to *Discourse Concerning Faith and Fervency in Prayer, and the Glorious Kingdom of the Lord Jesus Christ, on Earth, Now Approaching* (Boston, 1710), pp. 92–93.

21 "To the Christian Reader," in *The Banners of Grace and Love Displayed* (London, 1657).

22 John Cotton, *Discourse about Civil Government in a New Plantation* (London, 1663), p. 35. See also Chester E. Eisinger, "The Puritans' Justification for Taking the Land," Essex Institute Historical Collections, vol. 84 (1948), pp. 131–43.

23 John Winthrop, *Conclusions for the Plantation in New England* (1629), Old South Leaflets, vol. 2, no. 50 (Boston, 1883).

24 In *The Winthrop Papers,* ed. Allyn B. Forbes (Boston, 1929–47), 3: 182.

25 John Eliot, "Two Learned Conjectures," in Thomas Thorowgood, *Jews in America* (London, 1650), p. 14.

26 See Ralph H. Brown, *Historical Geography of the United States* (New York: Harcourt, Brace, 1948), pp. 11–16.

27 *Abstract of the Lawes of New England* (London, 1641), in Peter Force, *Tracts* 3, no. 9 (Washington, D.C., 1844); 8.

28 Cotton, *God's Promise to His Plantation,* p. 13; *Winthrop Papers,* 4: 101–02.

29 *Winthrop Papers,* 2: 115.
30 Winthrop, *Conclusions;* Thorowgood, *Jews in America,* p. 57; White, *Planter's Plea,* pp. 2–3.
31 Eliot, "Two Conjectures," p. 13; Winthrop, *Conclusions,*
32 *Winthrop Papers,* 4: 222; 3: 182–83.
33 Hubbard, *Present State of New-England,* p. 63.
34 Increase Mather, *An Earnest Exhortation to the Inhabitants of New-England* (Boston: John Foster, 1676), p. 9.
35 See Francis Higginson, *New-Englands Plantation* (London, 1630), and William Wood, *Wood's "New-England's Prospect"* (Boston: Publications of the Prince Society, 1865).
36 Yi-Fu Tuan, "Attitudes toward Environment: Themes and Approaches," in *Environmental Perception and Behavior,* ed. David Lowenthal (Chicago: University of Chicago Press, 1967), p. 16.
37 Edward Johnson, *The Wonder-Working Providence of Sions Saviour in New England,* ed. J. Franklin Jameson (1910; rpt., New York: Barnes and Noble, 1959), p. 154.
38 B[enjamin] T[ompson], "Uppon the Elaborate Survey of New England's Passions from the Natives, by the Impartial Pen of That Worthy Divine Mr. William Hubbard," in *Present State of New England.*
39 See Richard B. Holman, "John Foster's Woodcut Map of New England," *Printing and Graphic Arts* 8, no. 3 (September 1960): 53–92. For cartographical conventions of the seventeenth century, see Lloyd A. Brown, *The Story of Maps* (Boston: Little, Brown, 1950), and Edward Lynam, The *Mapmaker's Art: Essays on the History of Maps* (London: Batchworth, 1953), pp. 55–78. John Seelye discusses the "martial" and "epic" nature of this map; see *Prophetic Waters,* pp. 240–44.
40 Eisinger, "Puritans' Justification." See Alden T. Vaughan, *New England Frontier: Puritans and Indians,* 1620–1675 (Boston: Little, Brown, 1965), pp. 93–121.
41 *Winthrop Papers,* 3: 182–83.
42 The Puritans' apocalyptic state of mind has been well documented since the appearance of Helmut Richard Niebuhr's *The Kingdom of God in America* (1935; rpt., Hamden, Conn.: Shoe String Press, 1956) and since Harold Jantz remarked about "the transcendental, apocalyptic, millennarian, utopian tendencies which were so strong in many of the leaders (Cotton, Hooker, Davenport, Chauncy, the younger Winthrop, etc.)" in *The First Century of New England Verse* (1943; rpt., New York: Russell and Russell, 1962), p. 25. A useful encyclopedic survey of American eschatological writings is that of LeRoy Froom, *The Prophetic Faith of Our Fathers: The Historical Development of Prophetic Interpretation,* 4 vols. (Washington, D.C.: Review and Herald, 1946–51). The vitality of apocalyptic thought during the Middle Ages and early Reformation is demonstrated in Norman Cohn, *The Pursuit of the Millennium* (1957; rpt., London: Temple Smith, 1970). On the origins of English Puritan millennialism, see John F. Wilson,

"Comment on 'Two Roads to the Puritan Millennium,' " *Church History* 32 (1963): 339–43; and Peter Toon, *Puritans, the Millennium, and the Future of Israel: Puritan Eschatology 1600–1660* (Cambridge: Cambridge University Press, 1970). One work important in emphasizing the cultural pervasiveness of millennialism in seventeenth-century England is William M. Lamont, *Godly Rule: Politics and Religion, 1603–1660* (London: Macmillan, 1969). Some works addressed specifically to eschatological thought in Puritan New England are Jesper Rosenmeier, "The Teacher and the Witness: John Cotton and Roger Williams," *William and Mary Quarterly* 25, 3d ser., no. 2 (April 1968): 157–61; Everett H. Emerson, *John Cotton* (New York: Twayne, 1965), pp. 95–101; Robert Middlekauff, *The Mathers: Three Generations of Puritan Intellectuals, 1596–1728* (New York: Oxford University Press, 1971); Larzer Ziff, *The Career of John Cotton* (Princeton: Princeton University Press, 1962), pp. 170-202. Illuminating in its suggestion of the extent of apocalyptic thinking in Puritan New England is J. F. Maclear, "New England and the Fifth Monarchy: The Quest for the Millennium," *William and Mary Quarterly* 32, 3d ser., no. 2 (April 1975): 223–60. See also Aletha Joy Bourne Gilsdorf, "The Puritan Apocalypse: New England Eschatology in the Seventeenth Century" (Ph.D. diss., Yale University, 1965). Discussions of typology in early American literature are to be found in *Early American Literature* 5, no. 1, pts. 1 and 2 (Spring 1970), which includes essays on problems of criticism and on Roger Williams, Edward Taylor, and Jonathan Edwards by Sacvan Bercovitch, Thomas Davis, Stephen Manning, Richard Reinitz, Robert Reiter, Karl Keller, and Mason I. Lowance, Jr., in addition to an extensive checklist on typology. Of particular importance in revealing patterns of eschatological thought in American culture are Sacvan Bercovitch, "Horologicals to Chronometricals: The Rhetoric of the Jeremiad," in *Literary Monographs*, ed. Eric Rothstein (Madison: University of Wisconsin Press, 1970), 3: 3–124, and *The Puritan Origins of the American Self* (New Haven: Yale University Press, 1975). Most recently, John Seelye examines the mythic and political meanings of eschatology in Puritan culture; see *Prophetic Waters*, pp. 59–162 et passim.

43 Ernest Lee Tuveson, *Millennium and Utopia: A Study in the Background of the Idea of Progress* (Berkeley: University of California Press, 1949), pp. 113–203.

44 See David Minter, "The Puritan Jeremiad as a Literary Form," in *The American Puritan Imagination: Essays in Revaluation*, ed. Sacvan Bercovitch (London and New York: Cambridge University Press, 1974), p. 50.

45 See Maclear, "New England and the Fifth Monarchy," p. 226. Further scholarship is needed to reveal the integrity of Puritan New England world and spiritual life. As yet the social historian and literary critic have not synthesized their disparate findings. Indicative, however, is the conclusion of the social historian Kenneth Lockridge, *A New England Town: The First Hundred Years* (New York: Norton, 1970), who finds from his study of

politics, church polity, apportionment of land, distribution of wealth, etc., in Dedham, Mass., 1636–1736, that the town was a "Utopian Closed Corporate Community" (pp. 17–22). He finds in "some inscrutable chemistry" that bonded the Puritan and the peasant the motivation to create a utopian society, more, to establish " 'a new order on earth.' " Sacvan Bercovitch more recently explains the basis for that impulse when he writes of New England Puritan rhetoric that "the essence of colonial Puritan historiography was that... The New World, like Canaan of old, belonged wholly to God. The remnant that fled Babylon in 1630 set sail for the new promised land, especially reserved by God for them." See *Puritan Origins*, p. 100.

46 Roger Clap, *Memoirs*, ed. Thomas Prince, Dorchester Antiquarian and Historical Society Collections, no. 1 (Boston, 1844), pp. 20–24; and John Underhill, *Newes from America; or, a New and Experimentall Discoverie of New England,* Collections of the Mancester Historical Society, vol. 6, 3d ser. (1837), pp. 19–20.

47 *Puritan Origins*, p. 100.

48 Edmund Browne to Sir Simonds D'Ewes, September 7, 1638, in *Letters from New England: The Massachusetts Bay Colony, 1629–1638,* ed. Everett H. Emerson (Amherst: University of Massachusetts Press, 1976), pp. 224–25.

49 Underhill, *Newes from America,* pp. 12–13.

50 Quoted in Richard Slotkin, *Regeneration through Violence: The Mythology of the American Frontier, 1600–1680* (Middletown, Conn.: Wesleyan University Press, 1973), p. 73.

51 Anon., in *Letters from New England,* pp. 214–15.

52 Thomas Dudley, "Letter to the Countess of Lincoln," in *Chronicles of the First Planters,* ed. Alexander Young (Boston, 1846), pp. 303–41.

53 Richard Mather to William Rathband and Mr. T., June 25, 1636, in *Letters from New England,* p. 205.

54 Anon., in *Letters from New England,* p. 215.

55 Bercovitch, *Puritan Origins,* p. 120.

56 William Bradford, "A Relation or Journall" (1622), in Alexander Young, ed., *Chronicles of the Pilgrim Fathers* (Boston, 1841), pp. 117-19, 233, 165, 158.

57 See Jesper Rosenmeier, " 'With my owne eyes': William Bradford's *Of Plymouth Plantation,*" in *The American Puritan Imagination,* p. 82. See also David Levin, "William Bradford: The Value of Puritan Historiography," in *Major Writers of Early American Literature,* ed. Everett H. Emerson (Madison: University of Wisconsin Press, 1972), p. 25.

58 *Of Plymouth Plantation,* ed. Samuel Eliot Morison (New York: Knopf, 1966), pp. 25, 19, 105–06, 131, 3, 236.

59 Rosenmeier, " 'With my owne eyes,' " pp. 92–97.

60 *Of Plymouth Plantation,* p. 62. See also Alan B. Howard, "Art and History in Bradford's *Of Plymouth Plantation,*" *William and Mary Quarterly* 28, 3d ser., no. 2 (April 1971): 248.

61 *Of Plymouth Plantation*, pp. 213, 216.

62 Ibid., p. 62.

63 Ibid., pp. 62–63.

64 See George Williams, *Wilderness and Paradise in Christian Thought* (New York: Harper and Row, 1962); and Peter N. Carroll, *Puritanism and the Wilderness: The Intellectual Significance of the New England Frontier, 1629–1700* (New York: Columbia University Press, 1969). Other works on the scriptural meanings of wilderness include Eric C. Rust, *Nature and Man in Biblical Thought* (London: Lutterworth Press, 1953), and Alfred Haldar, *The Notion of the Desert in Sumero-Akkadian and West-Semitic Religions* (Uppsala: Lundequistska Okhandeln, 1950). Roderick Nash surveys Judeo-Christian attitudes toward wilderness in *Wilderness and the American Mind* (New Haven and London: Yale University Press, 1967), pp. 13–20. See also Slotkin, *Regeneration through Violence*, chaps. 1–6. Subject to subsequent revision, a valuable essay on Puritan conceptions of wilderness is that of Alan Heimert, "Puritanism, the Wilderness, and the Frontier," *William and Mary Quarterly* 26, 3d ser. (September 1953): 361–82.

65 *Of Plymouth Plantation*, pp. 82, 25.

66 *The Language of Canaan*, ed. Jesper Rosenmeier (Medford, Mass.: Trustees of Tufts University, 1976), p. 109.

67 See Bercovitch, "Cotton Mather," in *Major Writers of Early American Literature*, p. 141.

68 *Magnalia Christi Americana* (1702; rpt., Hartford, 1851–53), 1: 50; 2: 447, 490.

69 Bercovitch, "Cotton Mather," p. 99.

70 Ibid., pp. 140–48.

71 *Magnalia*, 2: 657.

72 *Magnalia*, 1: 44. See Cotton Mather, *India Christiana* (Boston, 1721), p. 23.

73 *Magnalia*, 1: 558–60; cf. pp. 363–64, 44.

74 Ibid. See also *India Christiana*, pp. 28–29.

75 See Bercovitch, *Puritan Origins*, pp. 40–55.

76 See Mather, *Successive Generations*, (Boston, 1715), p. 15; *The City of Refuge* (Boston, 1716), p. 25; *The World Alarm'd* (Boston, 1721), p. 3.

77 Bercovitch observes this to be characteristic of Puritan political sermons. See "Horologicals to Chronometricals," p. 20.

78 *Things To Be Look'd For . . .* (Boston, 1691), p. 10.

79 *The World Alarm'd*, p. 16; *Thoughts for a Day of Rain* (Boston, 1712), p. 26.

80 See *Agricola* (Boston, 1727), p. 204; *Successive Generations*, p. 2; *The City of Refuge*, pp. 3, 4, 12.

81 See "Bostonian Ebenezer," in *Magnalia*, 1: 90–105.

82 Ibid.

83 *Magnalia*, 2: 128–37, 660–61.

84 *Theopolis Americana* (Boston, 1710), pp. 1–3, 43, 50.

85 Ibid., pp. 6, 49, 50.
86 See *Successive Generations*, pp. 15ff.
87 Middlekauff, *The Mathers*, p. 325.
88 *Magnalia*, 1: 328.
89 See Bercovitch, "Cotton Mather," p. 147.

CHAPTER 2

1 William Hubbard, "To the Reader," in *The Present State of New-England, Being a Narrative of the Troubles with the Indians* (1677; facs. rpt., Bainbridge, N.Y.: York Mail-Print, 1972).
2 The definition of history as "theology exemplified" is of course that of Perry Miller. See *The Puritans*, ed. and rev. Perry Miller and Thomas H. Johnson (New York: Harper and Row, 1963), 1: 81–90.
3 Response to Johnson in modern scholarship has been mixed. Harold S. Jantz offers a warmly appreciative view in *The First Century of New England Verse* (1943; rpt., New York: Russell and Russell, 1962), pp. 23–29, citing Johnson's "Mastery of style and composition, his magnificent command of prose rhythm, his amazing sense of the truly epic." See also Helmut Richard Niebuhr, *The Kingdom of God in America* (1935; rpt., Hamden, Conn.: Shoe String Press, 1956), p. 47; Charles L. Sanford, *The Quest for Paradise* (Urbana: University of Illinois Press, 1961), p. 83; Peter Gay, *A Loss of Mastery* (Berkeley: University of California Press, 1966), p. 53; Miller and Johnson, *The Puritans*, pp. 1, 90; Moses Coit Tyler, *A History of American Literature, 1607–1765* (New York: Collier, 1962), p. 143; Richard S. Dunn, "Seventeenth-Century English Historians of America," in *Seventeenth-Century America*, ed. James Morton Smith (Williamburg, Va.: University of North Carolina Press, 1959), pp. 204–05; Michael Kraus, *The Writing of American History* (Norman: University of Oklahoma Press, 1953), pp. 27–28; and Kenneth Ballard Murdock, *Literature and Theology in Colonial New England* (1949; rpt., New York: Harper and Row, 1963), pp. 86–88. Johnson is called "vigorous," "imaginative." and "enthusiastic." but also a "rustic trumpet," "some minor player in the orchestra," "burdened by rhetorical flights," "verbose," "turgid," "crude in thought and style," "not an artist but a woodworker." Recent scholarship has focused upon the theological, especially typological, subtlety of Johnson's work. See Sacvan Bercovitch, "The Historiography of Johnson's *Wonder-Working Providence*," Essex Institute Historical Collections, vol. 104, no. 2 (1968), p. 142; see also Ursula Brumm, "Edward Johnson's *Wonder-Working Providence* and the Puritan Conception of History," *Jahrbuch fur Amerika Studiesn* 14 (1969): 140–51. Edward J. Gallagher, "An Overview of Edward Johnson's *Wonder-Working Providence*,"*Early American Literature* 3 (1971): 30–49, discusses the work "in relation to its contemporary purpose and cultural moment" (p. 30). In a subsequent essay,

"*The Wonder-Working Providence* as Spiritual Biography," *Early American Literature* 10, no. 1 (Spring 1975): 75–87, Gallagher demonstrates how Johnson's history conforms structurally to the pattern of the Puritan spiritual biography.

4 Johnson's self-depreciation is evidenced in *The Wonder-Working Providence of Sions Saviour in New England*, ed. J. Franklin Jameson (1910; rpt., New York: Barnes and Noble, 1959), pp. 51, 151, 128. All references in my text are to this edition.

5 See Harrison T. Meserole, ed., *Seventeenth-Century American Poetry* (Garden City, N.Y.: Doubleday, 1968), p. 147.

6 William Bradford, *Of Plymouth Plantation*, ed. Samuel Eliot Morison (New York: Knopf, 1966), p. 257.

7 John Winthrop, *Journal*, ed. James K. Hosmer (1908; rpt., New York: Barnes and Noble, 1966), 2: 144.

8 *Wonder-Working Providence*, p. 29.

9 Ibid., pp. 151, 29, 27.

10 For a thorough discussion of Johnson's literary clerkship, see William F. Poole, Introduction to *The Wonder-Working Providence of Sions Saviour in New England* (Andover, Mass., 1867), pp. lxxix–xc.

11 *Good News from New-England: An Exact Relation . . .* (London, 1648).

12 Cotton Mather, *Magnalia Christi Americana* (1702; rpt., Hartford, 1851–53), 1: 69.

13 *Wonder-Working Providence*, p. 271.

14 Gallagher, "Overview of Johnson's *Wonder-Working Providence*," p. 31.

15 As many of his readers have observed, Johnson was a better polemicist than he was a fastidious recorder, even though he became (in later life, at least) a collector of historical documents. Despite the *New England* rubric in its title, *The Wonder-Working Providence* is really confined to events of the Bay and lacks thoroughness in its account of events in which Johnson had no part. (The sketchy description of the Pequot War, for instance, has been attributed to Johnson's absence from New England during that Indian uprising.)

16 *Wonder-Working Providence*, pp. 112–15.

17 Cotton Mather, *Theopolis Americana* (Boston, 1710), p. 42.

18 *Wonder-Working Providence*, pp. 30, 25.

19 Ibid., p. 24.

20 Ibid., pp. 30, 34.

21 Ibid., pp. 29, 30, 34, 35.

22 Richard Baxter, *The Life and Death of Mr. Joseph Alleine* (London, 1672), pp. 1–2.

23 Gallagher, "Overview of Johnson's *Wonder-Working Providence*," pp. 32, 39–41.

24 See George A. Starr, *Defoe and Spiritual Biography* (Princeton, N.J.: Princeton University Press, 1965), pp. 17–23.

25 See Mather, *Magnalia*, 1: 81; rpt., *Wonders of the Invisible World* (Boston, 1693), n.p.; *A Brief Relation of the State of New England* (1689), in Peter Force, *Tracts*, vol. 4, no. 11 (Washington, D.C., 1846).

26 Sacvan Bercovitch, "Cotton Mather," in *Major Writers of Early American Literature*, ed. Everett H. Emerson (Madison: University of Wisconsin Press, 1972), pp. 93–148.

27 See Cotton Mather, *The Stone Cut Out of the Mountain* (Boston, 1716), p. 7.

28 William Hubbard, *A General History of New England from the Discovery to 1680* (Boston, 1848), pp. 96–97.

29 *Wonder-Working Providence*, pp. 51, 146, 210.

30 Ibid., p. 34.

31 See Cotton Mather, *Things To Be Look'd For. . .* (Boston, 1691); *Psalterium Americanum* (Boston, 1718); *Thoughts for a Day of Rain* (Boston, 1712); Increase Mather, Preface to *Discourse Concerning Faith and Fervency in Prayer. . .* (Boston, 1710). For a thorough discussion of the eschatology of the Mathers, see Robert Middlekauff, *The Mathers: Three Generations of Puritan Intellectuals, 1596–1728* (New York: Oxford University, Press, 1971).

32 In *Seventeenth-Century American Poetry*, p. 156.

33 *Wonder-Working Providence*, p. 156.

34 In *Seventeenth-Century American Poetry*, p. 170. See *Wonder-Working Providence*, p. 269.

35 Benjamin Lynde, *Lines Descriptive of Thomson's Island*, in *Seventeenth-Century American Poetry*, p. 493.

36 Grindall Rawson, *Upon the Death of His Much Esteemed Friend Mr. Jno Saffin Junr . . .*, in *Seventeenth-Century American Poetry*, p. 477.

37 William Bradford, *Of Boston in New England*, in *Seventeenth-Century American Poetry*, p. 388.

38 John Higginson, *The Cause of God and His People in New-England* (Cambridge, Mass.: Samuel Green, 1663), pp. 10–11.

39 *Wonder-Working Providence*, pp. 51, 65, 82, 85, 114–15, 180.

40 Ibid., pp. 209–10.

41 Ibid., pp. 211, 120, 175.

42 See C. W. Chalklin, *Seventeenth-Century Kent: A Social and Economic History* (London: Longmans, 1965), pp. 75, 90.

43 William Haller, *The Rise of Puritanism* (1938; rpt., New York: Harper and Row, 1957; Perry Miller, *The New England Mind: The Seventeenth Century* (1939; rpt., Cambridge: Harvard University Press, 1954); Alan Simpson, *Puritanism in Old and New England* (Chicago: University of Chicago Press, 1955); Sacvan Bercovitch, "Horologicals to Chronometricals: The Rhetoric of the Jeremiad," in *Literary Monographs*, ed. Eric Rothstein (Madison: University of Wisconsin Press, 1970), 3: 3–124. See also Sumner Powell, *Puritan Village* (Middletown, Conn.: Wesleyan University Press, 1963);

Michael Zuckerman, *Peaceable Kingdoms: New England Towns in the Eighteenth Century* (New York: Knopf, 1970); Kenneth Lockridge, *A New England Town: The First Hundred Years* (New York: Norton, 1970); Richard Bushman, *From Puritan to Yankee: Character and the Social Order in Connecticut, 1690–1765* (Cambridge: Harvard University Press, 1967).

44 Lewis Mumford, *Technics and Civilization* (1934; rpt., New York: Harcourt, Brace, 1962); *The Myth of the Machine: Technics and Human Development* (New York: Harcourt, Brace, 1967); *The Myth of the Machine: The Pentagon of Power* (New York: Harcourt, Brace, 1964).

45 Leo Marx, *The Machine in the Garden: Technology and the Pastoral Ideal* (New York: Oxford University Press, 1964).

46 Chalklin, *Seventeenth-Century Kent*, p. 12.

47 William Hubbard, "From Pascataqua to Pemmaquid," in *The Present State of New-England*, pp. 1–2.

48 *The Winthrop Papers*, ed. Allyn B. Forbes (Boston, 1929–47), 4: 103–04.

49 John Winthrop, *Conclusions for the Plantation in New England* (1629), in Old South Leaflets, vol. 2 no. 50 (Boston, 1883).

50 Herman Melville, *Israel Potter: His Fifty Years of Exile* (1855; rpt., New York: Warner, 1974), p. 168.

51 John Eliot, "Two Learned Conjectures," in Thomas Thorowgood, *Jews in America* (London, 1650), p. 3.

52 *Wonder-Working Providence*, p. 233.

53 *The Puritans*, 2: 729.

54 See Robert K. Merton, "Science, Technology, and Society in Seventeenth-Century England," *Osiris* 4 (1938): 360–624.

55 Richard Baxter, *The Christian Directory* (1664–65), in *Works* (London, 1825), 5: 535.

56 Quoted in *Science and Society, 1600–1900*, ed. Peter Mathias (London: Cambridge University Press, 1972), p. 61. See also A. Rupert Hall, "Science, Technology, and Utopia in the Seventeenth Century," in *Science and Society*, pp. 33–53. Hall writes, "It is clear that Hartlib's circle did not regard his 'attempts for a public good' as including, in any noteworthy way, the promotion of material riches or the attainment of a technological Utopia. If this is so, then we may effectively exclude the possibility that Utopian idealism mediated between science and technology in mid-seventeenth-century" (p. 43). Elsewhere, too, Hall challenges Merton; see "Merton Revisited; or, Science and Society in the Seventeenth Century," *History of Science* 2 (1963): 1–16. One scholar who identifies the consonance between Purtitanism and science as a European, neo-Platonic movement from the Renaissance onward is P. M. Rattansai, "The Social Interpretation of Science in the Seventeenth Century," in *Science and Society*, pp. 1–32.

57 Rattansai, "Social Interpretation of Science in the Seventeenth Century," p. 12.

58 See Poole, Introduction to *Wonder-Working Providence*, p. xci.
59 *Wonder-Working Providence*, p. 207.
60 Samuel Danforth, Sr., Almanac Verse ("January"), in *Seventeenth-Century American Poetry*, p. 417.
61 Poole, Introduction to *Wonder-Working Providence*, p. lxxxiv.
62 *Wonder-Working Providence*, p. 234.
63 John White, *The Planter's Plea* (London, 1630), pp. 2–3.
64 Eliot, "Two Learned Conjectures," p. 3.
65 In *Seventeenth-Century American Poetry*, pp. 166, 168.
66 Hubbard, "From Pascataqua to Pemmaquid," p. 4.
67 *Wonder-Working Providence*, pp. 73, 183, 245–46, 248.
68 Ibid., p. 248.
69 Ibid., pp. 61, 71, 201; see also Oliver Ayer Roberts, *History of the Ancient and Honourable Artillery Company of Massachusetts* (Boston: A. Mudge, 1895), 1: 13.
70 Edward Taylor, "Meditation 2.56," in *Seventeenth-Century American Poetry*, p. 135. See *Wonder-Working Providence*, pp. 256, 49.
71 *Wonder-Working Providence*, p. 33, 60.

CHAPTER 3

1 See *The Adams-Jefferson Letters*, ed. Lester J. Cappon (Chapel Hill: University of North Carolina Press, 1959), 2: 312.
2 See *Diary and Autobiography*, ed. Lyman H. Butterfield et al. (Cambridge: Harvard University Press, 1961), 1: 257.
3 Ibid., p. 34.
4 Philip Freneau, "The Millennium," in *Poems of Freneau*, ed. Harry Hayden Clark (New York: Harcourt, Brace, 1929), pp. 147–48. All citations of Freneau's verse are from this edition.
5 *Portico* 4 (1817): 240.
6 *Monthly Magazine and American Review* 3 (1800): 16–17.
7 Clarence J. Glacken, *Traces on the Rhodian Shore* (Berkeley and Los Angeles: University of California Press, 1967), p. 462.
8 Ibid., p. 657.
9 William Robertson, *The History of America* (London, 1777), 1: 248–64.
10 Peter Gay, "Enlightenment Thought and the American Revolution," in *The Role of Ideology in the American Revolution*, ed. John R. Howe, Jr. (New York: Holt, Rinehart, and Winston, 1970), p. 44.
11 Brooke Hindle, *The Pursuit of Science in Revolutionary America, 1735–1789* (1956; rpt., New York: Norton, 1974), pp. 190–91.
12 David Humphreys, *Poem on Industry* (Philadelphia: Matthew Carey, 1794), p. 14.
13 See John F. Kasson, *Civilizing the Machine: Technology and Republican*

Values in America, 1776-1900 (Harmondsworth, England, and New York: Penguin, 1977), pp. 3–51. See also Mercy Otis Warren, *History of the Rise, Progress, and Determination of the American Revolution* (Boston: E. Larkin, 1805), 3: 435.

14 Jared Eliot, *Essays upon Field Husbandry in New England and Other Papers, 1748-1762*, ed. Harry J. Carman and Rexford G. Tugwell (New York: Columbia University Press, 1934), pp. 96–97.

15 Adams, *Diary*, 1: 27, 34.

16 See Edward Malins, *English Landscaping and Literature, 1660-1840* (London: Oxford University Press, 1966), pp. 26–48, 97–141.

17 William Cowper, *The Task*, 3. 774–77, quoted in Malins, *English Landscaping*, p. 100.

18 A recent study that traces changing responses to the American landscape from the background of the Enlightenment into the Romantic period is that of Edward Halsey Foster, *The Civilized Wilderness: Backgrounds to American Romantic Literature, 1817-1860* (New York: Free Press, 1975).

19 Alexander Pope, "Epistle to Burlington," *Moral Essays*, 4. 47–49, quoted in Malins, *English Landscaping*, p. 37.

20 See *Columbian* 2, (1788): 399–400.

21 Eliot, *Essays*, pp. 96–97.

22 *Common Sense*, in *The Complete Writings of Thomas Paine*, ed. Philip S. Foner (New York: Citadel, 1945), 1: 45.

23 Bernard Bailyn, *The Ideological Origins of the American Revolution* (Cambridge: Harvard University Press, 1967), pp. 138–40. See also Ernest Tuveson, *Redeemer Nation: The Idea of America's Millennial Role* (Chicago: University of Chicage Press, 1968).

24 Timothy Dwight, *Travels in New England and New York* (New Haven, 1821–22), 1: 387.

25 See Ursula Brumm, *American Thought and Religious Typology* (1963; rpt., New Brunswick, N.J.: Rutgers University Press, 1970), pp. 91–92. This important work reveals the pervasive pattern of typological thinking in American literature from the seventeenth century to Faulkner.

26 Michael D. Bell, *Hawthorne and the Historical Romance of New England* (Princeton, N.J.: Princeton University Press, 1974), p. 8.

27 See *American Museum* 3 (1788): 20–21; *Massachusetts Magazine* 7 (1795): 560; Jedidiah Morse, *The Present Situation of Other Nations of the World, Contrasted with Our Own* (Boston, 1795), p. 7; *American Museum* 2, no. 1 (1787): 561.

28 *Literary Magazine and American Register* 7, no. 44 (1806): 324.

29 David Humphreys, *An Address to the Citizens of the United States* (n.d.), p. 25.

30 Morse, *Present Situation*, p. 34.

31 *Massachusetts Magazine* 4 (1792): 556–57; *American Museum* 3 (1788): 20–21; *Massachusetts Magazine* 7 (1795): 560, 4 (1792): 557.

32 Morse, *Present Situation*, pp. 36–37.

33 *Columbian* 2 (1788), 400.

34 Thomas Paine, *Common Sense*, in *Complete Writings*, 1: 45.

35 See Peter Gay "Enlightenment Thought," p. 49.

36 Dwight *Travels*, 2: 308; 1: 18. See Humphreys, *Poem on Industry*, p. 7.

37 *Massachusetts Magazine* 4 (1792): 558; *Literary Magazine and American Register* 7, no. 44 (1807): 324; *Massachusetts Magazine* 7 (1795):559–60.

38 See *American Museum* 2, no. 1 (1787): 560; *Literary Magazine and American Register* 2 (1804): 216; *American Museum; or, Universal Magazine* 4 (Paris, 1789): 332.

39 See Lewis Simpson, *The Dispossessed Garden* (Athens: University of Georgia Press, 1975), pp. 15–18.

40 In *America before the Revolution*, ed. Alden T. Vaughan (Englewood Cliffs, N.J.: Prentice-Hall, 1967), p. 177.

41 Dwight, *Travels*, 2: 140; see also *The Conquest of Canaan* (Hartford, Conn.: Elisha Babcock, 1785), p. 479.

42 See J. A. Leo Lemay, *Men of Letters in Colonial Maryland* (Knoxville: University of Tennessee Press, 1971), pp. 156–57, 167.

43 Ibid., pp. 275, 274.

44 Ibid., pp. 233, 128.

45 Ibid., p. 304.

46 Henry F. May, *The Enlightenment in America* (New York: Oxford University Press, 1976), p. 149; see also pp. 137–39.

47 See Leo Marx, *The Machine in the Garden* (New York: Oxford University Press, 1964), pp. 118–44; and Chester Eisinger, "The Farmer in the Eighteenth-Century Almanac," *Agricultural History* 28 (1954): 107–12. Loren Baritz, *City on a Hill: A History of Ideas and Myths in America* (New York: Wiley, 1964), writes that "the fear of the forest led to a virtual apotheosis of the farmer . . . In America the farmer was the essential instrument of humanization, and as such occupied a central position in the thought of the age. As American myth-making continued, most of the earlier ideas and many of the emerging ones began to coalesce around the farmer whose symbolic voice was heard in almost all categories of thought. He was *the* American, the savior of the nation that was to be the savior of the world. Recognizing the importance of the farmer, the men of the eighteenth century made his significance explicit" (pp. 100–01).

48 *Port Folio* 8, 3d ser. (1812): 569; *American Museum* 3, no. 1 (1788): 25, 4 (1788): 212; *Columbian* 2 (1788): 396.

49 Arthur O. Lovejoy, *The Great Chain of Being* (1936; rpt., Cambridge: Harvard University Press, 1964), pp. 183–92. See also Daniel Boorstin, *The Lost World of Thomas Jefferson* (1948; rpt., Boston: Beacon, 1960), pp. 41–55, 34–36. Glacken too discusses the eighteenth-century theory of plenitude (*Traces*, p. 511) and surveys the conflicting theories concerning the effect on man of divers climates and soils (pp. 594–605). These conflicting theories are the subject of Antonello Gerbi, *The Dispute of the New World: The History of a Polemic, 1750–1900*, trans. and rev. Jeremy Moyne (Pitts-

burgh: University of Pittsburgh Press, 1973), which surveys various theories presupposing the natural inferiority of America.

50 Dwight, *Travels*, 1: 107.

51 Adams, *Diary*, 1: 23–24.

52 See *Columbian* 2 (1788): 399–400.

53 *Literary Magazine and American Register* 7, no. 44 (1806): 324.

54 Dwight, *Travels*, 2: 297–98.

55 Humphreys, *Poem on Industry*, pp. 7, 20; see also *Valedictory Discourse* (Boston, 1804), p. 18.

56 Dwight, *Travels* 2: 297–98.

57 Mason L. Weems, *The Life of Washington*, ed. Marcus Cunliffe (Cambridge: Harvard University Press, 1962), p. 29.

58 Ibid., p. 6.

59 In *Poems*, p. 16.

60 Ibid., p. 13.

61 Ibid., pp. 92–95.

62 Ibid., pp. 113–14; see also "Crispin's Answer," p. 115.

63 Dwight, *Travels*, 2: 233; Warren, *History*, 3: 264.

64 Hector St. John de Crèvecoeur, *Letters from an American Farmer* (New York: Dutton, 1957), p. 61.

65 Russel B. Nye points out patterns of value in Crèvecoeur's recurrent words in "Michel-Guillaume de Crèvecoeur: *Letters from an American Farmer*," in *Landmarks of American Writing*, ed. Henig Cohen (New York: Basic Books, 1970), pp. 24–41.

66 See A. W. Plumstead, "Hector St. John de Crèvecoeur," in *American Literature, 1764–1789: The Revolutionary Years*, ed. Everett Emerson (Madison: University of Wisconsin Press, 1977), pp. 213–31.

67 Crevecoeur, *Letters*, pp. 65, 55–56, 35, 63.

68 Ibid., pp. 7, 8, 28–29, 39, 43, 52, 53, 63–64, 37.

69 Ibid., p. 35.

70 Ibid., p. 57.

71 Ibid., pp. 64–82.

72 Ibid., pp. 35, 8–9, 57.

73 I am thankful to Prof. Everett Emerson of the University of Massachusetts for furnishing me a typescript of this unpublished essay.

74 *Letters*, p. 39.

75 Ibid., p. 45.

76 Quoted in Ralph Brown, "The American Geographies of Jedidiah Morse," *Annals of the Association of American Geographers* 31, no. 3 (September 1941): 146.

77 Hugh Henry Brackenridge, *Modern Chivalry*, ed. Lewis Leary (New Haven: College and University Press, 1965), pp. 39, 140.

78 See William Dunlap, *Life of Charles Brockden Brown* (Philadelphia: James P. Parks, 1815), 2: 68, 85; and Brown, *A System of General Geography* (Philadelphia, 1809), pp. 6–7.

79 Quoted in Brown, *System*, p. 161.
80 Ibid., pp. 176, 181.
81 Jedidiah Morse, *American Universal Geography* (Boston: E. Lincoln, 1812), pp. 278, 208–10, 276–79.
82 Ibid., pp. 370, 505–06.
83 Ibid., pp. 285, 370–71, 495.
84 Ibid., pp. 211, 302, 355, 356, 370, 417.
85 Ibid., pp. 101, 521, 569.
86 Ibid., pp. 444, 454, 439, 579, 608–09.
87 Brown, *System*, pp. 147, 154.
88 Morse, *American Universal Geography* p. 599.

CHAPTER 4

1 See James Woodress, *A Yankee's Odyssey* (Philadelphia: Lippincott, 1958), p. 246. Woodress speaks of *The Columbiad* as a "face-lifting" of Barlow's earlier *Vision of Columbus* (Hartford, Conn.: Hudson and Goodwin, 1787). He adds that though "the two poems are the same under the skin, if anything the youthful blemishes are more attractive than the middle-aged remodeling."
2 See M. R. Adams, "Joel Barlow, Political Romanticist," *American Literature* 9 (1937): 113–53; Joseph L. Blau, "Joel Barlow, Enlightened Religionist," *Journal of the History of Ideas* 10 (1949): 430–44; Percy H. Boynton, "Joel Barlow Advises the Privileged Orders," *New England Quarterly* 12 (1939): 477–99; Merton A. Christensen, "Deism in Joel Barlow's Early Work: Heterodox Passages in *The Vision of Columbus,*" *American Literature* 27 (1956): 509–20.
3 Leon Howard, *The Connecticut Wits* (Chicago: University of Chicago Press, 1943).
4 The printer's copy of *The Columbiad* is in the collection of Barlow's writings, #Ca Barlow 1 and 2, Beinecke Library, Yale University, New Haven, Conn.
5 Letter to Ruth Barlow, 12 August 1782, Barlow Papers, #164, Houghton Library, Harvard University, Cambridge, Mass.
6 See Gordon E. Bigelow, *Rhetoric and American Poetry of the Early National Period*, University of Florida Monographs, Humanities no. 4 (Gainesville, Fla.; 1960), pp. 16, 43.
7 Brissot de Warville, *New Travels in the United States*, trans. Joel Barlow (New York: Berry and Rogers, 1792), pp. 62–63.
8 Buckminster to Barlow, 10 July 1780, Yale University MSS, Pequot M959.
9 *The Columbiad* (1806; rpt., Washington, D.C.: Joseph Milligan, 1825), p. 46. All references in my discussion are to this edition.
10 Barlow, *Prospectus for a National Institution* (Washington, D.C., 1806), p. 19.

11 *Columbiad,* p. 303.
12 Barlow, *The Prospect of Peace* (New Haven: Thomas and Samuel Green, 1778), p. 4.
13 Diary, 23 September–11 October 1788, Harvard University MSS.
14 William Robertson, *The History of America* (London, 1777), 1: 248–64.
15 These titles are among those Barlow listed in notebooks (Yale University MSS, uncatalogud Ca Barlow).
16 Barlow to Stiles, 24 May 1794, Harvard University MSS #529; and Barlow to Philips, 18 May 1807, Yale University MSS #Pequot 919.
17 The only letter on nationalistic themes during this period is that to Ruth from Paris on 1 January 1790: "I write now by the ship that carries my first cargo of settlers," he says proudly to Ruth: "They will be followed this spring by several thousands. I have taken infinite pains to make every arrangement for their agreeable reception & happiness. On this will depend our and their future prosperity. If the first 100 people find themselves happy, the stream of emigration will be irresistible, they may be followed by a million of European settlers into the Western country. This will greatly increase the value of all those lands, & enable congress to sink the national debt by the sale of lands. Many respectable and wealthy families are now making their purchases & are going this spring, among whom are several noble men & some members of the national Assembly" (Harvard University MSS #178).
18 Brissot de Warville, *New Travels*, p. 32. To find Barlow's corruption of De Warville's text I have collated the New York 1792 edition with *New Travels in the United States of America, 1788*, ed. Durand Echeverria, trans. Mara Soceanu Vamos and Durand Echeverria (Cambridge: Harvard University Press, 1964). Page references to passages which Barlow deleted in his translation are to this 1964 edition.
19 Ibid., p. 115.
20 Ibid., p. 215.
21 Ibid., p. 280.
22 Ibid., pp. 93, 120, 340.
23 Ibid., p. 42.
24 Ibid., pp. 74, 98, 86, 32.
25 Ibid., pp. 258, 263, 260; see also pp. 143, 256–57, 258, 262.
26 Roy Harvey Pearce, *The Continuity of American Poetry* (Princeton, N.J.: Princeton University Press, 1961), pp. 59–68.
27 *Columbiad,* p. 13.
28 Ibid., p. 346.
29 Ibid., p. 31
30 Ibid., pp. 32, 15, 16.
31 Ibid., pp. 32, 33.
32 Ibid., pp. 37-38, 129, 147, 285.
33 *Vision,* p. 33; *Columbiad,* p. 16.
34 *Columbiad,* pp. 44–45, 149–51.

35 Ibid., p. 302.
36 From manuscript entitled "Means of Subsistence," Yale University MSS #Ca Barlow 5; *Columbiad*, p. 135.
37 Howard, *Connecticut Wits*, p. 148; *Vision*, p. 82.
38 William Hayley and James Clark to Barlow, 25 March 1792, Yale University MSS #Pequot 986; *Columbiad*, p. 60.
39 *Columbiad*, pp. 129, 303.
40 Ibid., p. 131.
41 Ibid., pp. 141–42.
42 Ibid., pp. 161, 163.
43 Ibid., pp. 138, 283.
44 Sacvan Bercovitch, "Horologicals to Chronometricals: The Rhetoric of the Jeremiad," in *Literary Monographs*, ed. Eric Rothstein (Madison: University of Wisconsin Press, 1970), 3: 3–124.
45 *Columbiad*, p. 132.
46 Ibid., pp. 136, 126, 35.
47 Ibid., p. 153.
48 Ibid., p. 153; Barlow's account of the ascendant strength of the English colonies is to be found on pp. 151–52, 164.
49 Ibid., pp. 403–04.
50 Ibid., p. 405.
51 See William L. Hedges, "Towards a Theory of American Literature, 1765–1800," *Early American Literature* 4, no. 1: 4–14.
52 *Columbiad*, p. 434.
53 Barlow to Baldwin, 3 January 1801, Harvard University MSS #411.
54 Diary, 25 May–12 September 1788, Harvard University MSS; manuscript notes for projected history of the United States (Yale University MSS #Pequot 934, 935); *Columbiad*, p. 358.
55 Notes for history of the United States, p. 6 (Yale University MSS #Pequot 934).
56 Frederick Somkin, *Unquiet Eagle: Memory and Desire in the Idea of American Freedom, 1815–1860* (Ithaca, N.Y.: Cornell University Press, 1967), pp. 39–42.
57 *Columbiad*, pp. 275–76.
58 Ibid., pp. 198–99.
59 Diary, 23 September–11 October, 1788, Harvard University MSS; see also Woodress, *Yankee's Odyssey*, p. 191.
60 Notebook of 1802, Harvard University MSS; see Kenneth R. Ball, "Joel Barlow's 'Canal' and Natural Religion," *Eighteenth-Century Studies* 2, no. 1 (Fall 1968): 225–39. Ball's essay concludes with a printing of the entire 290-line fragment of "The Canal."
61 Ball, "Barlow's 'Canal'."
62 *Columbiad*, p. 282.
63 Notebook of 1802, Harvard University MSS.

64 Jedidiah Morse, *American Universal Geography* (Boston: E. Lincoln, 1812), p. 126.

65 "On the Discoveries of Captain Lewis," in Barlow to Jefferson, 12 January 1807, Library of Congress MSS. Barlow read the complete verse at a dinner given by Jefferson to honor Captain Lewis. An account of it appears in the *National Intelligence*, 6 January 1807; see *Columbiad*, p. 346.

66 *Columbiad*, pp. 346–47; "Oration Delivered at Washington, July Fourth, 1809," in *The Works of Joel Barlow*, ed. William K. Bottorff and Arthur L. Ford, (Gainesville, Fla.: Scholars' Facsimiles and Reprints, 1970), 1: 536; *Prospectus for a National Institution*, p. 10.

67 James Russell Lowell, "Nationality in Literature," in *Literary Criticism of James Russell Lowell*, ed. Herbert F. Smith (Lincoln: University of Nebraska Press, 1969), p. 129.

68 Notebook of 1802, Harvard University MSS.

69 I am thankful to Prof. Lenore O'Boyle for calling this point to my attention.

CHAPTER 5

1 James Russell Lowell, "Nationality in Literature," in *Literary Criticism of James Russell Lowell*, ed. Herbert F. Smith (Lincoln: University of Nebraska Press, 1969), pp. 129, 123, 118–19. On Lowell's relation to the Young America movement, see Perry Miller, *The Raven and the Whale* (New York: Harcourt, Brace and World, 1956), pp. 69–117.

2 *Western Monthly Review* 1 (May 1827): 25–27.

3 John James Audubon, "The Ohio," in *Delineations of American Scenery and Character* (1826; rpt., New York: Arno, 1970), p. 4.

4 See *North American Review* 39 (July 1834): 200, 38 (April 1834): 436; *Western Monthly Review* 1 (October 1827): 329; *Knickerbocker* 8 (August 1836): 193–94. See also "Atlantic and Michigan Railway," *Western Monthly Review* 3 (July 1829): 19; "Outline of an Essay on the Future Progress of Ohio," *Western Monthly Review* 3 (June 1830): 333; and "Darby's View of the U.S.," *American Quarterly Review* 5 (March 1829): 143–44.

5 *An Address Delivered at the Laying of the Corner Stone of the Bunker Hill Monument* (Boston: Cummings, Hilliard, 1825), pp. 36–37.

6 Ibid., p. 27.

7 *A Discourse, Delivered at Plymouth . . . in Commemoration of the First Settlement of New-England* (Boston: Wells and Lilly, 1821), pp. 60–61.

8 Ibid., pp. 60–61.

9 *Speech of Daniel Webster on the Subject of the Public Lands* (Washington D.C.: Gales and Seaton, 1830), pp. 6-9.

10 *Address at the Laying of the Corner Stone*, pp. 38, 26.

11 *Discourse at Plymouth*, pp. 9–10; *Address at the Laying of the Corner Stone*, p. 37.

12 J. H. Perkins, "Dangers of the West," *Western Messenger* 2 (September 1836): 92–93.

13 *Knickerbocker* 3 (February 1834): 95; 2 (September 1833): 161, 164; 9 (January 1837): 1; *United States Magazine and Democratic Review* 11, no. 49 (July 1842): 55. See also *North American Review* 38 (April 1834): 466–537.

14 Albert Gallatin to Frances Gallatin, 26 November 1824, in *Writings*, ed. Henry Adams (New York: Antiquarian Press, 1960), 2: 367; Orestes A. Brownson, "National Greatness," in *Works*, ed. Henry F. Brownson (Detroit: T. Nourse, 1884), 1: 537. Two important studies survey skeptical views of moral advancement in America during the first one-half of the nineteenth century. Arthur A. Ekirch, Jr., *The Idea of Progress in America, 1815–1860* (1944; rpt., New York: AMS Press, 1969), points out that the Panic of 1837 elicited strong criticism of American materialism by such writers as Brownson and Channing, though the ministers Horace Bushnell and George W. Burnap "foresaw a happier future for religion with some of the national faith in purely material and practical values destroyed by hard times" (pp. 76–79). More recently, Frederick Somkin, *Unquiet Eagle: Memory and Desire in the Idea of American Freedom, 1815–1860* (Ithaca, N.Y.: Cornell University Press, 1967), pp. 11–30, reviews the range of expressed fears on American material progress, concluding that "the principal complaint against prosperity was that it somehow turned a nation of God-fearing, freedom-loving idealists into a grasping horde of mercenary egoists" (p. 20). He observes that "this question of the influence of prosperity upon 'the heart' . . . often led into a thicket of unhappy introspection and misgivings" (p. 17). Recently, John F. Kasson has written that "as machine technology began to play an increasingly important role in ante-bellum America, the question of its relation to the development of republican culture and imaginative freedom grew critical." See his *Civilizing the Machine: Technology and Republican Values in America, 1776–1900* (Harmondsworth, England, and New York: Penguin, 1977), p. 110. Kasson illuminates the debate on the problem of technology and imaginative freedom with an extensive discussion of Ralph Waldo Emerson; see pp. 110–35.

15 Ralph Waldo Emerson, "The Transcendentalist," in *Works* (Boston: Phillips, Sampson, 1883), 1: 338; Thoreau quoted in Richard Lebeaux, "Young Man Thoreau" (Ph.D. diss., Boston University, 1975), p. 4.

16 Sacvan Bercovitch, "Horologicals to Chronometricals: The Rhetoric of the Jeremiad," in *Literary Monographs*, ed. Eric Rothstein (Madison: University of Wisconsin Press), 3: 3–124.

17 *Western Monthly Magazine* 1 (May 1827): 25–26.

18 "The Young American," in *Works*, 1: 345, 344.

19 Henry D. Thoreau, "Walking," in *The Portable Thoreau*, ed. Carl Bode (New York: Viking, 1964), p. 615.

20 F. O. Matthiessen, *American Renaissance* (Oxford: Oxford University Press, 1941), pp. 8, 11.

21 Emerson, "Man the Reformer," in *Works*, 1: 228; Thoreau, "Walking," p. 619.

22 Lawrence Buell, *Literary Transcendentalism* (Ithaca, N.Y.: Cornell University Press, 1973), p. 144; Alcott quoted in Matthiessen, *American Renaissance*, p. 160.

23 Quotations from "Paradise (To Be) Regained" are from Henry D. Thoreau, *A Yankee in Canada* (1892; rpt., New York: Greenwood, 1969), pp. 182–205.

24 *Walden* (Princeton, N.J.: Princeton University Press, 1973), p. 52.

25 *The Writings of Henry David Thoreau* (Boston and New York: Houghton Mifflin, 1906), vol. 3, *The Maine Woods*, pp. 5–6.

26 *Walden*, p. 264.

27 Ibid., p. 171.

28 Herman Melville, *Moby Dick*, ed. Harrison Hayford and Hershel Parker (New York: Norton, 1967), p. 97. One essay that pursues this point is Lewis H. Miller, Jr., "The Artist as Surveyor in *Walden* and *The Maine Woods*," *ESQ: A Journal of the American Renaissance* 21 (1976): 76–81.

29 *Walden* pp. 220, 313–17.

30 *Maine Woods*, 78.

31 Ibid., pp. 71, 68, 12, 88, 67.

32 Ibid., pp. 77–79, 90–92.

33 Matthiessen, *American Renaissance*, p. ix.

34 John L. Thomas, "Romantic Reform in America, 1815–1865," *American Quarterly* 17 (1965): 656–81.

35 James Fenimore Cooper, Preface to *Satanstoe* (New York: W. A. Townsend, 1860), p. v. With the exception of *The Pioneers*, all references to Cooper's fiction are to this F. O. C. Darley-illustrated edition of his *Works* (1859–61).

36 J. Perry Leavell, Jr., Introduction to *The American Democrat* by James Fenimore Cooper (1838; rpt., New York: Funk and Wagnalls, 1969), p. xxviii.

37 See *The Chainbearer*, p. 129; and *The Wept of Wish-Ton-Wish*, p. 243.

38 James Fenimore Cooper, *Notions of the Americans*, ed. Robert Spiller (New York: Ungar, 1963), 2: 347.

39 Preface to *The Spy*, pp. xi, xii.

40 *The Wept of Wish-Ton-Wish*, p. 242.

41 *The Spy*, p. 15.

42 William Sampson, Preface to *A Guide in the Wilderness* by William Cooper (Dublin, 1810), p. 3.

43 See E. Arthur Robinson, "Conservation in Cooper's *The Pioneers*," *PMLA* 82, no. 7 (December 1967): 564–78; and *The Chainbearer*, p. 97.

44 *Wyandotte*, pp. 42–43.

45 Of the gentleman-democrat, Cooper writes, "As society advanced, ordinary

men attained the qualifications of nobility, without that of birth, and the meaning of the word was extended. It is now possible to be a gentleman without birth .... the democratic gentleman must differ in many essential particulars, from the aristocratical gentleman. ... The democrat, recognizing the right of all to participate in power, will be more liberal in his general sentiments, a quality of superiority in itself" (*American Democrat*, pp. 112, 113, 90). Those critics who have discussed Cooper's gentlemen include John P. McWilliams, Jr., *Political Justice in a Republic* (Berkeley and Los Angeles: University of California Press, 1972), p. 239; Kay Seymour House, *Cooper's Americans* (Columbus: Ohio State University Press, 1965), p. 170; and Marius Bewley, *The Eccentric Design: Form in the Classic American Novel* (New York: Columbia University Press, 1959), p. 67.

46 Edwin H. Cady, *The Gentleman in America* (Syracuse, N.Y.: Syracuse University Press, 1949), p. 144.

47 A. N. Kaul, *The American Vision: Actual and Ideal Society in Nineteenth-Century Fiction* (New Haven: Yale University Press, 1963), writes of the Littlepage Trilogy (*Satanstoe, The Chainbearer, The Redskins*) that the novels are "all concerned with land: the ownership of land, and possible forms of social organization based upon land"(p. 86). Bewley observes that Cooper's purpose was "to praise landed wealth, transmitted through families ... [since] land wealth has a dignity, and carried certain values and responsibilities with it, that no other kind of wealth could claim" (*Eccentric Design*, p. 65). In *Political Justice* McWilliams finds the landscape to be related essentially to Cooper's characters. "Cooper's handling of setting is of prime importance," he remarks, because "the setting defines the political and national promise of the land." He adds that "Cooper's characters, like Hardy's, are remembered against a landscape" (pp. 23–24).

48 Roderick Nash, *Wilderness and the American Mind* (New Haven and London: Yale University Press, 1967), p. 60.

49 Joel Porte, *The Romance in America* (Middletown, Conn.: Wesleyan University Press, 1969), p. 47.

50 See Donald Ringe, "Cooper's Littlepage Novels: Change and Stability in American Society," *American Literature* 32 (1960): 280–90.

51 See *Home as Found*, pp. 187–90.

52 Robinson, "Conservation," p. 565. See also H. Daniel Peck, *A World by Itself: The Pastoral Moment in Cooper's Fiction* (New Haven and London: Yale University Press, 1977) pp. 61–62. Peck finds that the realistic portrayal of settlement in the novel is "uncharacteristic" of Cooper.

53 *The Pioneers*, ed. Leon Howard (New York: Holt, Rinehart, and Winston, 1959), pp. 298–99. All references to the novel are to this edition.

54 *American Democrat*, p. 89.

55 *The Pioneers*, pp. 232–38.

56 Ibid.

57   Ibid., pp. 328–29.
58   Ibid., pp. 32–33, 112–13, 92–94.
59   Ibid., p. 107.
60   Ibid., p. 29.
61   Ibid., pp. 29, 140, 180.
62   Ibid., p. 212.
63   Ibid., pp. 229, 98.
64   Ibid., pp. 229–30.
65   See Thomas Philbrick, "Cooper's *The Pioneers*," *PMLA* 79 (1964): 579–93.
66   *Political Justice*, p. 122.
67   *Cooper's Americans*, p. 167.
68   *American Democrat*, p. 91.
69   *Political Justice*, p. 368.
70   See Edgar A. Dryden, "History and Progress Some Implications of: Form in
     Cooper's Littlepage Novels" (*sic*), *Nineteenth-Century Fiction* 52 (March
     1974): 183.
71   *Political Justice*, p. 26.
72   Dryden, "History and Progress," p. 62.
73   See *The Crater*, chaps. 29, 30.
74   George Bancroft, *History of the United States from the Discovery of the
     American Continent* (Boston: Charles Bowen, 1834), 1: 436. All successive
     volumes were published in Boston by Little, Brown and appeared as
     follows: 2, 1837; 3, 1839; 4 and 5, 1852; 6, 1854; 7, 1858; 8, 1860; 9,
     1866; 10, 1874. References in my discussion are to these volumes.
75   Ibid., 3: 396–97.
76   See Sacvan Bercovitch, "How the Puritans Won the American Revolution,"
     Massachusetts Review, 17, no. 4 (1976): 597–630.
77   Quoted in Arthur A. Ekirch, Jr., *Man and Nature in America* (1963; rpt.,
     Lincoln: University of Nebraska Press, 1973), p. 24.
78   *History of the United States*, 1: 3–4.
79   Ibid., 2: 41, 218.
80   Ibid., 1: 249–51; 2: 164–65.
81   Ibid., 3: 152–53.
82   See Sacvan Bercovitch, *The Puritan Origins of the American Self* (New
     Haven: Yale University Press, 1975), pp. 161, 157.
83   *History of the United States*, 4: 136.
84   Ibid., 7: 394, 398; 6: 298–301.
85   Bancroft, *History of the Colonization of the United States* (Boston: Little,
     Brown, 1839), 1: 347.
86   *History of the United States* 5: 165; 4: 132, 135: 6: 297; 7: 167, 251.
87   Ibid., 2: 453–54, 300–01, 325, 328.
88   Ibid., 7: 21–22.
89   Ibid., 3: 162, 168; 4: 13; 3: 352.
90   Ibid., 2: 266–67.

91 Ibid., 2: 269–70.
92 David Levin, *History as Romantic Art* (Stanford, Calif.: Stanford University Press, 1959), p. 40. Levin emphasizes that Bancroft, along with other Romantic historians, felt obliged in sympathy and judgment to propound the view that his was the vantage point of "the highest station reached in human progress" (p. 24). From the extant records of royalty payments for Bancroft's *History* we get some sense of public acceptance of his beliefs. Russel B. Nye, *George Bancroft: Brahmin Rebel* (New York: Knopf, 1944), writes that within a year Bancroft's book (vol. 1) had taken its place in nearly one-third of the homes of New England and that his name was soon to be a household word. In the late 1830s Bancroft's publisher, Little, Brown and Co., paid him monthly royalties from the sale of the *History* ranging from $200 to $500 (from payments per volume at 50¢, 33¢, and 16¢ respectively in the United States, France, and Britain). In 1841, as Nye reports, Bancroft received a total of $4,250 in royalties. Though sales figures for the early volumes are lacking, Nye judges the extent of Bancroft's popularity "from the fact that forty-one years after the publication of Volume I of the *History* about six hundred copies of it were sold." He continues, "Bancroft's books filled shelves in thousands of American homes," and for more than twenty years Bancroft's "name had been very nearly synonymous with American history" (p. 187).
93 *History of the United States*, 3: 148–61; see also 2: 433; 3: 81, 122–23, 157, 206, 362.
94 Ibid., 1: 338.
95 Levin, *History as Romantic Art*, p. 17.
96 *History of the United States*, 5: 52.
97 Ibid., pp. 45–46. Russel Nye quotes from an early, untitled article by Bancroft ("written probably in 1832") in which he "discussed the function of the scholar in a world of action." In it Bancroft described the superlative scholar as the "greatest high-priest of nature who unfolds truths of universal importance, [and] discovers powers which give man mastery over his destiny." Among this species he includes Tacitus, Milton, Columbus, Galileo, and Copernicus (*George Bancroft*, p. 93). Indirectly, Bancroft evidently revealed his own ambitions.
98 *History of the United States*, 4: 556–57.

CHAPTER 6

1 See Floyd Stovall, *The Foreground of Leaves of Grass* (Charlottesville: University of Virginia Press, 1974), p. 137. Others similarly define Whitman's persona. See Gay Wilson Allen, *The Solitary Singer*, rev. ed. (New York: New York University Press, 1967), p. 221; Edwin Fussell, *Frontier: American Literature and the American West* (Princeton, N.J.:

Princeton University Press, 1965), p. 407; and Sacvan Bercovitch, *The Puritan Origins of the American Self* (New Haven: Yale University Press, 1975), pp. 182–84.

2   *Foreground*, pp. 45–46.

3   *Song of the Broad-Axe, Leaves of Grass*, ed. Harold W. Blodgett and Sculley Bradley (New York: New York University Press, 1965), pp. 184–95 (lines 121, 124). All references to the poetry of Walt Whitman are from this edition.

4   James E. Miller, Jr., *Walt Whitman* (New York: Twayne, 1962), pp. 66, 72. See Whitman, "Preface, 1855, to the first issue of *Leaves of Grass*," in *Prose Works* (1892; rpt., New York: New York University Press, 1965), 2: 456. See also *Democratic Vistas*, in *Prose Works*, vol. 2; and Richard Chase, *Walt Whitman Reconsidered* (New York: Sloane, 1955), p. 153.

5   Fussell, *Frontier*, pp. 397, 400; see Thomas Brasher, *Whitman as Editor of Brooklyn Daily Eagle* (Detroit: Wayne State University Press, 1970), pp. 85–95.

6   *Foreground*, pp. 146, 159.

7   *The Uncollected Poetry and Prose of Walt Whitman*, ed. Emory Holloway (New York: Peter Smith, 1932), 1: 187, 189.

8   Miller, *Walt Whitman*, p. 21; Fussell, *Frontier*, pp. 402–03.

9   See *Solitary Singer*, pp. 8, 23, 30–31, 56, 60–61, 154.

10   See Thomas L. Karnes, *William Gilpin: Western Nationalist* (Austin: University of Texas Press, 1970), p. 19.

11   Ibid., p. 56.

12   Henry Nash Smith, *Virgin Land* (New York: Random House, 1950), pp. 40–41.

13   William Gilpin, *The Central Gold Region: The Grain, Pastoral, and Gold Regions of North America* (Philadelphia: Sower, Barnes, 1860), p. 133.

14   Ibid., p. 136.

15   Ibid., pp. 132, 133.

16   Ibid., pp. 147–48.

17   Karnes, *William Gilpin*, pp. 346–47.

18   William T. Sherman, *Memoirs* (New York: Appleton, 1875), 1: 339–40; cf. 2: 109–10.

19   Edward Bellamy, *Equality* (New York: Appleton, 1897), pp. 272, 279, 301. I am thankful to Jan Seidler for calling these passages in *Equality* to my attention. In *Puritan Origins* (pp. 146–47), Bercovitch points out the millennial themes in Bellamy's *Looking Backward*.

20   See Laura Wood Roper, *FLO: Biography of Frederick Law Olmsted* (Baltimore and London: Johns Hopkins University Press, 1973), p. 403. My discussion of Olmsted is much indebted to this work.

21   Ibid., p. 401.

22   Frederick Law Olmsted, Jr., and Theodora Kimball, eds., *Frederick Law Olmsted: Landscape Architect* (1922; rpt., New York: Blom, 1970), 1: 77.

23 Ibid., p. 69.
24 Roper, *FLO*, pp. 82, 63.
25 Ibid., p. 249.
26 Olmsted and Kimball, *Frederick Law Olmsted*, 1: 37.
27 Frederick Law Olmsted, *Walks and Talks of an American Farmer in England* (1852; rpt., Ann Arbor: University of Michigan Press, 1967), p. 95.
28 Ibid., p. 68.
29 Ibid., p. 68.
30 Albert Fein, *Frederick Law Olmsted and the American Environmental Tradition* (New York: Braziller, 1972), pp. 3–10.
31 Albert Brisbane, *The Social Destiny of Man* (1840; rpt., New York: Kelley, 1969), pp. 239–40.
32 Whitman, *Democratic Vistas*, p. 363.
33 David Lowenthal, Introduction to *Man and Nature* by George Perkins Marsh (Cambridge: Harvard University Press, 1965), p. ix.
34 Marsh, *Man and Nature*, p. 40.
35 Ibid., pp. 36–37, 29.
36 Ibid., p. 44.
37 In Introduction to Marsh, *Man and Nature*, p. xxv.
38 William Dean Howells, *The Rise of Silas Lapham*, ed. Edwin H. Cady (1885; rpt., Boston: Houghton Mifflin, 1957), p. 13.
39 Stovall, *Foreground*, pp. 201–03.
40 Arnold Guyot, *The Earth and Man* (1849; rpt., New York: Arno, 1970), pp. 209–16, 298–301.
41 See Allen, *Solitary Singer*, p. 142; Stovall, *Foreground*, p. 203; and Whitman, "Preface, 1872," in *Prose Works*, 2: 460.
42 Ralph Waldo Emerson, "The Transcendentalist," in *Works* (Boston: Phillips, Sampson, 1883), 1: 338.
43 *Foreground*, p. 281.
44 *No Labor-Saving Machine*, p. 131.
45 Whitman, "Poetry To-day in America—Shakspere—The Future," in *Prose Works*, 2: 483; *Song of Myself*, p. 61, lines 715–16. See Charles Feidelson, *Symbolism and American Literature* (Chicago: University of Chicago Press, 1953), p. 4; Fussell, *Frontier*, p. 417; Whitman "Preface, 1855," p. 439.
46 *Language for America*, p. 630.
47 *Thou Mother with Thy Equal Blood*, p. 457, lines 34–39.
48 *Symbolism and American Literature*, p. 27.
49 *For you, O Democracy*, in *Calamus*, p. 117, line 1; *Song of Myself*, p. 74, line 1007; *Myself and Thine*, in *Birds of Passage*, p. 238, line 33; *A Woman Waits for Me*, in *Children of Adam*, p. 102, line 28; *Starting from Paumanok*, p. 18, lines 62–63.
50 *A Song for Occupations*, p. 215, lines 90–93.
51 *Starting from Paumanok* p. 27, line 258.
52 *Song of the Broad-Axe*, p. 189, line 117; *Starting from Paumanok*, p. 24,

line 193; *Spontaneous Me*, in *Children of Adam*, p. 103, line 8; *Song of the Answerer*, p. 169, lines 57, 61.

53   See Feidelson, *Symbolism and American Literature*, p. 20. In *Song of the Answerer* Whitman writes, "The maker of poems settles justice, reality, immortality, / His insight and power encircle things and the human race" (p. 169, lines 58–59).

54   Stovall, *Foreground*, p. 277.

55   See Alvin Rosenfeld, "The Eagle and the Axe: A Study of 'Song of the Broad-Axe,' " *American Image* 25 (1968): 354–70. Robin P. Hoople acknowledges Whitman's millennial themes in "Chants Democratic and Native American," *American Literature* 42 (1970): 181–96. Hawthorne's "unhappy fowl" appears in "The Custom-House," *The Scarlet Letter*, ed. Larzer Ziff (Indianapolis: Bobbs-Merrill, 1962), p. 3. In the following discussion of *Song of the Broad-Axe*, line references to passages in the poem will appear in the text.

56   *With Antecedents*, in *Birds of Passage*, p. 241, line 25; *A Song for Occupations*, p. 216, line 102.

57   *Whitman Reconsidered*, p. 158.

58   See Rosenfeld, "The Eagle and the Axe, pp. 360–61.

59   Tony Tanner, *The Reign of Wonder* (New York: Harper and Row, 1965), pp. 68, 67.

60   *Song of the Open Road*, p. 157, line 192; *Democratic Vistas*, p. 390.

61   Fussell's reading of this stanza is antithetical to mine. He writes, "The typical instrument of national progress sounds like a deformed baby resulting from a scarcely imaginable perversion, perhaps from the union of the old American nature and the new American industrialism" (*Frontier*, p. 423).

62   Lawrence Buell, *Literary Transcendentalism* (Ithaca, N.Y.: Cornell University Press, 1973), p. 169.

63   "The Function of the Poet," in *Literary Criticism of James Russell Lowell*, ed. Herbert F. Smith (Lincoln: University of Nebraska Press, 1969), p. 18.

64   *The Song of the Redwood-Tree* is to be found in *Leaves of Grass*, pp. 206–10. Line numbers are given in the text.

65   Frederik Schyberg, *Walt Whitman*, trans. Evie Allison Allen (New York: Columbia University Press, 1951), p. 232; Allen, *Solitary Singer*, p. 458.

66   Fussell, *Frontier*, pp. 433–34. Chase singles out *The Song of the Redwood-Tree* as one exception to his view that Whitman's later poetry "bespeaks a mind in which productive tensions have been relaxed" (*Whitman Reconsidered*, p. 148). Miller reads the poem essentially as a sexual symbol of the phallic tree in a fecund earth (*Walt Whitman*, pp. 131–132), while Roger Asselineau, *The Evolution of Walt Whitman* (Cambridge: Harvard University Press, 1960), sees the "optimistic conclusion" of the poem as reflective of Whitman's confidence that "the worst, that is, the Civil War, was over" (p. 218).

67 James Fenimore Cooper, *Home as Found* (1838; rpt., New York; W. A. Townsend, 1860), pp. 232–33.

68 See Roderick Nash, *Wilderness and the American Mind* (New Haven and London: Yale University Press, 1967), pp. 96–121. In the chapters, "Preserve the Wilderness!" and "Wilderness Preserved," Nash examines the basis and the chronology of the valuation of wilderness in America in the nineteenth century.

EPILOGUE

1 Charles Olson, *Maximus Poems IV, V, VI* (London: Cape Goliard Press, 1968), n.p.
2 Ezra Pound, *Selected Prose, 1909–1965*, ed. William Cookson (New York: New Directions, 1973), pp. 104, 111, 112.
3 Ibid., p. 121.
4 Sinclair Lewis, *Babbitt* (1922; rpt., New York: New American Library, 1961), p. 1.
5 Nathanael West, *Miss Lonelyhearts* and *The Day of the Locust* (1933; rpt., New York: New Directions, 1962), p. 27.
6 John Dos Passos, *The 42nd Parallel* (1930; rpt., New York: Washington Square, 1961), pp. 91–92.
7 John Steinbeck, *The Grapes of Wrath* (1939; rpt., New York: Viking, 1967), pp. 473–77.
8 F. Scott Fitzgerald, *The Great Gatsby* (1925; rpt., New York; Scribner's, 1953), p. 23.
9 William Faulkner, *Light in August* (1932; rpt., New York: Random House, 1959), pp. 2–3.
10 Thomas Pynchon, *The Crying of Lot 49* (1966; rpt., New York: Bantam, 1967), p. 12.
11 Pound, *Selected Prose*, p. 105.
12 Fitzgerald, *The Great Gatsby*, p. 69.
13 *The Collected Poems of Wallace Stevens* (New York: Knopf, 1964), p. 76.
14 See Benjamin Sankey, *A Companion to William Carlos Williams's "Paterson"* (Berkeley and Los Angeles: University of California Press, 1971), p. 4. I refer to the fifth printing of *Paterson* in the New Directions edition (New York, 1969).
15 Sankey, *Companion to Paterson*, p. 5.
16 Ibid., p. 222.

Index

Adams, Abigail, 80
Adams, John, 67-68, 70, 74, 76, 77, 80, 83
106, 158
Adams, John Quincy, 152-53
Addison, Joseph, 75
Agassiz, Louis, 221
Alcott, Bronson, 162
Allen, Gay Wilson, 209, 247
Alsted, Johann, 16
Amadas, Philip, 3
Ames, Nathaniel, 86
Audubon, John J., 153-54
Austen, Jane, 75

Bacon, Francis, 59
Bailyn, Bernard, 78
Baldwin, Elihu, 158
Bancroft, George, ix, 22, 38, 153, 157, 161,
167, 223, 231, 237, 242, 251, 253, 257;
History of the United States, 188–205
Baritz, Loren, 271
Barlow, Arthur, 3
Barlow, Joel, x, 22, 38, 77, 94, 106; early
life, 115–20; *Columbiad,* 81, 114–20, 128–
49, 153, 159, 160, 169, 186, 222; *Vision
of Columbus,* 115–17, 131, 133; *Prospect
of Peace,* 120–21; translates Brissot de
Warville, 124–28; environmental reform in,
134–45; "The Canal," 146–48; James Rus-
sel Lowell criticizes, 151–52; in literary
tradition of New Earth, 187, 203, 205,
218, 220, 223–24, 231, 237, 240, 242,
246, 251, 257
Baxter, Richard, 58
Beecher, Lyman, 158
Bell, Michael, 80
Bellamy, Edward, 214
Benton, Thomas Hart, 211
Bercovitch, Sacvan, xi, 16, 17, 21, 31, 54,
159, 186, 188, 192
Beverley, Robert, 86
Boone, Daniel, 192-95, 202, 212
Boorstin, Daniel, 90
Boyle, Robert, 59

Brackenridge, Hugh Henry, 97, 106
Bradford, William, 5, 21, 40, 51-52; escha-
tology in, 22–25, 26, 35, 36
Bradstreet, Anne, 38, 41
Brasher, Thomas, 208
Brereton, John, 4
Brightman, Thomas, 16
Brissot de Warville, Jacques Pierre, *New
Travels in the United States,* 117, 123–28
Brown, Charles Brockden, 107, 124
Brown, Eva Mae, xi
Brown, Lancelot, 74
Browne, Edmund, 19
Brownson, Orestes, 158
Brumm, Ursula, xi, 79
Buckminster, Joseph, 117, 118
Buell, Lawrence, 162, 240
Buffon, Georges Louis LeClerc, 71, 72, 107
Burke, Edmund, 75
Burnham, Daniel, 217
Bushman, Richard, 55
Bushnell, David, 110
Byrd, William, 86

Canby, Henry Seidel, 163
Carroll, Peter, 24–25
Chalklin, C.W., 55
Channing, William Ellery, 158
Chase, Richard, 234
Clap, Roger, 18
Clark, George Rogers, 212
Clay, Henry, 211
Cole, Thomas, 198
Collingwood, R.G., 246
Cooper, James Fenimore, ix, 22, 38, 153,
161; environmental reform in, 169–85;
The Pioneers, 174–85; repudiates New
Earth, 184–87; in literary tradition of
New Earth, 200, 205, 223, 231, 237, 238,
242, 247
Cooper, William, 172
Cotton, John, 7, 63, 80
Cousin, Victor, 221